Israel in the
Black American
Perspective

Israel in the Black American Perspective

ROBERT G. WEISBORD *and*
RICHARD KAZARIAN, JR.

Contributions in Afro-American and African Studies, Number 84

Greenwood Press
Westport, Connecticut • London, England

E
185.615
W345
1985

Library of Congress Cataloging-in-Publication Data

Weisbord, Robert G.
   Israel in the Black American perspective.

   (Contributions in Afro-American and African
studies, ISSN 0069-9624 ; no. 84)
   Bibliography: p.
   Includes index.
   1. Afro-Americans—Relations with Jews.   2. Israel—
Foreign opinion, American.   3. Afro-Americans—Attitudes.
4. Public opinion—United States.   I. Kazarian, Richard.
II. Title.   III. Series.
E185.615.W345   1985   956.94   84-12816
ISBN 0-313-24016-7 (lib. bdg.)

Library of Congress Catalog Card Number: 84-12816
ISBN: 0-313-24016-7
ISSN: 0069-9624

First published in 1985

Greenwood Press, 88 Post Road West, Westport, CT 06881
An imprint of Greenwood Publishing Group, Inc.

Printed in the United States of America

10 9 8 7 6 5 4 3 2

Copyright Acknowledgments

The eight lines from W.E.B. Du Bois' poem "Suez," which were quoted in Chapter III, were taken from Du Bois, W.E.B. *Creative Writings of W.E.B. Du Bois: A Pageant, Poems, Short Stories, and Playlets.* Edited by Herbert Aptheker. (*The Complete Published Works of W.E.B. Du Bois.*) Millwood, New York: Kraus-Thomson Organization Limited, 1985. Reprinted with permission of the publisher.

Portions of Chapter IV were previously published in an article entitled "Israel and the Black Hebrew Israelites," written by Dr. Weisbord for *Judaism: A Quarterly Journal of Jewish Life and Thought*, vol. 24, no. 1 (Winter Issue, 1975):23–38.

A portion of Chapter VII was previously published as "Israel and Black America: The Moshe Dayan Incident," *The Jewish Frontier*, vol. 36, no. 3 (January–February–March, 1982): 12–13.

Every reasonable effort has been made to trace the owner of copyright material for the poem from *Black Power* (p. 43), but this has proven impossible. The publishers will be glad to receive information leading to a complete acknowledgments in subsequent printings of this book, and in the meantime extend their apologies for any omission.

FOR CYNTHIA WEISBORD,

RICHARD KAZARIAN, SR., AND MARY MALIAN KAZARIAN

Contents

Acknowledgments

Many individuals have been of assistance to the authors in the preparation of this book. For their typing and/or proofreading skills we are indebted to Nancy Alling, Gail Sherman, Sue Rubinsky, Lorraine Hayes, Catherine Jo Shadd, John Richard Kazarian and Susan Rose. For sundry research tasks we would like to thank John Ciummo, Gerard Donley, Nancy Berg, Amy Boyle and Kevin Leff.

For their yeoman work, the Inter-Library Loan people in the University of Rhode Island Library, namely Sylvia Krausse, Roberta Doran and Vicky Burnett, richly deserve acknowledgment. Andrew Turyn and Abner Gaines were also of inestimable assistance.

For making it possible to do pertinent research in Israel, South Africa and various American cities, Professor Weisbord would like to thank the following for their generosity: Harry Starr and the Lucius N. Littauer Foundation the University of Rhode Island Foundation and the URICAS Faculty Support Committee.

Debts of gratitude are also owed to Robert A. Hill of the Marcus Garvey Papers (UCLA); Herbert Aptheker, Robert De Rusha and Katherine Emerson, University Archivist (University of Massachusetts, Amherst) for their help with the W.E.B. Du Bois Papers; and D. Louise Cook, Director of the King Library and Archives at the Martin Luther King, Jr. Center for Nonviolent Social Change in Atlanta for making available the papers of the SCLC, CORE and SNCC.

We are also grateful to officials of the American Jewish Committee, the American Jewish Congress and the Anti-Defamation League. David Neft of Lou Harris and Associates was most helpful also.

I

Introduction

On the night of July 17, 1984, in the course of his highly dramatic, emotion-stirring address to the Democratic national convention in San Francisco, the Reverend Jesse Jackson issued what was clearly intended to be an apology to American Jews. If in the "low moments" of his campaign to capture the Democratic party's nomination for President of the United States, "in word, deed or attitude through some error of temper or tone, I have caused discomfort, created pain or revived someone's fears, that was not my truest self," he said. Blacks and Jews had shared a passion for social justice, but the two communities were now in "anguish, anger and pain." It was necessary for them to turn from "finger-pointing to clasped hands." He added: "We must turn to each other and not on each other and choose higher ground."[1] On the Middle East Jackson declared that the American government's formula for peace was unworkable. He implied that U.S. policy had been one-sided in support of Israel and that it had to be able to influence twenty-two Arab nations. On many previous occasions Jackson had acknowledged the justice of Palestinian claims for an independent state. His advocacy of Palestinian rights had long been a bone of contention between Jackson and the Jewish community.

The San Francisco speech climaxed a long campaign which had been marred by accusations that Jackson was personally guilty of anti-Semitism. There were counteraccusations by his supporters that Jackson had been the victim of racism on the part of Jews. All would agree that Jackson's bid to become his party's standard-bearer in 1984 had brought out into the open the disturbing issue of Black-Jewish tensions.

In 1970 *Bittersweet Encounter*, a study of the manifold relationships between American Blacks and American Jews, was published.[2] That study included instances both of cooperation and of conflict. Although the civil rights movement received disproportionate political, moral and financial backing from Jews decades before the freedom struggle moved into high gear in the 1950's and 1960's, relations between Blacks and Jews were not always cordial. In fact, they were as often bitter as they were sweet.

The 1970 book contained only one chapter on Blacks and the Middle East. At that juncture psychological factors, specific local conflicts (such as the New York City school strike) and unequal status encounters in the ghettos seemed much more crucial to an understanding of escalating tensions between the two minorities. In the Black community Jews were frequently associated with wealth and "parasitism." Under the least propitious circumstance, Blacks usually met Jews as storekeepers and landlords—the most visible representatives of an oppressive economic system. Such meetings were not likely to promote good will and mutual respect.[3]

With the passage of time, as Jews have moved further up the economic, social and political ladders, Jewish visibility in Harlem and other Black neighborhoods has declined. Nevertheless, a corpus of stereotypical notions about Jews remains. Differences over thorny new issues, such as affirmative action, and events in the always volatile Middle East have sometimes brought these to the surface.

Shrill criticism of Zionism and of Israel had been heard during and after the Six Day War of 1967, most emanating from Black Muslim and Black radical groups. The general euphoria that the Israeli victory engendered among Jews in the United States and the steadfast support for Israel from moderate, integrationist-oriented middle-class civil rights organizations neutralized the criticism and assuaged Jewish hurt. However, since 1967, at least insofar as Black leaders are concerned, the Arab-Israeli dispute has figured more prominently in the Black-Jewish estrangement which has been one regrettable concomitant of the fragmentation of liberal opinion in this country. The fraying of Black support for Israel and its connection with that estrangement are the major concerns of this volume.

Chapter II looks at the response of various late nineteenth- and early twentieth-century Black thinkers (most notably Edward Wilmot Blyden, W.E.B. Du Bois, Marcus Garvey and Booker T. Washington) to the fledgling political Zionist movement. Most saw that movement as worthy of emulation by Black Americans. They saw Jews as a kindred suffering people and Zionism as a model for liberation. The role of some Blacks (e.g., Ralph Bunche, Paul Robeson, Walter White and Du Bois) in the Zionist struggle to create a Jewish state in the aftermath of the Holocaust is also examined. It is a role that few Americans, Blacks or whites, are familiar with today.

Chapter III traces the varied reactions of Black Americans to three Arab-Israeli wars (the Suez campaign of 1956, the watershed Six Day War of 1967, and the Yom Kippur War of 1973) in addition to the United Nations equation of Zionism and racism in November 1975. Support for Israel from the mainstream civil rights leaders of the National Association for the Advancement of Colored People and the Urban League as well as Martin Luther King, Jr., is contrasted with strident opposition from Elijah Muhammad's Black Muslims, the Oakland-based Black Panthers and the Student Non-Violent Coordinating Committee. Although at first only the most radical Third World-oriented Blacks identified with the Palestinian struggle, by the late 1970's several mainstream Black leaders reconsidered their backing for Israel.

Chapter IV on "Black Hebrew Israelites and Other Non-Whites in Israel" examines the origins and beliefs of the Black nationalist "sect" that migrated to Liberia and thence to Israel in the late 1960's. Very little has been written about this unusual group of expatriates even though their presence in Israel has stirred enough controversy to gain them special recognition among prominent Black leaders. Therefore close attention is given in this book to the friction that developed between the Black Hebrew Israelites and the Israeli government and Black American involvement in the dispute. Was that friction due to racism on the part of the Israeli government and populace? By looking not just at the Black Hebrew Israelites but at the experiences of Falashas (Ethiopian Jews) and other dark-skinned people in the Jewish state, an answer may be given to this provocative question.

In Chapter V the authors analyze the "normalization" of relations between the Republic of South Africa and the State of Israel in the 1970's and the corrosive effects this has had on Black American-Jewish American cooperation in the United States. Israel's ties with Black African countries, links between Arab and African nations and South Africa and alleged Israeli military and nuclear collaboration with the apartheid regime are a few of the subjects treated in this chapter.

Chapter VI deals with the 1979 events surrounding the forced resignation of Andrew Young as U.S. ambassador to the United Nations after he held an unauthorized meeting with the Palestine Liberation Organization (PLO) representative at the world body. The extent to which Zionist and American Jewish influence may have brought about the resignation will be gauged, and the degree to which Israel's standing among Black Americans was consequently eroded will be studied. Bound up with the highly charged controversy over Black immersion in the Middle East quagmire is the equally emotional domestic dispute over "quotas," which put Jews and Blacks at loggerheads.

Chapter VII chronicles the deepening involvement of American Blacks in the Middle East. It specifically looks at Black missions, led by Jesse Jackson and by Joseph Lowery and Walter Fauntroy of the Southern Christian Leadership Conference, to that troubled region. Several myths that surround another Black mission, this one to Libya and supposedly headed by a former aide to Dr. King, the Reverend Hosea Williams, are punctured. In 1980 in a period when Israel's stock was not very high in Afro-America and the old Black-Jewish alliance was in tatters, the redoubtable Moshe Dayan voiced a gratuitous slur against Blacks in the American armed services. That indiscretion and the furious response it elicited from Blacks in this country are also investigated. While Dayan spoke only for himself, his remark would have shocked and keenly disappointed those Black thinkers of previous generations for whom the Jewish people and the Zionist enterprise were deserving of high esteem.

NOTES

1. For the full text of the Jackson speech see the *Congressional Quarterly Weekly Report*, 42, no. 29, (21 July 1984): pp. 1785–1789.

2. Robert G. Weisbord and Arthur Stein, *Bittersweet Encounter: The Afro-American and the American Jew* (Westport, Conn.: Negro Universities Press, 1970).

3. In some cities, New Orleans and Newark to mention just two, Italian-Black relations were acrimonious for similar reasons. Of late, "exploitative" Korean merchants in Harlem have aroused the ire of Afro-Americans, some of whom have responded with "buy Black" campaigns and organized boycotts of the Korean businesses. And in Detroit, Arab grocers, mostly Iraqui Christians, have experienced picketing by Blacks who denounced profiteering outsiders. Burning and looting occurred in 1983 following the killing of a Black youth by an Arab storekeeper. Antagonism to the Arabs in Detroit was rooted in the frustrations Blacks feel when confronted by the more rapid economic progress made by first and second generation immigrants. Black hostility to the Iraquis in the Motor City is strikingly similar to that directed at the Jews in Gotham and elsewhere. See Abdeen Jabara and Noel J. Saleh, "Blacks and Iraquis Collide in Detroit," *Freedomways*, 23, no. 3 (1983): 182–183.

II

"That Marvellous Movement":
Early Black Views of Zionism

Even after the conclusion of the American Civil War, which brought political freedom to approximately four million bondsmen, most Blacks in the street or more commonly on the plantation had very little time to contemplate foreign affairs. Whether living in the North or the South, they were too preoccupied with the physical and emotional survival of themselves and their families in a hostile and racially prejudiced environment. Reparations in the form of forty acres and a mule for each ex-slave had been proposed but never delivered. Consequently, acquiring even the most basic necessities of life was a formidable, all-consuming task.

Yet, a few Black intellectuals and leaders were well aware of developments overseas in Africa, Europe and the Middle East, and some commented on obscure movements with what seemed to be only tenuous connections with the pressing realities of Black Americans. Zionism, which aimed at the establishment of a homeland for dispersed Jews in Palestine, their ancient homeland from which most had been expelled almost two millennia before, was one such movement. Jews drew the attention of some Black thinkers who had been raised on the Old Testament and saw a parallel between the enslavement and continuing travail of the "chosen people" and their own tragic history of thralldom and oppression. For some other Blacks the durable Jewish ethnic consciousness and Zionism's repatriationist answer to the questions of survival suggested paradigms for transplanted Africans in the Americas.

One nineteenth-century Black luminary, Edward Wilmot Blyden, fit into both categories. Born in St. Thomas in the Virgin Islands in 1832, Blyden enjoyed a remarkable multifaceted career. He was a true *uomo universale*, a Renaissance man. Blyden, who immigrated to West Africa in 1851, was an editor, a prodigious writer of books and pamphlets, an extraordinary linguist, a professor of classics, secretary of state of the newly established republic of Liberia, Liberian ambassador to the Court of St. James, and president of Liberia College. In addition, he was a Pan-Negro patriot and an apostle of diasporan Black repatriation to Africa. In the informed opinion of his biographer, Hollis Lynch, he was "easily the most learned and articulate champion of Africa and the Negro race in his own time."[1]

Blyden's curiosity about and attraction to Jews was at least partly traceable to his boyhood in Danish St. Thomas, where a majority of the white population was Jewish at the time. It was there that he became familiar with Jewish festivals and traditions. It was also there that he was first exposed to the Hebrew tongue. One of young Blyden's most ardent desires was to master Hebrew so that he could read the Old Testament and the Talmud in that ancient language.[2]

In 1866 Blyden spent three months visiting Lebanon, Syria and Palestine. Peripatetic by nature, he had developed a yearning to travel to "the original home of the Jews—to see Jerusalem and Mt. Zion, the joy of the whole earth."[3] He was deeply moved by his initial glimpse of Jerusalem and was particularly touched by the Western Wall, the holiest Jewish site in that holy city.

The sizeable Jewish population which then resided in Jerusalem and had done so for centuries was clearly a religious community bereft of political aspirations. At that period in history, political Zionism was only in embryonic form and was fated to be stillborn.[4] In 1862, four years before Blyden's journey, Rabbi Zvi Hirsch Kalischer, who lived under Prussian rule, had published a book entitled *Derishat Zion* (Seeking Zion). A classic in Zionist literature, that book meticulously outlined a program that would facilitate the purchase of villages, fields and vineyards in the land of the Bible. Kalischer also envisioned the organization of self-defense units to protect colonists from hostile Bedouins and the creation of an agricultural school to teach inexperienced Jewish youth the skills of farming.[5]

That same year Moses Hess, another pioneer Zionist, expounded his theory of Jewish nationalism in *Rome and Jerusalem*, which was also destined to become a fundamental document in Zionist annals.[6] Influenced by the various nationalist movements which were sweeping across Europe and stung by the persistence of anti-Semitism, Hess saw the Jewish future bound up with Palestine and became convinced that the political rebirth of the Jewish nation would be precipitated by the founding of Jewish colonies there. But the cries of the proto-Zionists, Kalischer and Hess, fell on deaf ears. European Jews pinned their hopes either on assimilation as a panacea or on an age-old messianic dream of divine redemption. As a general rule, Jews who travelled to Palestine in the nineteenth century went there to die, to be interred in holy soil, rather than to live and build a Jewish nation.

In point of fact, Blyden in the 1860's and 1870's was much more of a Zionist than most Jews. He advocated Jewish settlement in Palestine, a phenomenon which, in his judgment, would not have an adverse effect on the Arabs. Blyden reproved the sons of Abraham for remaining in the Diaspora and for not migrating to their ancient homeland, which the Ottoman Turks were misgoverning.[7] His words advising Jews to repatriate themselves, which were penned in 1873, would warm the hearts of today's frustrated Jewish Agency officials as they labor, frequently in vain, to promote immigration to Israel.

By the final decades of the nineteenth century, the recrudescence of anti-Semitism, both in Russia following the assassination of Czar Alexander II in 1881 and in western Europe (most notably in France and Germany), had led to a rebirth of political Zionism. Zionist associations had planted colonies in Palestine, and Theodor Herzl, a Vienna-based journalist, had emerged as the prime mover and central personality of the rejuvenated movement. In 1896 Herzl published his landmark volume, *The Jewish State*, which underlined the hopelessness of assimilation as a solution to the ubiquitous Jewish problem and offered nationhood as a viable alternative. Instead of being a vulnerable minority devoid of power and subject to the ravages of anti-Semitism, Jews would have a country of their own where they would constitute a power-wielding majority of the population.

The following year, 1897, 196 delegates from a score of nations and representing world Jewry gathered in Basle, Switzerland, to analyze the plight of the Jews and to forge a plan to guide Jewish destiny. One can argue that that first world Zionist Congress established the *national* character of the Jews. Without any doubt, it created a permanent international Zionist organization, the instrument which was to breathe life into a Jewish nation in Palestine in just half a century.

Blyden's response to Herzlian Zionism was set forth in *The Jewish Question*, published in 1898, the year after the Basle conclave. That twenty-four page booklet, avidly philo-Semitic and philo-Zionist, was dedicated to Louis Solomon, a Jewish acquaintance of Blyden's from his residence in West Africa. Blyden was familiar with Herzl's *Jewish State* and predicted that it propounded ideas which "have given such an impetus to the real work of the Jews as will tell with enormous effect upon their future history."[8] Blyden also commented on the powerful influence of the "tidal wave from Vienna—that inspiration almost Mosaic in its originality and in its tendency, which drew crowds of Israelites to Basle in August 1897...and again in 1898."[9]

Blyden, the Pan-Africanist, recognized Herzl's efforts to ingather the Jews as analogous to his own activities to effect a selective return of Afro-Americans to their fatherland. No wonder then that he described Zionism as "that marvellous movement"[10] and indicated his backing for a Jewish nation. If conditions were propitious in Palestine, the Jewish nation could be located there. Blyden was of the opinion that "There is hardly a man in the civilized world—Christian, Mohammedan, or Jew who does not recognize the claim and right of the Jew to the Holy Land."[11] His enthusiasm for Zionism was unbridled and he declared that there were very few "who, if the conditions were favorable would not be glad to see them return in a body and take their place in the land of their fathers as a great—a leading secular power."[12] Zionist pioneers were no less mistaken in expecting a warm welcome from the Arab inhabitants in Zion; but, it must be recalled, that Arab nationalism was in its infancy at the turn of the century.

If conditions were not favorable in Palestine, the Jewish nation could be built somewhere else. In not limiting Zionism's field of operations exclusively to Palestine, Blyden was echoing the sentiments of "territorialists" such as the

Russian-born Leo Pinsker. Pinsker, in 1882, had writen a pamphlet called *Auto-Emancipation* in which he argued that "The goal of our present endeavors must not be the 'Holy Land' but a land of our own. We need nothing but a large piece of land for our poor brothers; a piece of land which shall remain our property from which no foreign master can expel us."[13]

Geography was not crucial in Blyden's thoughts about Zionism. He was convinced that the Jewish destiny was not just to establish "a political power in one corner of the earth" but to achieve something far nobler. To the Jews had been "entrusted the spiritual hegemony of mankind."[14] He felt that Jews, along with people of African descent, were specially qualified to be spiritual leaders of a materialistic world by virtue of their heritage of suffering and sorrow. With this in mind he invited Jews to go to Africa. "Africa appeals to the Jew . . . to come with his scientific and other culture, gathered by his exile in many lands, and with his special spiritual endowments," he wrote in 1898.[15]

In a fascinating espisode this quixotic notion was almost fulfilled in 1903 when the British government offered the Zionist Congress territory in Kenya for developing a Jewish colony. The offer came at a time of deteriorating conditions in Russia, where the largest masses of downtrodden Jews dwelled. Acquisition of a haven was imperative. If Palestine were unavailable, some other place might have to do, at least temporarily. In addition to this humanitarian consideration, Herzl also understood the diplomatic advantage of not rejecting the British offer out of hand. With an international superpower such as Britain treating the Zionist movement as the spokesman for world Jewry, Herzl's concept of Jewish nationhood stood closer than ever to realization. A Britain committed to aiding the Zionists would have to provide a substitute for East Africa if the proffered territory there proved to be unsuitable and a Zionist-sponsored commission dispatched to Kenya found it seriously deficient. Palestinocentric Jews had from the start regarded even temporary conditional acceptance of East Africa as tantamount to treason and the acrimonious dispute over East Africa which ensued made necessary a tormenting reappraisal of the Zionist movement. By 1905 the offer was finally declined, and the Zionists were resolutely determined to found a Jewish state in Palestine and only in Palestine.[16]

Most prominent Black contemporaries of Blyden's did not share his Pan-Negro fervor or his African orientation. One who emphatically rejected back-to-Africanism in favor of a stay-at-home philosophy was Booker T. Washington. For at least twenty years, from 1895 when he delivered his famous Atlanta Exposition address until his death, Booker Taliaferro Washington was the best-known Black in white America. So great was the celebrity of Booker T. that, although he had been born a slave in western Virginia in 1856, he was asked to dine with Theodore Roosevelt in the White House (only once, however, because of the racist howls of protest) and invited to take tea with the venerable Queen Victoria. His path to fame was a torturous one. As a youngster he suffered numerous privations and often lacked the most basic necessities of life. He had to toil in saltworks but was determined to teach himself the alphabet and later managed, despite much hardship, to obtain an education at Hampton Institute. In 1881 with financial help from the Alabama state legislature, he founded Tuskegee Institute, which he headed for three and a half decades.

At a time of deteriorating conditions for Blacks, when racism was reaching its zenith, Washington, at least in public, exemplified the philosophy of accommodationism, of avoiding direct confrontations with the white power structure. In his 1895 Atlanta speech he appeared to accept the inevitability of racial segregation and described his aggrieved brethren as "the most patient, faithful, law abiding and unresentful people the world has ever seen."[17] Rightly or wrongly, later generations of Black Americans came to view Washington's posture as a cringing and groveling one, hardly appropriate at a time when Blacks were being disfranchised, Jim Crowed and lynched.

From childhood, Washington, like countless other Blacks weaned on Scripture, had a "special and peculiar interest in the history and progress of the Jewish race."[18] He frequently drew parallels between the tragic histories of Jews and Blacks. Speaking to a biracial audience in Little Rock, Arkansas, in 1905, he opined that ignorance and racial hatred had never solved a single problem and cautioned his Black listeners not to become discouraged or despondent because conditions for Blacks were becoming worse. "In Russia there are one-half as many Jews as there are Negroes in this country and yet I feel sure that within a month more Jews have been persecuted and killed than the whole number of our people who have been lynched during the past forty years." However, this was no excuse for lynchings, he added.[19] Even if Booker T.'s statistics about the victims of pogroms in czarist Russia were accurate, the comparison must have provided cold comfort to Afro-Americans. For in the "land of the free and the home of the brave," 60 Blacks were lynched in the year 1905 alone and from 1889 through 1905 lynch mobs claimed no fewer than 1,707 Black victims.[20]

Washington believed that salvation for Black Americans would be achieved through thrift and hard work. Racial solidarity would also contribute to Black progress, and Jews, Booker T. argued, could serve as a model in this respect. "There is, perhaps, no race that has suffered so much, not so much in America as in some of the countries in Europe. But these people have clung together. They have had a certain amount of unity, pride and love of race," he commented in 1899. He then prophesied, correctly as future events were to demonstrate, that Jews would become more and more influential in the United States, "a country where they were once despised and looked upon with scorn and derision." Booker T. admonished Blacks to follow the Jewish race in developing faith in themselves. Unless the Black learned to imitate Jews in this respect, he wrote, he could not expect to achieve a high degree of success.[21]

More than a decade later, after observing the Jewish condition in diverse locales—in London's East End, in Denmark, Germany and Austria, in the Russian Pale of Settlement and in the ghettos of Poland—Washington reiterated the same theme. In a 1901 manuscript for an article, he wrote that, prejudice and persecution notwithstanding, the Jew was advancing largely by dint of education.

Jews had struggled to the point where they occupied positions of power and enjoyed preeminence in civilization. Washington concluded that the "Negro has much to learn from the Jew."[22]

Undoubtedly, Washington knew about modern political Zionism, but he apparently did not take it very seriously. Perhaps he hoped that the Jewish community, the ethnic model to be emulated, would not take it very seriously. When he was asked in 1910 if there was any back-to-Africa movement among Afro-Americans comparable to the Zionist movement, Booker T. chuckled and replied: "I think it is with the African pretty much as it is with the Jews, there is a good deal of talk about it, but nothing is done, there is certainly no sign of any exodus to Liberia."[23] Washington was acutely aware of the repatriationist enterprises of Bishop Henry McNeal Turner, the leading apostle of back-to-Africanism in the 1890's and early 1900's,[24] but he could "see no way out of the Negro's present condition in the South by returning to Africa."[25] Washington, who never once visited the African homeland of his forefathers although he found ample time for several trips to Europe, preferred a future for Blacks in the United States where a satisfactory racial adjustment would have to be made. Given his staunch opposition to emigration as a solution to the "Negro problem," his disinterest in Zionism was predictable.

As far as Zionism was concerned, Washington's flippant remark about Jews paying only lip service to it was a half-truth. Virtually no *American* Jews were sailing to Palestine. In 1910 most Jewish inhabitants of the United States had just arrived from Eastern Europe during the previous two or three decades. On the other hand, the same despair born of resurgent anti-Semitism and chronic poverty, which had prompted in excess of a million and a half Jews to forsake the Czar's realms for western Europe and the New World, furnished the impetus for the Second *Aliyah*. *Aliyah*, which literally means "ascension," refers to waves of immigration to Palestine. The Second Aliyah, stimulated in part by the unsuccessful Russian revolution in 1905 and the concurrent pogroms, was well underway when Booker T. casually dismissed Zionism as a remedy for Jewish ills. It brought to Palestine many of those Socialist Zionist idealists who would begin to transform the Zionist vision into reality. Those adventurous *chalutzim* (pioneers) were destined to become Israel's establishment, the power elite in the future Jewish state, and the fruits of their labor—Zionist ideology (e.g., the kibbutzim, the moshavim and the Histadrut [labor federation])—are still vital elements in Israel today.

Booker T. Washington died in 1915 during the carnage of World War I. It was in the midst of that global cataclysm that political Zionism won an important diplomatic victory. Britain was eager to mobilize Jewish opinion in support of the Allied cause. With the new Bolshevik regime extricating itself from the sanguinary morass of the war, Jewish influence in the Soviet Union could be beneficial, or so Britain's Prime Minister David Lloyd George thought. If properly cultivated, American Zionist sentiment could also prove useful in stimulating the war effort. Therefore, in November 1917 British Foreign Minister Arthur

James Balfour, who not coincidentally also had a lifelong interest in Jews and a profound admiration for their culture, issued his famous declaration. In a letter to Lord Rothschild, a member of the fabulously wealthy and prestigious international banking family and a leader of British Jewry, Balfour asserted:

His Majesty's Government view with favour the establishment in Palestine of a national home for the Jewish people, and will use their best endeavours to facilitate the achievement of this object, it being clearly understood that nothing shall be done which may prejudice the civil and religious rights of existing non-Jewish communities in Palestine, or the rights and political status enjoyed by Jews in any other country.[26]

At that point in history, few people realized that Balfour's promise of a national home for the Jews conflicted both with the 1915 McMahon-Hussein agreement, which the British arranged to incite Arab opposition to the Ottoman empire, and with the Sykes-Picot agreement allocating Ottoman territory to France, Russia and Britain. For the Zionists the Balfour Declaration, which was subsequently incorporated in the League of Nations mandate for Palestine, was a solemn pledge to the Jewish people. For the Arabs it was treacherous, duplicitous and illegal. Thus, the seeds of future Middle Eastern conflict were sown during the Great War. Racial strife in the United States dramatically intensified during and right after the war. While Black troops were in Europe fighting to make the world safe for democracy, lynchings continued unabated in the United States; and race riots, which were actually pogroms against Black communities, occurred with unprecedented fury and frequency.

In those racially troubled times, the Black titan W.E.B. Du Bois emerged as a champion of Zionism as well as a tireless fighter for racial justice in this country. Even before the advent of World War I, Du Bois was a towering figure whose intellect and dedication to the cause of racial equality inspired hope in oppressed Black America and fear and awe in white America. Born in Great Barrington, Massachusetts, in 1868, Du Bois had a legendary career as both scholar and activist that spanned almost a century of turbulent racial history. Educated at Fisk University and the University of Berlin, Du Bois later earned a Ph.D. from Harvard University. Until his death in Ghana in 1963, his scholarly output was enormous. It included historical treatises, incisive sociological studies and essays on all the important issues of his day. But Du Bois' unflagging efforts as a crusader for first-class citizenship for the Black American at least equalled and probably surpassed in importance his academic accomplishments. In pursuit of that lofty and elusive goal, he relentlessly assailed the ears of his countrymen decade after decade. He worked to end lynchings and the humiliation of Jim Crowism. Even before the dawn of the twentieth century, his militant equalitarian philosophy was offered to Black Americans as a viable alternative to Booker T. Washington's racial accommodationism, which he found demeaning and subversive of Black manhood. Du Bois deserves much of the credit for founding the National Association for the Advancement of Colored People (NAACP) in

1910, and he was a driving force behind the Pan-African movement, which concerned itself with the plight of subjugated people of African descent on the African continent and in the far-flung African dispersion.

With the public disclosure of the Balfour Declaration, Du Bois recognized in the exertions of the Zionists a program and a policy that could possibly hasten the liberation of Africa. Africa's future, specifically the destiny of former German-controlled Africa, was to be determined after the armistice of November 1918. Du Bois dreamt of an independent free central African state which minimally would be carved out of German East Africa and the Belgian Congo.[27] If the triumphant Entente powers took into account the wishes of Blacks in Africa and those elsewhere, the victors would be given an "effective weapon" militating against restoration of African colonies to the vanquished Germans.[28] Alas, Du Bois and his Pan-African cohorts lacked the diplomatic leverage to persuade the Versailles peacemakers to sanction a Black African counterpart to the Balfour Declaration.[29]

Du Bois' ideas about the parallel between modern political Zionism and Pan-Africanism were tersely summarized in the *Crisis*, the organ of the NAACP, which he edited. Appearing as an editorial in February 1919, when Du Bois himself was in France to organize a crucial Pan-African conference, it stated:

The African movement means to us what the Zionist movement must mean to the Jews, the centralization of race effort and the recognition of a racial fount. To help bear the burden of Africa does not mean any lessening of effort in our problems at home. Rather it means increased interest. For any ebullition of action and feeling that results in an amelioration of the lot of Africa tends to ameliorate the conditions of colored peoples throughout the world. And no man liveth unto himself.[30]

Du Bois' philo-Zionism should not be seen simply as a political strategy. Nor was it an isolated, haphazard, fleeting thought. It was in keeping with his general sympathy for the liberation struggles of persecuted peoples around the globe.

As a student in Europe in the 1890's, Du Bois encountered the virulent bacillus of anti-Semitism in Germany and Poland and came to develop a genuine appreciation of Zionism as a solution to the Jewish problem. That appreciation ripened with the passing years and fully flowered following the Holocaust. In the intervening decades Du Bois closely monitored developments in Palestine under the British mandate.

Even in the pages of *The Brownie's Book*, a monthly magazine for Afro-American children which Du Bois started in 1919–1920, there were several selections dealing with the progress of Zionism. In the very first issue of that periodical, he directed the attention of young Black readers to the new Jewish state which was planned in the ancient Holy Land, " 'round about Jerusalem."[31] Eight months later he informed his juvenile readership that a "great Zionist congress of the Jews is meeting in London." Du Bois was particularly struck by proposals to "tax the Jews all over the world for the support of the new

Jewish government in Palestine."[32] In January 1921 he observed that blueprints for a Hebrew university on the biblical Mount of Olives in Jerusalem had been completed and remarked on urban planning in the "new Palestine."[33]

For Du Bois, imperial Britain, which had plundered Africa after the unjustified partition of the "dark continent," was the bête noire, or bête blanche, to be more precise. England retained many colonies by fostering religious and national jealousies and then presiding as a benevolent arbitrator, Du Bois wrote in his "As the Crow Flies" column published in the *Crisis*. He was speculating about the reason for what he described as the "murder of Jews by Arabs in Palestine" in 1929.[34] Tensions between Arab and Jew had smoldered for some time because of disagreement over access to the Western Wall in Jerusalem. In August defenseless Jews were massacred in Hebron and Safed by "ruthless and bloodthirsty evil-doers," as the malefactors were characterized by the British high commissioner.[35] That violence was but a foretaste of the bloodletting to come.

Zionism's trials and tribulations had also caught the eye of another important Black leader, a bitter rival of Du Bois', the redoubtable Marcus Garvey. In 1916, the year before the Balfour Declaration was issued, Garvey arrived in the United States. Although the Jamaican-born Garvey had been inspired by Booker T. Washington's autobiography, *Up From Slavery*, his own solution to the various problems that beset Black folk was very different from that of the sage of Tuskegee. Garvey arrived, armed with a Pan-Negroist/Black nationalist ideology that was to captivate millions of Blacks on the mother continent as well as in the African diaspora. In the course of a few years he was to build what the Black historian John Hope Franklin was to characterize as the "first and only really mass movement among Negroes in the United States."[36]

The era was a favorable one for his Black nationalist crusade. It coincided with an influx of West Indians, who comprised the nucleus of Garvey's Universal Negro Improvement Association (UNIA). Moreover, Afro-Americans who had migrated by the hundreds of thousands form the rural South to the urban North expecting a dramatic improvement in their fortunes, if not a racial utopia, were sadly disillusioned. They quickly discovered that discrimination in employment and housing knew no regional boundaries, and racial violence was commonplace in the frigid North.

Garvey's philosophy of race pride could raise their hopes, lift their spirits and reinvigorate their sagging self-esteem. Long before the slogan "black is beautiful" became *de rigeur*, Garvey preached the concept that Americans of African descent need not feel ashamed, not of their pigmentation nor of their heritage.

Day in and day out Garvey advocated the cause of self-determination for Africans, both those at home in Africa and those abroad. Africa was then controlled almost entirely by European colonialists. Garvey argued that it had to be transformed into a "Negro Empire where every Black man, whether he was born in Africa or in the Western world, will have the opportunity to develop on his own lines under the protection of the most favorable democratic institutions."[37]

In Garvey's view, which was strikingly similar to those of the political Zionists regarding Jews in the *galut* (dispersion), Blacks living as minorities in the New World faced bleak futures. Outside the confines of the land of their forefathers, "ruin and disaster" awaited Africans. Therefore, Garvey urged that Africa's dispersed and mistreated sons and daughters be restored to her. The stocky, ebony-skinned Jamaican asserted that Africa was the "legitimate, moral and righteous home of all Negroes,"[38] but he did not favor an immediate, wholesale repatriation. Even if the wherewithal were available, it would take half a century to largely depopulate the United States. Every Black was not wanted anyway. Lazy ones and those lacking self-reliance, for example, were not desired. Those whom Garvey wished to see immigrate to Africa were the adventurous and industrious Blacks, such as the members of his UNIA whose goal was an independent nationality. They numbered six million, Garvey claimed.

Even the stay-at-homes, those Blacks who remained outside of Africa, would benefit from the redemption of Africa. Garvey's widow, Amy Jacques Garvey, explained it this way: "Garvey saw Africa as a *nation* to which the African peoples of the world could look for help and support, moral and physical, when ill-treated or abused for being black."[39] Garveyite rhetoric here virtually duplicates that of the Zionists who argue to this day that a strong Jewish state enhances the security of Jews still in exile.

As a back-to-Africanist, Garvey failed. In 1924 he was conspicuously unsuccessful in his bid to establish settlements in Liberia. The next year the would-be Black Moses began to serve a prison term meted out to him following his conviction for using the U.S. mails to defraud investors in one of his Black nationalist commercial enterprises, the Black Star Steamship Line. His remaining days in this country were to be spent in a federal penitentiary in Georgia. After his sentence was commuted in 1927, he was deported to his native Jamaica as an undesirable alien, never to set foot in the United States again.

Throughout his checkered career Garvey was fond of pointing out the analogies between his brand of Black nationalism and other nationalisms, specifically those of the Irish, the East Indians, the Egyptians and the Jews. For example, in July 1920 Garvey told a UNIA meeting that Blacks in the aftermath of World War I were a new people: "A new spirit, a new courage, has come to us simultaneously as it came to other peoples of the world. It came to us at the same time it came to the Jew. When the Jew said 'We shall have Palestine!' the same sentiment came to us when we said 'We shall have Africa!' "[40]

William H. Ferris, a leading Garveyite who was both an educator and a journalist, repeated this analogy before the same gathering:

Our position in civilization for the last three hundred years has been the same position which the Jews have occupied during the past 2500 years. The Jews have been scattered all over the world and been suppressed by one race and then another. But the Jews have now realized that it is necessary for them to build up an empire and a republic in their native land of Palestine. In this stage of the world's history it is necessary for the Negro to build up some sort of republic and empire in Liberia so that there will be some land which he can call his own.[41]

Although Garvey and many of his disciples felt an affinity for Zionism, he sometimes displayed his pique over the shabby treatment accorded Black nationalism compared with other nationalist movements. Speaking in London in 1928, he lamented the fact that when the Versailles peacemakers distributed the spoils of war: "You gave to the Jew, Palestine; you gave to the Egyptians, a large modicum of self-government; you gave to the Irish Home Rule Government and Dominion status; you gave the Poles a new Government of their own." When he inquired rhetorically what had been given to the Negro, an anonymous voice rang out from the throng gathered at London's Royal Albert Hall: "Nothing."[42] It is clear though that Garvey's animosity was not directed at either the Zionists and the Egyptian nationalists or the Polish patriots and the Irish home rulers but at Britain and the other European powers which denied Africans the right to their continent.

Garveyite philo-Zionism was sometimes reciprocated. Louis Michael, a Jew from Los Angeles, sent the UNIA a telegram in August 1920 which read as follows: "As a Jew, a Zionist and a Socialist I join heartily and unflinchingly in your historical movement for the reclamation of Africa. There is no justice and no peace in the world until the Jew and the Negro both control side by side Palestine and Africa."[43]

Garvey and Garveyism stirred the curiosity of much of the Yiddish press in the United States; and they received accolades from pro-Zionist Yiddish newspapers (such as the *Morgen Journal* and the *Tageblatt*), which saw the UNIA as a kindred nationalist undertaking. Those publications sometimes applied Zionist nomenclature to Garvey's movement. To cite just one illustration, his anthem, "Ethiopia—Thou Land of Our Fathers," which had been composed by Arnold Ford, a West Indian-born Black rabbi and Garvey apostle, was dubbed "The Negro Hatikvah." "Hatikvah" or "Hope" was the Zionist anthem and is now the national anthem of Israel.[44]

Despite his support for Zionism, an example which he urged his followers to emulate, Garvey harbored ambivalent feelings about Jews. He believed that it was the Jews' obsession with money that was the root of their difficulties in Germany and later in Palestine.[45] He subscribed to more than one unflattering stereotype of Jews and had been guilty of anti-Semitic utterances at his trial over which a Jewish jurist, Judge Julian Mack, had presided. But to label him as an anti-Semite is to be guilty of gross oversimplification.

Initially, at least, Garvey seems not to have recognized the dangers posed by Adolf Hitler's accession to power. In this respect the Jamaican was not unique. Garvey admired the Fuhrer as a German patriot and a fervent nationalist, but he realized Hitler had outrageously mistreated the Jews and was antagonistic toward Blacks.[46] In 1935 Garvey prophesied that it was only a matter of time before the Jews destroyed Nazi Germany as they had allegedly destroyed Russia. "Jewish finance is a powerful world factor,'' Garvey observed and added, ''It can destroy men, organizations and nations.''[47] Yet, in the pages of *The Blackman*, his monthly journal published for a short while in Jamaica and then beginning in the spring of 1935 in London, Garvey frequently expressed his sympathy for Jews as a despised and oppressed minority.[48] As he had done years before in his American heyday, he lauded their efforts to rebuild their Zion in Palestine. Praise was due the Jews because they recognized the ''only safe thing to do is to go after and establish racial autonomy.'' So wrote the Black Moses in 1936.[49]

By 1936 Palestine was in turmoil. There was rioting and sporadic fighting, which claimed both Arab and Jewish lives. Hitlerite persecution had escalated *aliyah* from Germany and Austria, and certain Palestinian Arab leaders voiced strenuous objections. A general strike, which aimed at terminating the immigration of Jews and halting the further purchase of land by them, was called. It too was marked by bloodshed.

Faced with a rapidly worsening state of affairs, the British appointed a commission of inquiry, one of several which sought to no avail to reconcile conflicting Jewish and Arab aspirations in the Holy Land. In their report made public in July 1937, the so-called Peel Commission advocated that the country be partitioned into a British mandatory zone, an Arab state and a Jewish state. Arab opinion overwhelmingly opposed partition; but the Zionists were divided, some believing that half a loaf was better than none.

Writing from Britain, in the twilight of his career, Garvey admonished the Jews not to throw away their opportunity to establish a state of their own. What was important was not the size of a Jewish state but the chance to have an independent government that could enjoy diplomatic and economic relations with other nations. Garvey speculated that the Black man's case for a country might be strengthened by the success of the Jewish cause. In Garvey's judgment the Negro had even ''more right to a free state of his own in Africa than the Jew in Palestine;'' and Black unwillingness to line up behind the UNIA the way Jews supported Zionism, explained why the world did not take the Black seriously.[50]

Territorial compromise, as recommended by the Peel Commission, did not bring peace to Palestine. Arab-Jewish frictions did not diminish in the late 1930's as ominous war clouds gathered over Europe and the plight of German Jewry was further aggravated. In May 1939 publication of the British ''White Paper'' dealt a cruel blow to Zionist hopes. At the very moment when the need for a refuge was most desperate, the British, in response to Arab agitation, decided to curtail Jewish immigration into Palestine. Only seventy-five thousand Jews would be admitted over a five-year period. Jewish land purchases were to be restricted as well. British policy in Palestine on the eve of World War II, which was clearly calculated to mollify the Arabs, had the tragic effect of denying sanctuary to untold numbers of Jewish refugees in flight from Nazism.

Whereas an influx of Jews into Palestine would have heightened tensions in that troubled land and added to the herculean British task of maintaining the peace, diverting a productive white population to British Guiana would have strengthened the British position there. Consequently, Prime Minister Neville Chamberlain announced in May 1939 that his government would contemplate the settlement of Jewish refugees in that South American colony. Garvey reacted with alacrity and anger. In this instance, Black rights were being subordinated to those of Jews. British Guiana was a "Negro country," Garvey exclaimed, a description with which the sizeable East Indian community would have vehemently disagreed. Jews had no claim on Guiana, and their presence there would only serve to turn Blacks and Jews into enemies. The correct goal for Jews was a Jewish nation but not in Guiana, which Garvey insisted was the property of Blacks. At that juncture Garvey was so incensed by the Guiana plan and so irritated by what he perceived as British concern with Jews that he commented that an injustice had been done the Arab in Palestine. Ostensibly, Garvey's endorsement of Zionism was predicated on the notion that Zionism's chief value was as a model for victimized diaspora Blacks to copy.[51] When it appeared to preempt Black rights, it earned his animosity. In June 1940 Garvey died in London in relative obscurity. As for Guiana, it never materialized as a refuge for Jews. Indeed precious few havens were available at that critical juncture in the history of the Jews. After Hitler's army invaded Poland on September 1, 1939, it grew increasingly difficult for Jews to escape. The lives of millions, especially those dwelling in eastern Europe, were imperilled by the Fuhrer's mad racial schemes.

Early in 1941 W.E.B. Du Bois wrote that American Jews were proposing to raise millions of dollars for Palestine, "the only refuge that the harassed Jewry of Europe had today." Although Jews didn't really believe in segregation, they were going to make segregation in Palestine both possible and profitable and simultaneously work for an unsegregated humanity. In the process Zionism was providing Blacks who believed "someone else is going to do our fighting for us" with a constructive lesson in self-help. It is regrettable that during the war the Zionists were incapable of opening the gates of Palestine to those few harassed European Jews who managed to slip through the Nazi grip.[52]

When the war ended in 1945, a stunned world learned the grisly truth about the Holocaust which dramatized, as no event in modern history has, the necessity for a Jewish homeland. Hitler had unwittingly convinced skeptics of the logic of Zionism. The converts included most Diaspora Jews who, until then, had been lukewarm at best and downright hostile at worst towards the Zionist movement.

World War II had also dealt a serious blow to the British empire. After 1945 Britain was more favorably disposed to relinquish parts of the empire, particularly when they were costly and troublesome, owing to local agitation for independence. Palestine was a case in point. Arab-Jewish strife had not vanished miraculously. In fact, as the Jewish claim for unlimited immigration to Palestine by Holocaust survivors grew more raucous, Arabs felt still more threatened.

By 1947 Britain, caught between the conflicting claims of Arab and Jew, was not just willing to depart from Palestine. It was eager to leave and consequently presented its dilemma to the young United Nations. The plan eventually adopted by the United Nations called for the partition of Palestine into an independent sovereign Jewish state and an independent sovereign Arab state. There was to be a third entity: an international zone under United Nations trust which would encompass Jerusalem and its suburbs, including Bethlehem. Despite vociferous Arab objections to the plan, which they deemed unfair and unworkable, the General Assembly voted for it as a means of reconciling the seemingly irreconcilable national aspirations of the two peoples. Support from two-thirds of the members voting was necessary for approval. Only frantic eleventh-hour lobbying by Zionist sympathizers made possible the thirty-three for, thirteen against, ten abstention vote.[53]

One Afro-American who was lobbied intensively and heavy-handedly by advocates of partition was Walter White, the very fair-skinned executive director of the NAACP. Zionists hoped that White could persuade two Black nations, Haiti and Liberia, to reverse their previously announced anti-partition stance. In his autobiography White recounted his doubts about both the "wisdom and practicability" of dividing the territory in dispute. But no other feasible solution had been advanced. As an unflagging believer in racial integration, White "did not like the self-segregation of Zionism, nor...approve of the attitude of many Jews who had made it a sacred cult."[54] White took umbrage at some of the Zionist pressure which he found imperious and racially condescending. Nevertheless, his reluctance notwithstanding, he supported partition "because Palestine seemed the only haven anywhere in the world for nearly one million Jews of Europe."[55] In the end, Liberia, Haiti and the Philippines, whom White had also attempted to influence, voted for the United Nations resolution. As matters turned out, their votes were crucial to the creation of Israel. After a gestation period of approximately half a century, the Jewish homeland of which Herzl had written and dreamt would become a reality. The Rubicon had been crossed, if not the Jordan.

In the months following the fateful November 1947 United Nations vote to partition Palestine, there was a resurgence of battling between Jews and Palestinian Arabs. Jews in the *Yishuv* (the Jewish community in prestate Palestine) were jubilant to learn that after two thousand years a Jewish state would reemerge in at least a portion of their ancient homeland. By contrast, Arabs were livid. They constituted a sizeable majority—two-thirds, in fact, of Palestine's entire population—and they believed that Zionist intrigue had caused the world body to forsake them. Arabs vented their spleen by atacking Jews, who then retaliated in kind. Intercommunal fighting, i.e., civil war, threatened to violently tear the country asunder. It was the very state of affairs the United Nations had sought to avoid.

Although outnumbered, the Jews were better organized and their community services operated more efficiently that those of the Arabs, many of whose leaders fled to safer Arab locales. The Jewish armies proved superior as well. Punctuating the bitter fighting were atrocities committed by both sides. Word of the notorious Deir Yacin massacre of Arabs near Jerusalem in April 1948 spread quickly and led to panic among the already anxious and often leaderless Arabs. It was this panic that touched off the exodus of terrified Palestinians and, in large measure, created the still unresolved Arab refugee problem. When the war finally ended at the beginning of 1949, approximately three-quarters of a million Palestinians found themselves in the Arab countries surrounding the triumphant "Zionist entity."

When the British withdrew and, at long last, extricated themselves from the Palestine morass, military forces of five Arab nations (Iraq, Jordan, Lebanon, Egypt and Syria) invaded the fledgling Jewish state, which David Ben-Gurion had proclaimed on May 14, 1948. What had theretofore been a civil war was broadened into an international conflict. Given their vast manpower, the Arabs prophesied a quick victory; but, as a result of poor coordination among the Arab commanders and low morale among their troops, the anticipated triumph eluded them.

It was in the midst of the sanguinary first Arab-Israeli war that Israel's fate became entwined with the career of one extraordinary Black American—Ralph Johnson Bunche. When Count Folke Bernadette, the Swedish diplomat who was serving as the United Nations mediator, was assassinated by members of the extremist Stern Gang in September 1948, Bunche, who had been secretary of the peacekeeping Palestine Commission, was appointed acting mediator. Born in Detroit in 1904, Bunche, as a youth, was outstanding both as a scholar and an athlete. He was the first Black American to earn a doctorate in political science, which he received from Harvard in 1934. He subsequently assisted the Swedish scholar Gunnar Myrdal in researching his monumental opus on the Afro-American, *An American Dilemma*.[56] In the early 1940's Bunche had argued that anti-Semitism among Blacks and the irrational fear and dislike of Blacks on the part of Jews were nonsensical examples of the pot calling the kettle black. He expressed a hope that Jewish and Black leaders and organizations would strive to improve the strained relations which existed between the two minorities. "In large measure," he maintained, "their problems—their grievances and their fears are cut to a common pattern."[57]

It was Bunche's statesmanship which facilitated the termination of the first Arab-Israeli war. Ensconced in his headquarters on the lovely Greek island of Rhodes, Bunche mediated negotiations between King Farouk's Egypt and Israel, which resulted in an armistice agreement in February 1949.[58] Agreements between Israel and other Arab belligerents were also concluded. For his efforts in hastening the end of hostilities, in 1950 Dr. Bunche became the first Afro-American to be awarded the Nobel Peace Prize.

On at least one occasion, the fact that Bunche was a Black American colored his outlook on the clash between Arabs and Jews. When matters were still precarious in Palestine, Bunche thought it advisable to consult Menachem Begin, then the wanted chieftain of the Irgun, an underground "terrorist" faction. After a clandestine meeting between United Nations officials and those of the Irgun, Begin thanked Dr. Bunche for his diligence and toil in preparing a report on their dialogue.[59] In his personal memoir, *The Revolt*, the future prime minister characterized Dr. Bunche as the warmest of the United Nations team. As Begin remembered the conclusion of their meeting, Bunche shook his hand and exclaimed emotionally, "I can understand you. I am also a member of a persecuted minority."[60] Begin also paid tribute to Bunche as "undoubtedly a brilliant mind."[61]

Bunche's mediating role in nurturing Israel in its fragile infancy is also recalled by Afro-Americans, who often invoke his name to justify Black involvement in the Middle East conflict.[62] However, in 1978 one Black columnist bewailed the fact that "although there are monuments in New York to Bunche, not one stands to his memory in Israel. Not even a tree."[63]

In view of Bunche's contribution, it is hard to believe that as late as the fall of 1948 his work as mediator in Palestine was judged insufficiently pro-Zionist by the erudite W.E.B. Du Bois. Speaking to the American Jewish Congress on November 30 of that year, Du Bois apologized in the name of fifteen million Black Americans for "the apparent apostasy of Ralph Bunche...to the clear ideas of freedom and fair play, which should have guided the descendant of an American slave." Count Bernadette, who represented the nefarious combination of European aristocracy and American money to Du Bois, could not be expected to "judge Israel justly and without bias." But from Bunche, Du Bois hoped for more than consistent adherence to State Department directives which prevented him from playing "a great role for freedom." In Du Bois' estimation the State Department was guilty of compromise, vacillation and betrayal. On the other hand, he had hoped that Bunche "would have stood fast for justice, freedom and the good faith of his nation and race."[64]

Even before the Nazis capitulated, Du Bois, as editor of *Phylon*, wrote that millions of Jews had perished in Hitler's pogroms and millions more were in peril of extermination. America's doors had been closed to Jewish immigrants and, worse still, "Great Britain has assumed the right to limit Jewish migration to Palestine and to support the nationalism of the Arabs."[65]

From Du Bois' prolific pen came articles and columns trumpeting the cause of the Zionists in their hour of need. In the wake of the Holocaust, Du Bois wrote that there "was one refuge, a little thing, a little corner of the world where the Jews anciently had lived."[66] A Zionist homeland there in Palestine was a sine qua non for displaced and homeless Jews. There was no other place for them. Persecution was the only real alternative to migration to Zion. In a 1948 piece published as "A Case for the Jews," Du Bois depicted the objective of the Zionist movement as follows: It was a question of "young and forward thinking Jews, bringing a new civilization into an old land and building up that land out of the ignorance, disease and poverty into which it had fallen, and by democratic methods to build a new and peculiarly fateful modern state."[67]

Du Bois excoriated British Foreign Secretary Ernest Bevin for his "half hidden dislike of Jews," for reneging on the Balfour Declaration, for using British troops against the Jews, for training Arab soldiers for future use against them and for utilizing the Royal Navy to block the immigration of displaced persons into Palestine.[68] Uprooted Jews were being allowed to rot in Europe while the United States discussed "unworkable possibilities for the partition of Palestine," wrote Du Bois, employing words that echoed the maximalist sentiments of the Vladimir Jabotinsky-Begin Revisionists who envisioned a Jewish state on both banks of the Jordan River.[69]

Du Bois further castigated President Harry Truman for not keeping his promise to back the establishment of a Jewish state and for not allowing weapons to be dispatched to the beleaguered Jews. Because of "sordid commercial" factors, Britain betrayed the Zionists in tandem with the United States. Under intense pressure from the State Department, which was eager to safeguard Middle East oil supplies and apprehensive about potential Soviet penetration of the Arab world, Truman had vacillated. United States repudiation of its partition position and substitution of a United Nations trusteeship was seriously contemplated for a while. "If there is one act for which President Truman and his advisors can be utterly and finally condemned and refused the support of all decent thinking people, it is this reversal of stand in the matter of Palestine," wrote Du Bois in an article to be published in the Black press.[70] Between April 30, 1948, when Du Bois mailed the article to the *Chicago Defender* and its publication on May 15, 1948, Truman reversed himself again and came out in favor of the Zionist demands. Indeed, the United States was the first nation to extend official recognition to Israel.

Du Bois had been closely associated with Jews in the creation of the NAACP, which in June 1948 expressed its gratification that Israel had come into being. At its thirty-ninth annual conference, which was held in Kansas City, Missouri, on June 26, the NAACP adopted the following resolution: "The valiant struggle of the people of Israel for independence serves as an inspiration to all persecuted people throughout the world. We hail the establishment of the new State of Israel and welcome it into the family of nations."[71]

By no means was Du Bois the only Black militant with a reputation for challenging tyranny against great odds who was counted among the sympathizers of Zionism. At that time there were many in the Afro-American community. Take Paul Robeson, for instance. Truly versatile, Robeson was an all-American football player at Rutgers University, an attorney, an accomplished actor and a soul-stirring vocalist. Until he openly professed his affinity for the Soviet Union and for Communism, Robeson was a national hero, venerated by millions and held up by the United States government as an example of the heights to which a talented, industrious Black could rise. During the Cold War, however, Robeson was persona non grata, and he was denied a passport.

Robeson, whose father had been a slave, was, by his own admission, especially close to the Jewish people.[72] On many occasions he took uncompromising stands against the evil of anti-Semitism and the persecution of the Jews. In 1933 he had sung in Britain to aid Jewish refugee children and after the war had witnessed the horrors of Dachau first hand.[73] Robeson saw Jews as a "race without a nation;" and in a March 1948 speech in Honolulu, he said that should an all-out war start in Palestine he would travel there to sing for the Jewish troops just as he had entertained the anti-Franco Loyalists during the Spanish Civil War. To Robeson this intention was in keeping with his ongoing worldwide fight for the oppressed.[74]

When the Palestine question came before the United Nations in 1947, it received some space in the Black press. But then, as now, there was no unanimity of opinion among Black Americans. For example, columnist George Schuyler called upon Blacks to follow the model of Zionism. At the same time he took Palestinian Jews to task for their "imperialistic spirit" and "Hitler-like" methods. Jews, Schuyler argued, had "no more claim on Palestine than the Alpha Kappa Alpha." It was the "Arab aborigines" tarbrushed with Negro blood who were truly entitled to the land. The Bible, which he called the "Jewish Mein Kampf," provided no justification whatsoever for Zionism.[75] He informed his readers that procuring the Holy Land was only the immediate objective of the Zionists. Their long-range goal was to once again build a great political state and "to become one of the richest and most powerful groups in the world today."[76] Such strong sentiments were rarely expressed by the Black press and, as far as can be determined, virtually never by Black leaders.

Schuyler, who was something of an iconoclast and later became a leading, perhaps the preeminent, Black conservative in the United States, denied the accusation made by several "Zionist fanatics" that he was anti-Semitic. He added that Arabs are "far more Semitic than most of the Zionists now in Palestine or abroad."[77] Of course, the scholarly Schuyler was playing linguistic tricks. He knew full well that the term "anti-Semitic" referred to animosity toward Jews and that the fact that both Hebrew and Arabic are classified as "Semitic" languages was quite irrelevant.

It is significant that in March 1948 the *Pittsburgh Courier*, which had carried Schuyler's columns, published a long editorial in which it argued strongly for the legitimacy of a Jewish state. Entitled "Persecution and Doubletalk," the editorial demanded that "the lust for Arabian oil" not be allowed to interfere with the United Nations' pledge to partition Palestine. "Not only do the Jews have the legal right to a part of Palestine based on years of international commitments," the editorial stated, "they also deserve the heartfelt sympathy and support of everyone who hates cruelty and tyranny."[78]

*   *   *

Middle Eastern geography, not to mention history, was drastically altered by the 1948 Arab-Israeli war or what the Israelis have dubbed the "War of Independence." Not only did a Jewish nation emerge like a phoenix from the ashes of the Holocaust, but it was one-third larger than the political entity envisaged by the General Assembly partition plan. The projected Palestinian Arab state never came into being nor did the international zone ever materialize. King Farouk's Egypt occupied the Gaza Strip, and King Abdullah's Hashemite Kingdom of Jordan seized the West Bank, including East Jerusalem. Both areas were crowded with frustrated, disillusioned refugees. They yearned to return to their homes, fields, vineyards, shops and factories, but the envenomed politics of the Middle East made that well-nigh impossible. From the Israeli perspective they were potential fifth-columnists, and their readmission would be an act of suicide for the infant Jewish state. In a few short years their abandoned lands and other property were taken over by Jewish immigrants in dire economic straits, the bulk of whom had left Arab countries because Arab hatred toward Zionism had been directed against the local Jewish populations. That seemingly irreversible exchange of population was to enormously complicate the search for a solution to the Arab-Israeli dispute.

The whole Arab world seethed with anger over its defeat in 1948, an event they viewed as an unprecedented humiliation, an unparalleled catastrophe. Cries for justice and revenge reverberated throughout the Middle East. Even the most irrepressible optimist would not forecast peace in the area.

NOTES

1. Hollis R. Lynch, *Edward Wilmot Blyden, Pan-Negro Patriot 1832–1912* (London: Oxford University Press, 1967), p. vii.

2. Edward W. Blyden, *The Jewish Question* (Liverpool: Lionel Hart and Co., 1898), p. 6. Also see Hollis R. Lynch, "A Black Nineteenth Century Response to Jews and Zionism: The Case of Edward W. Blyden, 1832–1912." (Unpublished paper presented at the spring symposium of the Afro-American Studies Program, University of Pennsylvania, 25–27 March 1982).

3. Blyden, *Jewish Question*, p. 6.

4. One of the proto-Zionists whose ideas and efforts were generally scorned and/or ignored was a Serbian-born rabbi, Yehudah Alkalai. Writing in the 1840's, Alkalai likened Jewish residence outside Palestine to life on the edge of a volcano. He anticipated the World Zionist Congress by almost half a century when he spoke of a representative body for world Jewry. See Yehudah Alkalai, "The Third Redemption," in *The Zionist Idea*, ed. Arthur Hertzberg (Garden City, N.Y.: Doubleday and Co., Inc. and Herzl Press, 1959), pp. 105–107.

5. Zvi Hirsch Kalischer, "Seeking Zion," in *The Zionist Idea*, ed. Hertzberg, pp. 111–114.

6. Moses Hess, *Rome and Jerusalem—A Study in Jewish Nationalism*, trans. Meyer Waxman (New York: Bloch Publishing Co., 1945).

7. Lynch, "A Black Nineteenth Century Response," p. 7. See Edward W. Blyden, *From West Africa to Palestine* (Freetown, Manchester and London, n.p., 1873), pp. 192–193, 199.

8. Blyden, *Jewish Question*, p. 7.

9. Ibid., p. 8.

10. Ibid., p. 7.

11. Ibid., p. 8.

12. Ibid.

13. Leo Pinsker, *Auto-Emancipation* (Masada Youth Zionist Organization, 1935), p. 22.

14. Blyden, *Jewish Question*, p. 8.

15. Ibid., p. 23.

16. For the full story of the East African episode in early Zionist history, see Robert G. Weisbord, *African Zion—The Attempt to Establish a Jewish Colony in the East Africa Protectorate 1903–1905* (Philadelphia: Jewish Publication Society, 1968).

17. Booker T. Washington, "The Atlanta Exposition Address," in *Booker T. Washington and His Critics—The Problem of Negro Leadership*, ed. Hugh Hawkins (Boston: D. C. Heath and Co., 1962), p. 16.

18. Louis Harlan, ed., *Booker T. Washington Papers*, vol. 11 (Champagne-Urbana: University of Illinois Press, 1972), p. 390.

19. Ibid., vol. 8, p. 442. This is from an account of Emmett J. Scott of a speech delivered by Washington in Little Rock. It appeared in the *Boston Evening Transcript*, 4 December 1905.

20. *Thirty Years of Lynching in the United States 1889–1918* (New York: National Association for the Advancement of Colored People, 1919), p. 28.

21. Booker T. Washington, *The Future of the American Negro* (New York: Negro Universities Press, 1969), pp. 181–183.

22. Harlan, *Papers*, vol. 11, pp. 390–397.

23. Ibid., vol. 10, p. 382.

24. After Bishop Turner had dispatched two boatloads of Afro-Americans to Liberia, Washington said that whites were mistaken in concluding that a majority of Blacks were committed to returning to Africa. See Washington, *Future*, pp. 163–164.

25. Ibid., p. 159.

26. Don Peretz, *The Middle East Today* (New York: Holt, Rinehart and Winston, 1978), p. 101.

27. *Crisis*, 15 (January 1918): 114.

28. *W. E. B. Du Bois Papers*, University of Massachusetts (Amherst), Reel 6, Frame 1096.

29. See Robert A. Hill, "Jews and the Enigma of the Pan-African Congress of 1919." (Unpublished paper presented at the spring symposium of the Afro-American Studies Program at the University of Pennsylvania, 25–27 March 1982.)

30. *Crisis*, 17 (February 1919): 166.

31. Herbert Aptheker, ed., *Writings in Periodicals Edited by W. E. B. Du Bois— Selections from The Brownie's Book* (Millwood, N.Y.: Kraus-Thomson Organization Ltd., 1980), p. 6. This was taken from *The Brownie's Book*, 1, no. 1 (January 1920): 23–25.

32. Ibid., p. 52. See *The Brownie's Book*, 1, no. 8 (August 1920): 234–235.

33. Ibid., p. 83. See *The Brownie's Book*, 2, no. 1 (January 1921): 16–17.

34. *Crisis*, 36 (October 1929): 329.

35. Walter Laqueur, *A History of Zionism* (New York: Holt, Rinehart and Winston, 1972), p. 256.

36. John Hope Franklin, *From Slavery to Freedom* (New York: Vintage Books, 1969), p. 492.

37. Amy Jacques Garvey, ed., *Philosophy and Opinions of Marcus Garvey or Africa for the Africans* (London: Frank Cass and Co., 1967), p. 53.

38. Ibid., p. 122.

39. Beverly Reed, "Black, Beautiful and Free," *Ebony* (June 1971): 48.

40. *Marcus Garvey Papers*, UCLA. This statement appeared in a report of a UNIA meeting which was published in Garvey's organ, *The Negro World*, 17 July 1925.

41. Ibid. See report of UNIA meeting in *The Negro World*, 31 July 1920.

42. Marcus Garvey, "The Case of the Negro for International Racial Adjustment, Before the English People" (London: Poets' and Printers Press, n.d.), pp. 17–18. This was from a speech delivered by Garvey at Royal Albert Hall on 6 June 1928.

43. *Marcus Garvey Papers*. This telegram was read at a rally by Garvey. It is contained in a report of a Madison Square Garden meeting in the *Negro World Convention Bulletin*, (3 August 1920).

44. Hasia R. Diner, *In the Almost Promised Land—American Jews and Blacks 1915–1935* (Westport, Conn.: Greenwood Press, 1972), pp. 54–55, 76.

45. *The Blackman*, II, no. 2 (July/August 1936): 3.

46. Ibid., I, no. 1 (December 1933): 2, and I, no. 4 (March/April 1934): 2–3.

47. Ibid., I, no. 9 (late July 1935): 9.

48. Ibid., I, no. 9 (August/September 1935); 10.

49. Ibid., I, no. 12 (late March 1936): 3.

50. Ibid., II, no. 7 (August 1937): 2.

51. Ibid., IV, no. 1 (June 1939): 5–6. Less than a year earlier he did not remark on possible injustices perpetrated against Arabs. In a speech delivered in Nova Scotia, he simply stated, "Our obsession is like that of the Jews. They are working for Palestine. We are working for Africa...." Ibid., III, no. 10 (July 1938): 10.

52. *W. E. B. Du Bois Papers*, Reel 84, Frames 324 and 325. These ideas were published in the *New York Amsterdam News*, 25 January 1941.

53. For the atmosphere of the United Nations at the time, see Peter Grose, "The Partition of Palestine 35 Years Ago," *New York Times Magazine*, 28 November 1982, 88ff.

54. Walter White, *A Man Called White—The Autobiography of Walter White* (New York: The Viking Press, 1948), p. 353.

55. Ibid.

56. Gunnar Myrdal, *An American Dilemma*, 2 vols. (New York: McGraw-Hill Book Company, 1964).

57. Lunabelle Wedlock, *The Reaction of Negro Publications and Organizations to German Anti-Semitism* (Washington, D.C.: Howard University Press, 1942), pp. 8, 10.

58. J. C. Hurewitz, *The Struggle for Palestine* (New York: Schocken Books, 1976), p. 319.

59. Menachem Begin, *The Revolt* (New York: Dell Publishing Co., 1978), p. 388.

60. Ibid., pp. 393–394.

61. Ibid., p. 387.

62. See the editorial, "Middle East Powder Keg," *New York Amsterdam News*, 20 October 1973.

63. Bill Lane, "people—places 'n' situwayshuns," *Los Angeles Sentinel*, 6 April 1978. In 1951 Israel's first president, Chaim Weizmann, paid tribute to Bunche on the occasion of a dinner given by the NAACP: "Dr. Ralph Bunche will always be honored in the memory of the people of Israel for his objectivity, tenacity and his devotion to the aims of the United Nations....He is a distinguished champion of the cause of equality and fought against all manifestations of discrimination and bigotry. In this struggle my

people and the people of Ralph Bunche have long been allies...." Chaim Weizmann Archives, Letter from Weizmann to Walter White, 8 January 1951. This letter was published in Chaim Weizmann, *The Letters and Papers of Chaim Weizmann*, vol. XXIII, Series A, ed. Barnet Litvinoff (Jerusalem: Israel Universities Press, 1980), Doc. 341, p. 295.

64. *W. E. B. Du Bois Papers*, Reel 80, Frame 1158. (Unpublished speech on "America's Responsibility to Israel," delivered 30 November 1948.)

65. W.E.B. Du Bois, "Jews and Arabs," *Phylon*, V, no. 1 (1944): 86. Early in 1941 Du Bois thought that Zionism provided Blacks who believed "someone is going to do our fighting for us" with a constructive lesson in self-help.

66. *W. E. B. Du Bois Papers*, Reel 83, Frames 1543 and 1544. See Du Bois, "Winds of Time," *Chicago Defender*, 15 May 1948.

67. *W. E. B. Du Bois Papers*, Reel 82, Frame 575. The manuscript which was entitled "The Ethics of the Problem of Palestine" was retitled "A Case for the Jews" in the *Chicago Star*, 8 May 1948.

68. Ibid.

69. Ibid., Reel 83, Frames 1543 and 1544.

70. Ibid.

71. *NAACP Papers*, Film 246, Reel 12, Part I.

72. See the author's foreward to Paul Robeson, *Here I Stand* (Boston: Beacon Press, 1958), p. 4.

73. Philip Foner, ed., *Paul Robeson Speaks—Writings, Speeches, Interviews 1918–1974* (New York: Bruner/Mazel Publishers, 1978), p. 462.

74. Ibid., p. 183.

75. *Pittsburgh Courier*, 24 May 1947.

76. Ibid., 27 December 1947.

77. Ibid., 27 March 1948.

78. Ibid., 13 March 1948.

III

Middle Eastern Wars and the Tarnishing of Israel's Image

A second round in which the Jews would surely be driven into the Mediterranean Sea was impatiently awaited by the Arab world, eager to atone for the ignominious defeat of 1947–1948. Israel's continued presence in the Middle East fanned the flames of Arab nationalism in the early 1950's, during which time Abdel Gamal Nasser emerged as its most charismatic spokesman. Against the backdrop of a series of incidents on Israel's borders, incidents for which both sides bore some responsibility, the situation deteriorated in the mid-1950's. Israel had long chafed over being denied unhindered passage through both the Gulf of Aqaba and the Suez Canal. To make matters worse Egypt concluded an arms deal with the Soviet bloc in 1955. The escalation of Egyptian *fedayeen* (guerrilla) raids into Israel and the 1956 unification of the military commands of Jordan, Syria and Egypt further heightened tensions and precipitated an Israeli military buildup. On October 29, 1956, Israeli troops invaded Egypt and, in short order, conquered almost all of the vast Sinai Desert.

Irate over Nasser's nationalization of the Suez Canal in July 1956, Britain and France sent their forces to bomb and capture the waterway and to seize Port Said two days after the Israeli incursion. Despite official denials, it was clear that the three invading countries, all nursing grudges against Nasser, had coordinated their military plans. Under pressure from the Eisenhower administration, Paris and London agreed to evacuate Egyptian territory in December 1956. But David Ben-Gurion, Israel's prime minister, did not withdraw the last Israeli troops from the Gaza Strip until the following March.

Very little animosity was expressed toward Israel by the Black media after the tripartite invasion of Egypt. Writing on this point in the Communist party paper, the *Daily Worker*, an Afro-American, Abner Berry, noted with some hyperbole that he could not find any evidence in the Negro press or statements by Black leaders indicative of hostility toward Israel in the wake of the Sinai campaign.[1] Criticism of the invasion was mainly directed against British and

French imperialism and was related to their colonial policies in sub-Saharan Africa. One editorial in the *Afro-American* coupled British bloodletting in Port Said and in Kenya, then the site of the anti-colonial agitation known as Mau Mau. There was no mention whatsoever of Israel. Referring to the furor in the United States and the United Nations over the Russian intervention in Hungary, the editor inquired: "Are the Hungarians, because they are white entitled to any more self-determination and freedom than East Africans and Egyptians who happen to be colored?"[2] An unsigned article in the same newspaper flagellated the British and the French for the "high handed manner" in which they attempted to reassert their authority over the Suez Canal. Israel was judged guilty of "bare aggression" but was assigned a secondary role. In fact, the Jewish state, in the opinion of the *Afro-American*, was allowing itself to be used as a pawn by the old imperial powers. The crux of the problem was that France and England could not accept the fact that the era of colonialism had ended.[3]

Editorial comment in the *Norfolk Journal and Guide* was clearly sympathetic to Israel, "this little democracy—the only one in the Middle East." While Britain and France attacked "to save their tottering empires," Israel acted in self-defense. "When the little Zionist nation struck, it was a blow of desperation, for the Arab nations were mobilizing armed forces for a push against Israel."[4]

Colonialist Europe was also the major target of Du Bois' wrath, which was ventilated in his poem "Suez," first published in December 1956. In that poem Israel was portrayed as a dupe of racist, capitalist, imperialist powers fearful of the socialist Soviet Union.

> Young Israel raised a mighty cry
> "Shall Pharoah ride anew?"
> But Nasser grimly pointed West,
> "They mixed this witches' brew!"
>
> ...Israel as the West betrays
> Its murdered, mocked, and damned,
> Becomes the shock troops of two knaves
> Who steal the dark man's land.[5]

One minor instance of Black-Jewish friction in the United States which occurred in the aftermath of the Suez crisis was reflected in a *Pittsburgh Courier* editorial. "Despite the provocations suffered by Israel," the *Courier* cautiously observed, "there are many persons of integrity who question the wisdom of Israel's attack (or counterattack) on Egypt." The overriding issue, however, was freedom of the press in America. Unidentified Jewish groups were accused of trying to thwart free discussion of the Middle East problem. The editor was distressed because the anti-Zionist opinions of some of the *Courier*'s columnists were being confused with the newspaper's official policy. Jews were also counseled to avoid "imputing anti-Semitism to individuals who might differ strongly with them about Israel."[6]

One of those anti-Zionist columnists was the iconoclastic George Schuyler. True to form, Schuyler had written that the "unabashed aggression" against Egypt proved not only the uselessness of the United Nations but also "why Israel was set up against the wishes of Palestine's inhabitants (most of whom were chased into the desert and their bank accounts sequestered)."[7]

Jamaican-born Joel Augustus Rogers was another Black who opposed the Israeli assault. Despite his lack of academic credentials, Rogers' lifetime output of pamphlets and books was truly prodigious. In November 1956 he called the invasion of Suez "asinine" and said that anti-Semitism had increased throughout the world because of Israel. He asked whether the United States could trust France, Britain and Israel after their joint aggression.[8]

Other columnists in the same newspaper were sympathetic to Israel. For example, the distinguished scholar Horace R. Cayton wrote: "The fact of the matter is that Israel is fighting for her life. Egypt and the rest of the Arab countries have openly avowed their purpose of destroying the country."[9] Foreshadowing subsequent Black nationalist identification with the Arab world are Cayton's observations about Nasser's effect on some Blacks in the fall of 1956: "A brilliant and talented Negro painter...greeted Nasser's seizure of the Canal with the same enthusiasm he had for the Montgomery bus strike. And this was not an unsophisticated man politically."[10]

When President Nasser thumbed his nose at the British and French, he assumed heroic proportions in the eyes of some Black Americans as well as in much of the Third World, then struggling for political freedom. According to Bayard Rustin, Nasser's gesture of defiance was the crucial incident that sparked the escalation of Black American interest in the Middle East. Nasser, a "non-white," captured the Black imagination by doing to the white world what Black Americans were impotent to do themselves.[11]

Nevertheless, a sizeable segment of the Black press editorially ignored events unfolding in Egypt in the fall of 1956. For example, the *Chicago Defender* gave the issue a wide berth, limiting itself to commentary on Ralph Bunche as the United Nations' experienced peacemaker in that troubled region.[12] In general, except for the Black Muslims, Black Americans did not then evince much concern for Middle East developments. At that juncture the battle for equal rights at home absorbed most of their energies. While there was a growing consciousness of the striving toward political and economic independence by colonial peoples, there was not, by and large, a sense of immediate identification with the Palestinian Arabs.

Not quite eleven years elapsed before the third Arab-Israeli conflagration occurred. Respites from belligerence were ephemeral after the battling of 1956. Guerrilla forays across the Syrian and Jordanian frontiers were usually answered by Israeli reprisals and served to aggravate the chronically tense state of affairs. When the United Nations Emergency Force was removed from the Egyptian border at Nasser's request—Israel had refused United Nations troops to be stationed on her side of the border—the situation went from bad to worse. It became still more critical when the Egyptian leader excluded Israeli shipping from the Straits of Tiran, in effect denying the Israeli port of Eilat access to Asian markets and petroleum from Iran.

War erupted on June 5, 1967, when the Israelis devastated the air forces of Iraq, Jordan, Syria and Egypt in a surprise attack. When the fighting came to a close six days later, Israel occupied the entire Sinai peninsula and the Gaza Strip, Syria's Golan Heights (including its most important city, El Quneitra) and the West Bank of the Jordan River. From an emotional perspective, the most significant of all the captured territory was East Jerusalem, especially the "old city" within which stood the Western Wall and several other Jewish holy places from which Jews had been excluded since 1948. To demonstrate their determination never to relinquish "Arab" or East Jerusalem, the Israelis officially annexed the area and administratively united the two parts of the city. Israeli sovereignty over the entire city was non-negotiable, the Israeli government declared in 1967. It is a position from which they have not retreated since, much to the consternation of the Arabs who assert that for Muslims, Jerusalem (the site of two venerated mosques: the silver-domed El-Aksa and the Dome of the Rock) is the third holiest city in the world.

As a result of the Six Day War, a new configuration of power seemed to exist in the Middle East. Because of the enormity and swiftness of the Israelis' victory, the image of vulnerability that the Jewish state had projected to much of the outside world since 1948 was now grossly distorted. Although twenty Arab states were still arrayed in opposition to its very existence, Israel was no longer perceived as the engulfed underdog. Its physical annihilation, a real threat prior to June 1967, appeared to be only a very remote possibility thereafter. Post-1967 Israel was an expanding nation, an occupying power ruling over hundreds of thousands of Arabs in Gaza and in Judaea and Samaria, the biblical names by which the Israelis called the West Bank. For countless millions of onlookers, David had suddenly become Goliath, the superpower of the region. Who could sympathize with the new Middle Eastern Goliath? Some Blacks whose relationship with the gargantuan white Goliath of America had been that of horse to rider found it increasingly difficult to do so. Their hostility toward Israel, America's surrogate in their view, was made explicit.

Best publicized of all the anti-Zionist assaults unleashed by the June war was the statement issued by the Student Non-Violent Coordinating Committee (SNCC). The expressed purpose of the SNCC newsletter was to shed light on "the Palestine problem." It explained that Afro-Americans are an integral part of the Third World and as such had to appreciate what their brothers were doing in their native lands. To this end, photographs of "Gaza Massacres 1956" were reproduced with the following provocative caption: "Zionists lined up Arab victims and shot them in the back in cold blood. This is the Gaza Strip, Palestine, not Dachau, Germany." Another photograph showed "Zionist Jewish Terrorists." Two rough sketches accompanied the text. One was of Moshe Dayan, who was portrayed with dollar signs on his epaulets. The second depicted Nasser and the

American boxer Muhammad Ali (Cassius Clay), each with a noose around his neck. Holding the rope was a hand marked with a Shield of David and a dollar sign. An arm labeled "Third World Liberation Movement" holding a scimitar was poised to cut the rope.[13]

Some thirty-two "points of information" about the Palestine issue were offered for the readers' edification as answers to the question, "Do you know?" Among these were:

That the Zionists conquered the Arab homes and land through terror, force, and massacres? That they wiped out over 30 Arab villages before and after they took control of the area they now call "Israel" . . .

Israel was Planted at the Crossroads of Asia and Africa Without The Free Approval Of Any Middle-Eastern, Asian Or African Country![14]

That Israel segregates those few Arabs who remained in their homeland, that more than 90 per-cent of these Arabs live in "Security-Zones" under Martial Law, and are not allowed to travel freely within Israel, and are the victims of discrimination in education, jobs etc.

That dark skinned Jews from the Middle East and North Africa are also second-class citizens in Israel, that the color line puts them in inferior positions to the white European Jews?

That the U.S. Government has worked along with Zionist groups to support Israel so that America may have a toehold in that strategic Middle-East location, thereby helping white Aemerica [sic] to control and exploit the rich Arab nations?

That several American and European Jews, who are not Zionists and cannot support the horrors committed by Zionists in the name of Judaism, have spoken out and condemned the Zionist distortions of the Jewish religion; but their opinions are never printed in the Zionist controlled press or other communcations media?

That the famous European Jews, the Rothschilds, who have long controlled the wealth of many European nations, were involved in the original conspiracy with the British to create the "State of Israel" and are still among Israel's chief supporters. That The Rothschilds Also Control Much Of Africa's Mineral Wealth.[15]

From its founding in 1960, SNCC had attracted much Jewish support. Jews were disproportionately represented in the ranks of the "new abolitionists," whose ideal was that of philosophical pacifism. When the anti-Zionist polemic appeared, the withdrawal of Jewish support for SNCC, which had already begun because the organization had drifted away from biracialism and non-violence, was sharply accelerated. Such noted figures as Theodore Bikel, the folk singer and actor, and Harry Golden, the humorist and social critic, discerned anti-Semitic overtones in SNCC and announced that they were quitting. For its part SNCC said their letters of resignation were "hypocritical" and were designed by the authors to obtain a hearing for their anti-SNCC views in the media. The resignations were also superfluous, declared the SNCC newsletter. As of 1966 SNCC was an all-Black organization which was unaware that Bikel and Golden were members. Golden, it alleged, did not even know the correct SNCC address and mailed his letter of resignation to Martin Luther King, Jr.'s, Southern Chris-

tian Leadership Conference (SNLC).[16] Among the suggested replies to anticipated questions about SNCC's position on Israel, which may be found in the
SNCC papers, is the following: "Theodore Bikel's resignation from SNCC is
the same as if I announced my resignation as President of the United States.
Incidentally, exactly who is Theodore Bikel?"[17]

SNCC also expressed irritation at the fact that both Golden and Bikel had
invoked the names of Andrew Goodman and Micky Schwerner, two young
Jewish civil rights activists who, along with a Black, James Chaney, were
murdered by racists in Mississippi. SNCC deplored what it called the crass use
of their names in the furor over the anti-Zionist stance it had taken. It was an
"insult to their martyrdom" to discuss Schwerner and Goodman in that context
because, SNCC implied, they died as people trying to promote social justice
rather than as Zionists.[18] Also implicit in the SNCC response was annoyance
that Blacks were expected to uncritically back Israel as a quid pro quo for Jewish
liberal backing of the civil rights movement. Failure to do so was construed by
Jews as ingratitude or worse.

In the weeks that followed publication of SNCC's anti-Israel article, much
abuse was showered upon the civil rights group. B'nai B'rith's Anti-Defamation
League described SNCC as racist and anti-Jewish as well as anti-Zionist. The
League asserted that the newsletter parroted anti-Israeli diatribes produced by
the Palestine Arab Delegation and the Palestine Liberation Organization. The
latter was then led by the vitriolic Ahmed Shukairy.[19]

Both the illustrative material and the text of the newsletter seem to have been
borrowed from Arab propaganda sources. Ralph Featherstone, SNCC program
director, admitted that Arab embassies had furnished some data; but SNCC, he
steadfastly maintained, was not anti-Semitic. Not Jews per se, only oppressors,
in which category he put Israel and "those Jews in the little Jew shops" in the
ghettos, deserved severe condemnation.[20] H. Rap Brown, successor to Stokely
Carmichael as SNCC chairman, contended that "we are not anti-Jewish and we
are not anti-Semitic. We just don't think Zionist leaders in Israel have a right
to that land."[21] Especially ironic is the fact that SNCC's screed closely paralleled
an onslaught on Israel featured in *Thunderbolt*, the official organ of the white
supremacist National States Rights party.

Virtually without exception, Jewish spokesmen rejected the disclaimer of anti-
Semitism. The reaction of Rabbi Israel Miller, head of the American Zionist
Council, was representative of Jewish feeling. He saw the SNCC publication as
an example of "crude and unadulterated anti-Semitism."[22] Many Black public
figures agreed. Bayard Rustin, organizer of the 1963 march on Washington, and
A. Philip Randolph were both "appalled and distressed by the anti-Semitic
article." Whitney M. Young, Jr., executive director of the National Urban
League, was struck by the similarity of SNCC's views on the thorny Middle
East problem with those of the anti-Semitic and anti-Black American Nazi party.[23]

Obviously stung by the charge of anti-Semitism, SNCC resorted to semantic
sleight of hand. Although they knew full well that the term "anti-Semitism"

connotes antipathy to Jews as such, they labelled the charge "ridiculous" because Arabs were as Semitic as Jews. Indeed they were more "Semitic than the European, Ashkenazim Jews who recently migrated to Israel and form the ruling circles that control the dark-skinned, native, Middle-Eastern Jews and Arabs...the true Semites."[24]

Undoubtedly, SNCC's analysis was one-sided and superficial. Unquestionably, many of its statements were inaccurate and misleading. But was it really anti-Jewish as well as anti-Zionist? Because of their tragic history, Jews are acutely sensitive about direct assaults on the State of Israel. This sensitivity has been heightened in recent years because anti-Semitism is often paraded in the guise of anti-Zionism. Certainly, all sympathy for the Arabs is not veiled anti-Semitism. Still, a content analysis of the SNCC pronouncements suggests anti-Semitic along with anti-Zionist sentiments.

References to the Rothschilds, associated as they are with enduring myths about worldwide Jewish financial domination, raised nagging doubts about SNCC's real intent. And whereas SNCC may have meant the dollar signs on Dayan's epaulets to reflect American backing of Israel, sensitive Jews saw them as an anti-Semitic linkage of Jews and money. Still others asked why there was a Star of David and a dollar sign on the hand which held the rope choking Ali and Nasser. Nasser, of course, was Israel's archenemy in the Arab world; but what did Muhammad Ali, then dethroned as the heavyweight boxing champion of the world because of his refusal to serve in the United States military, have to do with the relative merits of the Arab and Israeli cases? SNCC subsequently explained that the Star of David, which symbolized Zionism, was strangling the Arab or Muslim world. The dollar sign symbolized the United States, which was killing Ali and through its proxy, Israel, was killing Arabs too. Surely, it was at least an error of judgment to juxtapose the wrong perpetrated against Ali with the Middle East dispute. To avoid confusion it would have been much wiser to show one hand with a Star of David representing Israel and a second hand with a dollar sign hanging Ali. After all, Israel or the American Jews had nothing whatsoever to do with the callous mistreatment of Ali. SNCC's answer contained in the next issue of the newsletter explained that it placed the two symbols on one hand to dramatize the close bond between Israel and the United States. That explanation probably mollified very few Jewish critics, a couple of whom had already written flagrantly racist epistles to SNCC.[25]

Needless to say, SNCC could easily have steered clear of the Arab-Israeli conflict. Within the organization thinking about the wisdom of taking a stand on the issue was far from unanimous. Militating against entanglement was reluctance to unnecessarily alienate either Arabs or Jews. Because of the Black power question then confronting many Afro-American groups, i.e., the question of remaining biracial in makeup, SNCC already had its fill of controversy. James Forman, then SNCC's director of international affairs, thought it imprudent for SNCC to take an anti-Israeli stand, for to do so would hurt it financially and isolate it from the media. Certainly until SNCC was independent of Jewish monetary support and until its staff was knowledgeable about the Middle East, it should take no public stand.[26]

In view of the foregoing, how did the provocative article come to be? According to Clayborne Carson, a young Black historian and an authority on SNCC, Ethel Minor, who edited SNCC's newsletter, agreed to research the Arab-Israeli conflict. Carson has written that Minor, by virtue of her involvement with Black Muslims and her friendship with Palestinians during her student days, was not unbiased on the subject. What was published in the newsletter was intended to provide the SNCC staff with "documented facts" that could not be gleaned from the white press. Though supposedly earmarked for internal communication, the explosive piece was projected into the spotlight of the press in short order. A hornet's nest had been penetrated, and disunity surfaced almost immediately in SNCC's ranks. SNCC disclaimers that the article did not reflect their official position were issued, but to no avail, for Ethel Minor and other personnel in headquarters repeated their criticism of Israel. Although vexed by the tactical mistake that had been committed, in public Forman stood behind the newsletter's position.[27]

In actuality, Forman saw the Middle East dispute in global terms as part of the ongoing struggle between capitalism and socialism, between colonizing white peoples and oppressed darker peoples. According to this somewhat simplistic formulation, because socialist nations lined up behind the Arabs while the Israelis found favor with the United States, Britain and France, SNCC was bound to aid the Arabs in "their fight to restore justice to the Palestinian people." Forman later wrote that Israel was an extension of imperialistic American foreign policy as well as a "violation of territory of the Arabs." SNCC's anti-Israel stance took it "one step further along the road to revolution."[28]

Trinidadian-born Stokely Carmichael was the leading light in SNCC until May 1967 when he was replaced by H. Rap Brown as chairman of SNCC. While travelling in the Arab world in September 1967, Stokely Carmichael, an exponent of Black power, lashed out at "Zionist aggression." In Syria he accused "high officials" in America of being in league with Zionism; and, according to the Damascus radio, he pledged military aid by American Blacks to the Arabs. Eleven months later in his keynote address to an Arab students' convention in Michigan, Stokely informed his audience that militant Afro-Americans were ready to fight and die if necessary to aid the Arabs in freeing Palestine. He employed such phrases as the "trickery of Zionism" and the "evil of Zionism," called the United States the "greatest de-humanizer in the world," and argued that "Israel is nothing but a finger of the United States of America." A further point was that the "aggression [Israel's] of June 6th was for several reasons; one of them was to destroy the revolutionary governments of the Arab world." Also meaningful in Stokely's Michigan speech was his statement that "the same Zionists that exploit the Arabs also exploit us in this country. That is a fact. And that is not anti-Semitic."[29]

In his book *Stokely Speaks*, which included a chapter entitled "The Black

American and Palestinian Revolutions,'' Carmichael elaborated. Zionist propaganda had once deceived him, but he had come to the realization that the "so-called State of Israel" is an "unjust and certainly immoral state." He also suggested that Israel was a proxy for the Western imperialists who had planned that role for Israel at the time of the Balfour Declaration.[30] Carmichael also sounded a theme which frequently recurred in the Black American community after Israel's 1967 conquest of the Sinai peninsula, namely that Sinai was part of the African motherland. Black people were prepared to fight for and defend Egypt, Carmichael asserted. "Egypt is in Africa and Africa is our homeland. The oldest civilization in the world comes from Egypt. We must feel we are part of it. . . . We intend to fight imperialism wherever it is, in the United States or in our homeland.''[31]

Israel's continued occupation of the Sinai unquestionably subverted her popularity among Afro-Americans, who viewed Egypt as an authentically African nation from both a historical and a geographical perspective. Despite the Caucasian world's repeated attempts in the nineteenth and twentieth centuries to deprive non-whites of credit for the remarkable cultural achievements of ancient Egypt, Black American scholars have long claimed such credit—and with good reason. Typical were the arguments of J. A. Rogers, who wrote that the testimony of eyewitnesses such as Herodotus and Aristotle as well as that of modern science is that the "Egyptians were Negroid, that is to say, largely mulatto.''[32]

After the June war Shirley Graham Du Bois, the widow of W.E.B. Du Bois who had died in 1963, authored an article entitled "Egypt Is Africa" in which she maintained that the fate of Egypt and the fate of the rest of Africa were inextricably intertwined. Nasser's Egypt was a bulwark against imperialist aggression. "Egypt defends Africa," she wrote in The Black Scholar. "Should her defenses fall Africa would be in danger of being ground under the heel of those who are determined to dominate and hold in subjugation not only this continent [Africa], but the entire colored world.''[33]

Lacking her deceased husband's sympathy for Israel, Mrs. Du Bois in another article cried out against the "imperialist philosophy embedded in Zionism." Then residing in Egypt, she lambasted Israel as a "white supremacist, imperialist base at the most strategic crossroads between Africa and Asia" which was planted there to serve the undeserving cause of western empire building. She further bracketed the Palestinians with the "enslaved peoples of Southern Africa" as groups needing liberation.[34]

Three months after the lightning Israeli victory, in the midst of the "Black revolution" and anti-Vietnam War activism, the anti-establishment National Conference for New Politics met in Chicago and turned the "windy city" into a stormy one. In exchange for their continued participation in the conclave, Black militants, eager to flex their untried political muscle and to "prove our manhood," demanded that young white leftists agree to a thirteen-point program which they propounded. Ten of the thirteen points were more or less unobjectionable. Of the remaining three, the most troublesome was the one which condemned the "imperialist Zionist war." Sweeping aside an amendment that would have called upon the Jewish state to return captured Arab land, the convention overwhelmingly accepted the resolution.[35]

The Black caucus denied that the anti-Israel motion implied any anti-Semitism. Despite this disclaimer, which was becoming a ritual, several Jews in attendance were profoundly upset. One reportedly exclaimed in disgust, "*Goyim* [Gentiles] do not understand Zionism."[36] When a second tried to express a few words in support of Israel, her words evoked a chorus of boos. An undetermined number of Jews walked out of the conference in protest. Still others were sorely tempted to follow suit.

The Black caucus' condemnation of Israel in connection with the Six Day War caused considerable consternation among Jewish groups, many of which scorned the resolution. To cite just one example, while meeting in Miami Beach, Hadassah, the Women's Zionist Organization, objected to the language and the intent of the Chicago statement. Its president, Mrs. Mortimer Jacobson, called the Zionist movement "one of the great forces for political liberation in this century." She also assailed Black extremists for fostering "racial divisiveness."[37]

Although spokesmen for the Urban League and the NAACP repudiated the Chicago declaration, Jewish anger was not soothed. Ten Jewish agencies wired Dr. Martin Luther King, Jr., to convey their distress over the destructive and "irrational anti-Israel resolution." It was in conflict with everything Dr. King stood for, the Jewish organizations stated, and they requested that he publicly disavow "the malevolence which found expression in the resolutions."[38]

There was no doubt in the minds of the Jewish leaders that Dr. King could be relied on. King, the founder of the Southern Christian Leadership Conference (SCLC) in 1957, had been catapulted to national and international prominence by the Montgomery, Alabama, bus boycott a few years earlier. As a tireless advocate of first-class citizenship for all Americans, regardless of race, and as an apostle of non-violence, King had achieved moral stature that few have equalled in modern history. Almost from the inception of his crusade for social justice, he had established close ties with the Jewish community, which assid-uously supported him. "Our Jewish friends have demonstrated their commitment to the principle of tolerance and brotherhood in tangible ways, often at great personal sacrifices," he wrote in a SCLC newsletter in 1964.[39] Dr. King spoke out on behalf of Jews wherever they were oppressed. In 1966, long before most American Jews were aware of the plight of Russian Jews, he championed the cause of Soviet Jewry, whom he described as the victims of cultural and spiritual genocide.[40] He had rallied to Israel's cause in her hour of need. As war clouds gathered in early June 1967, Dr. King joined several other prominent Christians in asking the United States government to champion Israel's independence, its integrity and its right to unimpeded passage through the Straits of Tiran.[41] Consequently, the ten Jewish agencies had reason to be optimistic about Dr. King's response to their telegram.

In his 1967 reply addressed to Morris Abram, then president of the American

Jewish Committee and one of the signatories to the telegram, Dr. King, who had delivered the opening speech to the convention and then departed, insisted that the SCLC staff members who attended were the "most vigorous and articulate opponents of the simplistic resolution on the Middle East question." He praised the SCLC's spirited opposition spearheaded by Reverend Hosea Williams, its director of voter registration and political education, for endeavoring to moderate the anti-Zionist thrust. Dr. King reassured Morris Abram, a fellow Georgian, that, had he personally participated in formulating policy at the Chicago gathering, he would have rejected any motion which unequivocally endorsed the position of the Arab powers and rebuked Israel.

He then reiterated the SCLC's stand on the Israeli-Arab conflict, stating that "Israel's right to exist as a State in security is uncontestable."[42] Simultaneously, he voiced humanitarian concern for the impoverished in Arab countries and chided unnamed Arab feudal rulers for neglecting their own people. For Dr. King oil was the crux of the matter, and he observed that United States policy in the Middle East was shaped by anxiety over protecting two and a half billion dollars in investments by American oil companies.

Dr. King also strongly condemned anti-Semitism, not only because it was "immoral" but also because it undermined Jewish-Black amity and was detrimental to Afro-Americans by virtue of the fact that it strengthened the doctrine of racism. In concluding, Dr. King hoped that he had helped to clear up what he termed "an unfortunate misunderstanding."[43]

But was it simply an unfortunate misunderstanding or was it more? It can be argued retrospectively that the adoption of the anti-Israeli resolution at the Chicago convention dramatized a significant schism between the older, established SCLC leadership, personified by Dr. King, and a "Young Turk" element, more unwilling to calculate the response of Jewish supporters before developing positions on issues. A similar generational and ideological gap may have been opened in the larger Black community. At that juncture in history, it must be recalled, Jews were important contributors to SCLC, the more so because of their disillusionment with SNCC. However, it would be cynical to ascribe Dr. King's reply just to pecuniary motives. It is most likely that his statement was a blend of pragmatism and idealism. Undoubtedly, he valued Jewish backing, financial and other. At the same time he was dismayed by the anti-Zionism and anti-Semitism of some Black power extremists.

To John A. Williams, a Black writer of fiction and non-fiction, what had happened in the aftermath of the New Politics convention was that "Jewish leaders used King as a 'house Negro' to refute the allegations of other more militant Negroes." Williams interpreted the telegram sent to Dr. King by the ten Jewish organizations as a "thinly veiled threat" to withhold donations to SCLC.[44]

To the end of his life Dr. King maintained his friendship for Jews and for Israel. On one occasion, not too long before his untimely death, Dr. King appeared in Cambridge, Massachusetts, at a dinner given in his honor. Curious to find out what Black students at Harvard thought about a broad range of questions, he quizzed them at great length. When one young Black expressed a view hostile to Zionism, Dr. King impatiently responded: ''Don't talk like that! When people criticize Zionists, they mean Jews. You're talking anti-Semitism.''[45]

On March 25, 1968, just a week and a half before an assassin's bullet ended his life and amazing career, Dr. King appeared before the annual convention of the Rabbinical Assembly and made a pro-Zionist statement, which is chiefly remarkable for its ardor and its unambiguity.

Peace for Israel means security, and we must stand with all our might to protect its right to exist, its territorial integrity. I see Israel...as one of the great outposts of democracy in the world, and a marvelous example of what can be done, how desert land can be transformed into an oasis of brotherhood and democracy. Peace for Israel means security and that security must be a reality.[46]

In 1967 Dr. King was planning a pilgrimage to the Middle East,[47] but the tour did not materialize because of the Six Day War. Nevertheless, the government of Israel and many of its citizens were aware of his friendship. A decade later Dr. King's humanitarianism and his philo-Zionism were appreciatively remembered when the first saplings were planted in the Martin Luther King, Jr. Forest. It is located in northern Israel, in the Galilee, and was sponsored by both Black and Jewish members of Congress. Established under the auspices of the Jewish National Fund, the King Forest is part of a large wooded area which commemorates and honors ''righteous Gentiles,'' i.e., non-Jews committed to Israel, to Jews and to human rights.[48]

Although Coretta Scott King perpetuated her late husband's pro-Israeli, pro-Jewish philosophy, the SCLC would never be quite the same again without Dr. King at the helm.[49] After his assassination several of its most outstanding personalities would find themselves at odds with Israel and its American Jewish advocates in the years ahead.

The widening chasm in the Black American community over Israel was brought into sharper focus by advertisements which appeared in 1970. On June 28 the *New York Times* carried a full-page message from the A. Philip Randolph Institute. It was signed by more than sixty Black opinion molders, including members of the Congressional Black Caucus and several civil rights notables. In essence it was an appeal by Afro-Americans for the United States to support Israel. Specifically, it urged the American government to bring the Arabs and the Israelis to the bargaining table to negotiate a just settlement. With a view to safeguarding Israel, the sponsors of the advertisement, which was also published in the *Washington Post*, implored President Nixon to furnish the Jewish state with the full number of jet planes it had requested.[50]

What was, in effect, a rejoinder appeared in the *New York Times* of September 1, 1970. It took the form of an ''Appeal By Black Americans Against United States Support of the Zionist Government of Israel'' and was paid for by the

"Committee of Black Americans for Truth about the Middle East." The signatories, many of whom were identified with socialist or Black nationalist organizations, affirmed their solidarity with their "Palestinian brothers and sisters, who like us, are struggling for self-determination and an end to racist oppression." Advanced in the appeal was a world view which held that in opposing the "Palestinian Revolution" the United States was opposing the anti-colonial movements in such far-flung places as Vietnam, Laos, Brazil, Mozambique, Angola, Zimbabwe and South Africa. Zionism was an objectionable "reactionary, racist ideology;" and Israel, an "outpost of American imperialism in the Middle East." A cessation of all military and other aid to Israel was demanded, and Black Americans were summoned to identify with the "Palestinian Peoples' Struggle For National Liberation And To Regain All Of Their Stolen Land."[51]

At various Black American conferences, such as the Atlanta gathering of the Congress of African Peoples in September 1970, anti-Zionist themes were repeated, especially by the younger, more radical, Third-World-oriented delegates. A good illustration is contained in the remarks made by Howard Fuller, at the time president of Malcolm X Liberation University in Durham, North Carolina, and a member of SOBU, the Student Organization for Black Unity. For Fuller, Israel was a settler colony. "There is no such place as Israel. It is Palestine and so that all of you, all of you niggers who saw fit to sign that document that you support Israel, you are supporting nothing. We must understand that those Europeans who called themselves Jews moved into Palestine, took the land in 1948. This is what it's all about."[52] Fuller then went on to explain that America too was a settler colony because it displaced the indigenous population of Indians.

The summer and fall of 1970 were a particularly gory time for the Palestinians. If anything, the debacle of 1967 had deepened divisions between Palestinian refugees and their Arab host countries. Palestinian national consciousness was fostered in the process. Long-simmering tensions between Palestinian guerrillas, bent on using Jordan as a staging area for raids into Israel, and King Hussein boiled over in the summer. Arab killed Arab in the already blood-soaked Middle East. Among the thousands of casualties were countless Palestinian women and children. Ironically others escaped certain death at Jordanian hands by finding sanctuary on the Israeli-occupied West Bank!

In the midst of the carnage, on September 6, one of the most intransigent of the guerrilla organizations, the Marxist Leninist Popular Front for the Liberation of Palestine (PFLP), founded and led by a Christian Arab physician, George Habash, stunned the world by hijacking three commercial planes in midair. Two of the aircraft, one from Swissair and one from TWA, were flown to a "revolution airport" in the Jordanian desert. On September 9 the same fate befell a BOAC plane, its crew and its passengers. Under the broiling sun 475 passengers were held hostage on board the aircraft while the PFLP demanded the release of Arab prisoners held in Israel and Europe. Before the crisis ended—the planes were eventually blown up—the Palestinian guerrillas separated the Jewish passengers from the non-Jewish passengers and released the latter.

This blatant discrimination affronted Roy Innis, the Virgin Island-born national director of CORE, the Congress of Racial Equality, who observed that Blacks could not ignore what had happened in Jordan. He wrote in the *Manhattan Tribune*, a small, independent newspaper of which he was the co-publisher, that "The sight. . . this week of fathers being separated from their families because they were American Jews. . . vividly illustrates the irresponsible tactics of certain guerillas [sic]." Obviously Innis had the Holocaust in mind when he commented further that "The taking of Jewish hostages. . . the holding of innocent men, women and children merely because they worship in a synagogue. . . is a symbolic and frightening reminder of a disease which too many people ignored in Germany."[53] He saw a parallel with the heartless separation of members of slave families in the antebellum South. Innis remarked, quite correctly, that the terrorists' segregation of Jewish passengers undercut the Arabs' oft-repeated insistence that their battle was against Zionism and not against Jews per se.[54]

American Jewish agencies were particularly delighted by Innis' spirited attack on the conduct of the PFLP because he was well-known as a Black nationalist. By 1970 the dichotomy within the Black community on the Palestinian issue was becoming more pronounced. Backers of Israel could still rely on the so-called "moderates"—establishment, integrationist-minded civil rights leaders such as Roy Wilkins, executive director of the NAACP,[55] and Whitney M. Young, Jr., the head of the Urban League.[56] But the so-called "radicals," those who categorized themselves or were categorized as militants, Marxists, Black power advocates, Black nationalists or Pan-Africanists, were presumed to be identified with the Palestinian Arabs and hostile to Israel. It is worth remembering that prior to 1948 much of the enthusiasm for Zionism had emanated from the more radical elements in the Black community.

Representative of the Black radical animus towards Israel which surfaced in the post-Six Day War period was that displayed by the Black Panther party. It had come into being in Oakland, California, in 1966 due to the efforts of two young Blacks: Huey P. Newton, who became minister of defense, and Bobby G. Seale, who assumed the title of chairman. Ostensibly organized to promote the self-defense of Afro-Americans against police brutality, the Panthers were typical of younger, more assertive Blacks who broadened their political vision to include Southeast Asia, Africa and the Middle East, where they identified in no uncertain terms with those they conceived of as fellow victims of a brutal colonialism perpetrated by Caucasians.

For several years the Panthers adhered to a strong, often crude, anti-Zionist line. Editorials and articles in their weekly organ, *The Black Panther*, and in its predecessor, *Black Power*, spelled out, often in highly strident terms, the reasons for their bitterness towards the Jewish state and often towards Jews.

A vicious poem published in *Black Power* in 1967 was flagrantly anti-Semitic as well as anti-Zionist. It included such patently offensive lines as "couldn't kill the Jews too soon," "So I won't rest until the Jews are dead" and "In Jew-land Nailing Rabbis to a cross." The sources of their hatred, which they unashamedly cited, were that Jews had "stolen all our bread" and their "filthy women tricked our men into bed." Moreover, Jews were white. Readers were admonished not to be Uncle Toms siding with Israel. Even the timeworn deicide argument was trotted out along with threats couched in vulgar insulting language.

> Really, Cause that's where Christ was crucified,
> No-no-no-no
> We're gonna burn their towns and that ain't all
> We're gonna piss upon the Wailing Wall
> And then we'll get Kosygin and DeGaulle
> That will be ecstasy, killing every Jew we see
> Jew-Land, Not another day should pass
> Really, Without a foot up Israel's ass
> No-no-no-no
> Jew-land, Uh-huh-uh-huh, Jew-Land[57]

Linking Israel with the United States was obviously the goal of much Panther rhetoric re: the Middle East. Arab resistance to Israel's "fascist type repression" was comparable to the resistance movement in Vietnam, wrote a special correspondent in a piece provocatively titled "Palestine Guerrillas vs. Israeli Pigs."[58] Whenever possible the Panthers characterized Israel as an extension of the same United States that practiced racism. "The Israeli government is an imperialist, expansionist power in Palestine.... There are many non-Jews who support what Israel is doing. Pig Johnson [President Lyndon B. Johnson] is one of them. The term, Israel, is like saying racist United States, and it has the same policy as the U.S. government has in the Middle East."[59]

Zionism or "Kosher nationalism" plus imperialism equaled fascism, screamed a 1969 headline in the *Black Panther*, which stated flatly that the "Zionist fascist state of Israel is a puppet and lackey of the imperialist and must be smashed."[60] If readers were unaware of the identity of the imperialist behind the "Zionist Menace," they were informed that "Behind Israel with her arrogant contempt for the Arab peoples and her dream of establishing a religious Jewish state... stands the world's most powerful and imperialist state, the U.S.A."[61]

Sometimes it seemed that the Panthers were bent on opposing Israel *mainly* because it was allied with the United States government, which they despised because it had subjugated Black people. Their logic was whomever the enemy (the American government) supported, merited opposition; whomever the enemy opposed, deserved support. One is almost driven to the conclusion that, had the United States befriended the Palestinians instead of the Israelis, the Panthers would have become Zionists.

Ray "Masai" Hewitt, the Black Panther minister of education, trumpeted his party's coalition with Al Fatah and laid the woes of Afro-Americans and Palestinians at the same door—that of the United States.[62] On another occasion Hewitt said that Black folk were not anti-Semitic. Rather they were "anti-landlord, anti-pig, anti-demagogic lying politicians."[63] However, more than once in disavowing anti-Semitism and in differentiating between anti-Semitism and anit-Zionism, the Panthers blurred the distinction. They were in "total support of the people of Palestine's righteous struggle against Zionist imperialism that works hand in glove with U.S. imperialism," a *Black Panther* article stated in 1970. The only right that "Zionist clique," headed by Golda Meir and Moshe Dayan, had to Israel was a "robber's right." They were against Zionist expansion in the Arab world and against "Zionist exploitation here in Babylon," the Panthers wrote, using their derogatory nickname for the United States. Zionist exploitation was "manifested in the robber barons that exploit us in the garment industry and the bandit merchants and greedy slumlords that operate in our communities."[64]

To many Jews, including some who avidly defended the Panthers' civil liberties when they were shamelessly violated by the government in the 1960's, the most scurrilous anti-Semitic tirade came from the pen of Connie Matthews. Identified as the Panthers' "international coordinator," Matthews wrote that a substantial segment of the white left, which was supposedly abandoning the Panthers because of their pro-Palestinian stand, were "Zionists and. . .therefore racists." She went on to revile the "Zionist" jurist, Judge Friedman, who had sentenced Huey P. Newton to a jail term and the "Zionist" Judge Julius Hoffmann, who "allowed the other Zionists to go free" but kept Bobby Seale incarcerated and sentenced him for contempt of court. Seale's fellow defendants in the so-called Chicago "Conspiracy 8" trial, "the other Zionists," to use Matthews' loaded and inaccurate phrase—only two were Jewish—allegedly sacrificed Seale to gain publicity. Her use, perhaps careless, perhaps calculated, of the term "Zionist" as a synonym for Jew incensed Jews at least as much as her call for the assassination of Moshe Dayan, Tel Aviv's "one-eyed bandit."[65]

One Black Nationalist group whose anti-Zionist sentiments were manifested long before the June war was the Nation of Islam or the Black Muslims, as the organization is commonly referred to. For approximately four decades, from the mid-1930's until his death in 1975, Elijah Muhammad, a native Georgian, led the movement from his Chicago headquarters. Given the religious nature of the movement, it was only logical that the Black Muslims would identify with the Arab world. With that world they share a corpus of Islamic doctrine despite some disparate practices. In common they use Arabic for religious worship. Shared also is a distasteful historical experience with fair-skinned Westerners. Lastly, there is a common psychological plight: they both sense an oppression by powerful and often uncontrollable forces, whether white or financed by whites. The American Black has long felt the imprint of the white man's boot; the Arab perceives that his brother has been dispossessed from his lands by an expansionist Israel.

Black Muslim thinking about Zionism has been communicated through many channels.[66] Muslim views on Zionists and on Jews were perhaps best articulated by Malcolm X, the most renowned disciple of Elijah Muhammad until their falling out in the early 1960's. Born in Omaha in 1925, Malcolm was the son of a Baptist minister who served as an organizer for Garvey's UNIA and who was slain at the hands of white racists. Malcolm's turbulent life led him into underworld crime, but after having been converted to the Black Muslim movement, he was rehabilitated in prison.

Interviewed by C. Eric Lincoln, Malcolm voiced resentment at "the Jews who with the help of Christians in America and Europe drove our Muslim brothers (i.e., the Arabs) out of their homeland, where they had been settled for centuries and took over the land for themselves."[67] The religious and linguistic reasons for Black Muslim identification with the Arabs have already been alluded to. Malcolm appears to have had a particular affinity for Egypt as a revolutionary state.[68] He thought Nasser's seizure of the Suez Canal significant because for the first time the waterway was "under the complete jurisdiction of an *African* nation." [italics added][69] He found Cairo unusually congenial. "More so than any other city on the African continent, the people of Cairo look like American Negroes—in the sense that we have all complexions, we range in America from the darkest black to the lightest light and here in Cairo it is the same thing; throughout Egypt it is the same thing."[70] The object of Malcolm's admiration, Nasser's Egypt, the Arab world's most prestigious and populous country, was still Israel's main antagonist in the Middle Eastern cockpit.

For Malcolm there were local as well as international implications of Israel's creation and maintenance. By perpetuating Israel, its military and "its continued aggression against our brothers in the East," Malcolm told C. Eric Lincoln, "the Jews sap the very lifeblood of the so-called Negroes."[71] Christian assistance to Zionism was predicated on the expectation of promoting Jewish emigration to Israel. Jewish businesses could then be taken over. But the "American Jews aren't going anywhere," Malcolm disclosed. "Israel is just an international poor house which is maintained by money sucked from the poor suckers in America."[72] An unidentified militant Black in Watts put it this way: "You know them trees you got planted all over Israel from the Jews in Los Angeles, well they should have our names on them, not the Jews' names. The money for them trees came out of my back, out of the back of every Black brother in the ghetto!"[73] According to this thesis, ghetto merchants and slum landlords use their ill-gotten gains to sustain a Zionist state. As a consequence "colored people" thousands of miles apart suffer a common fate: exploitation by parasitic Jews.

Clearly, the ghetto situation and the Middle Eastern quandary cannot be separated in analyzing Black nationalist antipathy to Jews. In his autobiography Malcolm asserted that "in every Black ghetto, Jews own the major businesses. Every night the owners of those businesses go home with that Black community's money, which helps the ghetto to stay poor."[74] In a speech given in 1965 he talked of absentee landlords who often reside near the Grand Concourse, a Bronx thoroughfare heavily populated by Jews. On an earlier occasion before his split with Elijah Muhammad, Malcolm had denied that his movement was hostile toward Jews qua Jews. Such tensions as existed were between the Muslims and those who exploited, and degraded Black people, be they Jews or Christians.

But the Muslims seemed to single out Jews when blame was being apportioned for the plight of inner-city Blacks. "New York Zionists are constant bloodsuckers of the world's Black ghettos and slums," the Muslims charged. Because "Zionist" and "Jew" were pejoratively used synonyms in the Black Muslim lexicon, the American Jewish Committee pronounced the Muslims a "source of anti-Semitic infection."[75]

For many years *Muhammad Speaks* (later renamed the *Bilalian News*), the Muslim's weekly newspaper, published articles and editorials—the distinction between the two has never been very clear—overtly unfriendly towards Israel. Indeed, an analysis done in 1972 by the American Jewish Committee stated that the Muslim publication displayed a "pathological hatred of Israel," which it traced to the period just before the 1956 Suez crisis.[76] A regular column written by Ali Baghdadi, a former president of the Organization of Arab Students in the United States, gave an impassioned tone to the treatment of the Middle East conflict. Inflammatory phrases such as "Nazi-like Zionists" and "racist Israel" were by no means unusual. Baghdadi declared that under Israeli occupation the "holy cities of Israel" had been transformed into "Sodoms and Babylons."[77]

Alienation from the United States predisposed the Muslims to flagellate Israel, which it termed an offshoot of this country. They viewed the United States, Israel, South Africa and even the Vatican as integral elements in an "international conspiracy" plotting against Black Africa.[78]

Muhammad Ali, the flamboyant and world famous boxing champion who announced his membership in the Nation of Islam right after winning the heavyweight title in 1964, often voiced the anti-Zionist propaganda of the Muslims. Visiting Beirut during the course of a Middle Eastern tour, Ali declared his support and that of all Muslims for the "Palestinian struggle to liberate their homeland and oust the Zionist invaders." He also remarked that the "United States is the stronghold of Zionism and imperialism."[79] It was not for his amazing pugilistic skills alone that Ali received an ecstatic greeting from the Palestinian refugees in Lebanon. As late as 1980 Ali, his boxing career at an end, was reported to have said that Zionists controlled America and the world.[80]

Paradoxically, on other occasions Ali had gone out of his way to praise Jews. "There's gonna be whites who'll escape Allah's judgment, who won't be killed when Allah destroys this country—mainly some Jewish people who really mean right and do right," he told a *Playboy* interviewer.[81] In addition, a New York home for elderly Jews, some of them Holocaust survivors, is alleged to have been the recipient of a one hundred thousand dollar donation from Ali, whose generosity is legendary.[82]

To many historically aware people, identification with Arabs by Blacks is rather remarkable. Although Islamic cultural influences are of enormous significance in West Africa, Arabs were also the most important slave traders in East Africa. Countless Africans were forcibly transported to Arabia and other Muslim lands. Black slaves were a major commodity on which was based the economic well-being of Arab settlements dotted along the Indian Ocean.[83] It is not insignificant that within a few weeks after the Arab-dominated island of Zanzibar, once the leading slave market in the world, became independent in December 1963, an indigenous Black revolution exiled the Sultan, massacred large numbers of Arabs, and sent many others packing to the Arab countries. These facts have not escaped the notice of all Blacks. As one reader of *Ebony* wrote to the editor of that Black periodical:

For any Black man to think of himself as being a natural ally of the Arabs is comparable to the final thread of the screw being turned...the Arabs, in league with the Portuguese, were the chief instigators and the main profiteers of the slave trade, the ones who set tribe against tribe in bloody massacre and then sat back and collected the human debris; the ones who raped and razed defenceless villages, enslaving men, women and children, after slaughtering the aged, infirm and those considered unsalable....Indeed, it was the Arab who showed the white man what a fortune could be made in Black flesh....I do not see how any Black brother with even a passing acquaintance with our history, can proclaim himself in spiritual league with the Arab.[84]

Apparently new vogues in racial nomenclature in the 1960's facilitated the solidarity between some Black nationalists and Arabs. More and more militant Black Americans, especially the young, eschewed the term ''Negro.'' Sometimes ''Negro'' was used disdainfully to stigmatize one regarded as unduly moderate or compliant. Ordinarily the preference was for ''Afro-American'' or ''Black.'' Until the mid-1960's ''Black'' had a pejorative connotation for many Negroes. For most nationalists the concept ''Black'' became synonymous with non-white, thus making it possible to characterize the ancient Egyptian and the Moorish civilizations as well as Christ and Hannibal as Black.[85] It was in this vein that Malcolm, echoing Elijah Muhammad, observed, ''The red, the brown and the yellow are indeed all part of the Black nation. Which means that black, brown, red, yellow, all are brothers, all are one family. The white one is a stranger. He's the odd fellow.''[86]

Having redefined the meaning of Black, it is possible to include Arabs in the same racial family as Afro-Americans. Thus, a soapbox orator in Harlem, haranguing his listeners about Zionist expropriation, can talk glibly of his colored brothers or his Black kinsmen, the Arabs. And in treating the hostilities in June 1967, *Muhammad Speaks* can talk of Black men endemic to the population invaded by Israel.[87] Pragmatic diplomatic advantages aside, many color-conscious Arabs would not welcome news of this racial consanguinity.

If Arabs are perceived as Black, then Israelis are seen as white. For Afro-Americans the Jew is a Central or East European—a white man. Oriental Jews, who now comprise slightly more than half of Israel's population, have never been seen by American Blacks. Those Jews from North Africa and the Middle East are often physically indistinguishable from the Arabs in whose midst they lived for centuries. In other words, they too are "Black" given the broadened connotations of that word.

It should not be inferred that anti-Zionism in some radical Black groups just flows from ignorance of the historical and ethnological complexities of the Middle East. At the core of their outlook are grievances against the white West in general and the United States in particular. Unable to make appreciable progress toward economic, political and social equality in America, their strategy has been to forge ties with the Third World. They find inspiration in the revolutionary words of Che Guevara and Frantz Fanon and strive to internationalize their struggle by linking arms with liberation movements across the seas.

Periodically the strained relations between Zionists and some Black Americans erupted in controversy. This happened early in 1972 as a consequence of an anti-Israeli resolution adopted by the National Black Political Convention, held in Gary, Indiana, and attended by a few thousand delegates. Proposed from the floor by Reverend Douglas Moore, head of the Black United Front of Washington, D.C., in the closing minutes of the convention, the resolution asserted that the "establishment of the Jewish State of Israel constitutes a clear violation of the Palestinians' traditional right to live in their own homeland" and alleged that "thousands of Palestinians have been killed and thousands made homeless by that illegal establishment." Israel was taken to task because her agents were "working hand in hand with other militaristic interests in Africa, for example, South Africa." By a voice vote the convention resolved that the government of the United States ought forthwith end its "economic and military support of the Israeli regime." Lastly, they favored negotiations that would lead to the creation of a second state based on the "historical right of the Palestinian people for self-government in their own land."[88]

Whether Imamu Baraka, the mercurial Black poet formerly known as Leroi Jones who was co-chairman of the convention, had a role in framing the resolution is not known. What is known is that on several occasions Baraka had made remarks scornful of Jews.[89] A second co-chairman, Richard G. Hatcher, the Black mayor of Gary, dissociated himself from the anti-Israeli motion. Hatcher, who was one of the principal architects of the meeting, remarked that the resolution was adopted "late in the day when few people were on the convention floor" and, in his judgment, the majority of delegates actually opposed it.[90] Hatcher was quoted as saying that the resolution was "snuck through" with only 200 of the 3,456 convention delegates present.[91] H. Carl McCall, then editorial board chairman of the *Amsterdam News*, also found the resolution on Israel unrepresentative of the thinking of most Blacks at the conclave and said it would not be part of the final report.[92]

Sharply critical of the resolution were thirteen Black members of the United States House of Representatives who reaffirmed their position fully respecting the "right of the Jewish people to have their own state in their historic homeland" and vigorously opposing the "efforts of any group that would seek to weaken or undermine Israel's right to existence."[93] In addition, the Congressional Black

Caucus stated that Israel's example had stimulated national liberation among colonized African people and had provided financial and technical assistance to new African states. They noted that even Black Americans had been inspired to "strive for self-respect and dignity and to revive their own cultural heritage" by the centuries-old struggle of Jews against oppression.[94]

While Black leaders publicly and privately debated the Arab-Israeli dispute, matters in the strife-torn Middle East went from bad to worse in the fall of 1973. On October 6 another war started. It was the fourth, if one does not count the war of attrition that raged across the Suez Canal in the late 1960's. Frustrated by his fruitless efforts to regain Egypt's lost patrimony, Anwar Sadat, who had succeeded Nasser after the latter's death in 1970, coordinated invasion plans with Syria, another implacable foe of Israel. Fighting commenced in the midst of Ramadan, the Muslim holy month of fasting, and on Yom Kippur, the day of atonement which is the most sacred in the Hebrew calendar.

The suprise attack launched by the much maligned Egyptian armed forces enabled them to cross the Suez Canal, to overrun the vaunted Bar-Lev line and to hoist the Egyptian flag on the east bank of the French-built waterway. Syrian troops managed to regain some of the land on the Golan Heights that they had lost in the humiliating defeat of 1967. Before the hostilities, so costly in blood and treasure, were ended, the fiercest tank battles since World War II had been fought. Resupplied by the United States, the Israeli army had counterattacked on the Golan and had encircled the Egyptian Third Army west of the canal.

However, a decisive victory was denied the Israelis by the United States government, which believed that a rout of the Egyptians would cause further embarrassment and thereby diminish prospects for peace. Despite its desperate position when the cease-fire materialized on October 24, Egypt interpreted the war as a military triumph, which bolstered its sagging national pride. In the ensuing months Henry Kissinger's shuttle diplomacy yielded a series of disengagement agreements which left Israel still in control of most of the Sinai and the lion's share of the Golan Heights.[95] Of course, with King Hussein playing the role of an interested bystander in 1973, the October war did not directly change the status of Jerusalem or the West Bank of the Jordan River, which remained under Israeli jurisdiction.

As had been the case with previous wars, the Black community did not speak with a single voice about the Yom Kippur War. A survey of the Black press carried out by the American Jewish Congress on the heels of the war revealed that with few exceptions Afro-American newspapers were either favorably disposed towards the Jewish state or were adjudged to be "evenhanded" in their coverage.[96] Classified as sympathetic to Israel were the *Atlanta Inquirer*, the *Chicago Daily Defender*, the *Los Angeles Sentinel*, the *Minneapolis Spokesman* and the *St. Louis Argus*. Categorized as "mixed" or "neutral" were the *Atlanta Daily World*, the *Baltimore Afro-American*, the *Norfolk Journal and Guide*, the *Philadelphia Tribune* and the *New York Amsterdam News*. The last named weekly boasted a circulation of seventy-five thousand, the highest of all the newspapers monitored. In an editorial aptly called the "Middle East Powder Keg," the *Amsterdam News* asserted, "To us the survival and existence of the state of Israel is non-negotiable" but pleaded for a cease-fire to be followed by face to face negotiations between the warring parties rather than a settlement imposed by the superpowers. It expressed the fear that the failure to resolve the conflict peaceably could transform the Middle East into another Vietnam.[97]

The *Afro-American* was editorially apprehensive because it thought that Israel would learn the wrong lesson from the war, namely that the lands captured in June 1967 had to be retained as buffer zones. "That could be a dangerous, even fatal, calculation," it opined.[98] For James S. Tinney, a columnist in the same paper, the color question in the Arab-Israeli altercation was paramount. Not only would Black American soldiers have to put their lives on the line in the event of a Middle Eastern war, but they would have to fight against people regarded as fellow Africans by some Afro-Americans. "If and when the U.S. Army settles in to support Israel as a nation," he wrote, "our soldiers will find themselves confronting and killing half-brothers." Tinney said that although Caucasians had tried to artificially differentiate Egypt from Africa and to distinguish between North Africa and sub-Saharan Africa, it remained true that the same spectrum of coloration found among Black Americans was also found among Arabs. Although he conceded that Oriental Jews were dark-skinned, in aiding Israel white America and white Europe were really "protecting white folks transplanted on land formerly belonging to non-whites." Tinney asked rhetorically, "Who then would dare to become a pawn in white American hands to slaughter our black brothers and their wives and little children, in the name of 'pro-Israel' alignment?" U.S. military involvement in the Arab-Israeli dispute could serve other nefarious aims of the Nixon administration, Tinney claimed. It could undercut burgeoning support for African liberation movements and generate fratricidal warfare among Pan-Africanists. He even speculated that it could provide the government with a pretext for genocide directed at those "treasonous" Afro-Americans who opted to back the anti-American Arabs.[99]

The American Jewish Congress rated only one of the fifteen publications evaluated, the *Los Angeles Herald-Dispatch*, as antagonistic. However, *Muhammad Speaks* and the *Black Panther*, both distinctly unfriendly to Israel, were excluded from the survey because they were ideological journals rather than community newspapers. For Naomi Levine, executive director of the American Jewish Congress, the survey was encouraging. She commented that the results challenged the "frequently-expressed view that the black community is at best indifferent to Israel and at worst hostile to the Jewish state."[100]

Data from another survey were anything but encouraging. In January and February of 1975, a little more than a year after the Yom Kippur War, a Yankelovich poll was conducted among one hundred Black grass roots leaders in eleven representative but geographically dispersed cities across the United States. Blacks who were recruited and trained locally did the interviewing to determine how Afro-American leaders felt about Jews and about Israel. In general, the results were a source of consternation to the American Jewish Committee for whom the survey was carried out. A disturbingly large number of those polled appeared to subscribe to negative economic stereotypes of Jews as a people who controlled banks and other media and who were unscrupulous in business dealings. The findings on the Middle East seemed contradictory. While four of five Black leaders interviewed expected Israel to exist as a Jewish state,[101] roughly two-thirds thought it made no difference to Black Americans whether Israel endured.[102] More than six of ten admired Jewish American support for Israel,[103] but 43 percent believed it fair to fault Jews for being more concerned with Israel than with underprivileged Americans.[104] If war were to erupt again in the Middle East, more of the respondents, 23 percent, anticipated that Israel would be the main aggressor.[105] In the event of war 41 percent expected Blacks in the United States to support the Arab nations.[106] Slightly more than a third of those questioned believed that Blacks sympathized with the PLO. Thirty-two percent were of the opinion that there was more sympathy for Israel. Another third was unsure.[107] From these data compiled by Yankelovich, the American Jewish Committee drew the unhappy conclusion, which was consistent with earlier polls, that "Blacks are less sympathetic to Israel and somewhat more hostile to American Jews than whites, and younger blacks more than older ones."[108]

To mobilize Afro-American public opinion in defense of the Jewish state, the Black Americans In Support Of Israel Committee (BASIC) was formed in June 1975. Bayard Rustin became the organization's director. On its membership rolls were distinguished Black Americans—athletes, entertainers, educators, clergymen, businessmen, labor leaders, writers, editors, publishers, civil rights chieftains and elected officials. In retrospect it is noteworthy that some of the early members of BASIC have since tempered their enthusiasm for Israel and two, Congressmen Walter Fauntroy and Andrew Young, later clashed with Zionists.

In its statement of principles, BASIC proclaimed its backing for "democratic" Israel's right to exist: "Only in Israel, among the nations of the Middle East, are political freedoms and civil liberties secure. All religions are free and secure in their observance." BASIC condemned the anti-Jewish blacklist and castigated the oil policies of the Arabs which it charged had had disastrous effects on Africans and Afro-Americans. Mutual acceptance and reconciliation were the path to peace in the Middle East, and BASIC identified the Arab failure to recognize the legitimacy of Israel as a fundamental obstacle. Expressing compassion for the suffering Palestinian people, BASIC championed their right to "genuine self-determination but not at the expense of the rights of Jews to independence and statehood."[109] It found the PLO representatives unrepresentative of the Palestinian people and it chided the "terrorist" PLO for its "unbridled violence." Needless to say, the foregoing statement was a resounding endorsement of Zionism at a critical juncture when it was under siege.

As the fall 1975 session of the United Nations General Assembly approached, there was anxiety among Israel's supporters due to rumors that the Arab states would make a determined effort to oust Israel from the international body. A conference of Islamic foreign ministers had previously passed a resolution calling for the removal of Israel.

In anticipation of proposals to expel or suspend the Zionist state, ten Black Congressional leaders on August 1, 1975, issued a statement expressing their shock at the move to "ostracize this small, Democratic nation." Such action, they averred, would be "morally untenable" and would increase the probability of fighting in the Middle East. The Black solons compared the plight of the Israelis with that of the subjugated Bantu in South Africa, a comparison which is ironic in view of subsequent criticism of Israel's normalization of relations with the apartheid republic. But, in the summer of 1975 the Black Congressional leaders stated, "Just as the Southern African liberation movements seek the right of self-determination and nationhood for the oppressed Black majority, the State of Israel fights for the same rights for the Jewish people."[110] They backed Israel's struggle to keep alive its own national identity; and, just as they refused to permit business interests to supersede moral concerns where U.S. policy in Africa was concerned, they would not dilute their pro-Zionism for the sake of Arab oil. So strong were the feelings of the Black congressmen that they recommended that the United States and other nations reevaluate their United Nations membership should the bid to suspend Israel succeed. In light of future controversies which could not be foreseen in 1975, it should also be recalled that among the Black Congressional contingent that approved of the statement were Andrew Young, then a representative from Georgia, and Walter Fauntroy, the non-voting delegate to Congress from Washington, D.C.

Vernon Jordan, Jr., executive director of the National Urban League since Whitney Young's tragic death in 1971, also sided with Israel. He said that his organization, a biracial one since its founding in 1911, "considers the State of Israel the sole, legitimate representative of its people. Therefore we cannot support any consideration of their expulsion from the U.N." He emphatically opposed attempts to oust U.N. members on what he regarded as "flimsy and parochial political bases."[111]

Echoing the sentiments of Jordan and the elected Black officials was the *Philadelphia Tribune*, which is published twice weekly for the benefit of the sizeable Black population in the "City of Brotherly Love." In a lengthy editorial the *Tribune* asserted that if the United Nations becomes "so outrageous as to vote to expel Israel, it will be clear that they have completely outlived their usefulness." Israel's banishment would constitute "an outrage and an injustice of monstrous proportions." A majority of the United Nations' member states were military dictatorships which deny basic freedoms, the *Tribune* charged. Other countries murdered citizens in cold blood, and in still others enormously wealthy oligarchies kept their countrymen in grinding poverty; but, except for South Africa, there was no move to expel them from the United Nations. The *Tribune* also reprimanded the Arab states for their "shameful treatment" of the Palestinian refugees and reminded its readers that there were also eight hundred thousand penniless Jewish refugees who had been forced to leave Arab lands.[112]

The *Chicago Defender*, one of the two Black daily newspapers, branded the Islamic foreign ministers' motion "a crude and emotional gesture of contempt toward the United Nations." Should the Arabs succeed in their campaign to eject Israel, the *Defender* said withdrawal of America's significant financial contribution would be in order.[113]

When the Organization of African Unity assembled in Kampala, Uganda, it refused to endorse the idea of expelling Israel, The *Kansas City Call* was delighted. In an editorial entitled "Africa and Israel," the *Call* commented that "African states should have no part in any resolution, however mild, which condemns the state of Israel for acts or action taken in self-preservation." Israel was a friend of African states and had dealt generously with them. Africa was obligated to "lend much moral support to Israel which like black Africa has had to go through a baptism of fire and sacrificial blood spilling to establish a homeland free of persecution and racism, and take her place in the family of nations." Furthermore, ousting Israel from that family would destroy the effectiveness of the U.N. in resolving the Middle East problem.[114]

On November 10, 1975, in an atmosphere crackling with tension, the United Nations General Assembly, which had authorized the birth of Israel twenty-eight years earlier, determined Zionism to be a "form of racism and racial discrimination." It did so after a debate replete with recrimination and invective. Following the abortive attempt to banish Israel from the U.N. or at least to suspend her membership, the Arab states sought and found a face-saving measure. They would officially denigrate Zionism and the state of Israel. In this their efforts would succeed. The highly controversial "Zionism equals racism" resolution was adopted by a vote of seventy-two in favor, thirty-five against and thirty-two abstaining.

Debate over the resolution in the international media was as heated as it had been in the Assembly hall. Public opinion in the United States, including Black opinion, was appalled for the most part. The *Dallas Post Tribune* called it "an act of gigantic hypocrisy" and the *Defender* found it "malicious."[115] "Zionism and racism are about as far apart as the two poles and as different as night is from day," editorialized the *Call* in Kansas City. To the *Call* Zionism reflected the Jewish peoples' desire for a homeland, Israel. Dismissing the Assembly's vote as "ridiculous" and "obnoxious," the Black weekly recommended that the U.S. government seriously consider withholding its sizeable financial contributions from the U.N. and even contemplate withdrawing from the organization entirely unless the resolution was rescinded.[116]

A spokesman for CORE concurred with New York's Senator Patrick Moynihan who had flatly pronounced the Zionism-racism equation a "lie." Edward H. Brown, Jr., CORE's director of political affairs and its chief U.N. representative, asserted that "Zionism is a healthy form of nationalism."[117]

For Urban League executive director Vernon Jordan, the U.N. action was reminiscent of the 1936 failure of the old League of Nations to aid Ethiopia and its Emperor Haile Selassie in their hour of need. In his syndicated column which appeared in many Black newspapers, Jordan said the resolution was "obscene" and an "insult to intelligence." Zionism, in his estimation, was an expression of the nationalist yearnings of the Jewish people, a genuine national liberation movement. Anti-Zionism in the context of the U.N. vote was in reality anti-Semitism in Jordan's opinion, and most of the countries that denounced Zionism were themselves racist. He unequivocally judged the Arab nations who were the driving force behind the Assembly motion to be "the most guilty of discrimination." By turning the true definition of racism on its head and diluting it with untruths, the anti-Zionist resolution compromised the vital struggle against real racism. November 10, therefore, was a "day that will live in infamy."[118]

Impassioned praise for Zionism came from what would have been a most unlikely source just a few years before: Eldridge Cleaver. The one-time Black Panther luminary and author of the celebrated *Soul on Ice* had fled the United States in 1968 rather than face charges stemming from a gunfight with Oakland police. He took up residence in Castro's Cuba for a short while before moving to Algeria. Eventually he went to France. It was in Paris that the fugitive Cleaver allegedly underwent a religious experience which prompted him to forsake Marxism for Christianity. After a seven-year exile, he returned to the United States, spiritually reborn and politically reformed, a promoter of the American dream which the old Cleaver had denounced as the American nightmare.

Cleaver was shocked by two facets of the United Nations resolution which he considered "repugnant to human reason and historical fact." He wrote from a California prison cell early in 1976 that first of all, Jews had not just been victimized by racial persecution. "They have done more than any other people in history to expose and condemn racism."[119] He was also of the opinion that to vilify Zionism, the Jews' ideology for their survival, was a "travesty upon the truth."[120] Secondly, the Arab initiative in yelling racism surprised Cleaver because "it can so easily and so righteously be turned against them." Based on his personal experience of living among Arabs, he knew them to be "among the most racist people on earth. No one knows this better than black Africans living along the edges of the Sahara."[121]

As might have been expected, there was no Black unanimity on the U.N. resolution, and Cleaver's former Black Panther colleagues replied with alacrity and anger to his fierce defense of Zionism. They excoriated the "not-so-new 'red, white and blue,' Bicentennial model" of Eldridge Cleaver as an opportunist who should fool nobody.[122] They suggested that Cleaver's newly discovered pro-Zionism was motivated by a desire for Jewish financial help and recollected that in his Algerian incarnation Cleaver had "viciously attacked world Jewry." In point of historical fact, to the cheers of Algerian youth who surrounded him, Cleaver had reviled Israel as a "puppet and pawn" of the United States. Zionists, he exclaimed, had usurped the land of the Palestinian people. "We recognize that the Jewish people have suffered," Cleaver conceded, but that did not justify making the Arabs suffer.[123] Of course, those negative views of Zionism were expressed in July 1969 and by 1975 they were, as we say redundantly, past history.

In late November 1975 the Panthers, somewhat enfeebled and no longer in the limelight, remarked that the "hysterical reaction" of Zionists and Zionist sympathizers to the General Assembly resolution "clearly revealed the racist character of this jingoistic political ideology and those who adhere to it." One issue of their newspaper contained several pieces illustrative of the "racist character of the Zionist 'state of Israel.' "[124] Consistent with earlier disavowals, there was a strenuous denial that anti-Zionism was in reality anti-Semitism.

The *Hilltop*, Howard University's student newspaper, was in general agreement with the Panthers. It construed the resolution as a condemnation not of Jews or Judaism but of "a political ideology used to justify continued displacement and subjugation of Arab Palestinians in their own land, Palestine, part of which is now Israel." Israel was seen as "intransigent in recognizing Palestinian rights, restoring seized Arab land" and in maintaining "substantial economic and military ties with racist South Africa."[125] By the mid-1970's the relationship between Israel and the Republic of South Africa was being discussed in Black American circles with increasing frequency and no little emotion. At that juncture it was clear that Afro-Americans were becoming increasingly involved in the Middle East dispute. Black American-Jewish American relations would be influenced in turn.

NOTES

1. *Daily Worker*, 2 April 1957.
2. *Afro-American*, 1 December 1956.
3. Ibid., 10 November 1956.
4. *Norfolk Guide and Journal*, 10 November 1956.
5. W.E.B. Du Bois, "Suez", in *Black Titan—W. E. B. Du Bois*, ed. John Henrik Clarke, Esther Jackson, Ernest Kaiser, J. H. O'Dell (Boston: Beacon Press, 1970), pp. 296–298. This poem, which originally appeared in *Mainstream*, has been republished in W.E.B. Du Bois, *Creative Writings of W.E.B. Du Bois: A Pageant, Poems, Short Stories and Playlets*, ed. Herbert Aptheker (Millwood, N.Y.: Kraus-Thomson Organization Ltd., 1985).
6. *Pittsburgh Courier*, 29 December 1956.
7. Ibid., 10 November 1956.
8. Ibid., 24 November 1956.
9. Ibid., 10 November 1956.
10. Ibid., 24 November 1956.
11. Bayard Rustin, Personal interview with the author, 16 June 1983.
12. *Chicago Defender*, 10 November 1956.
13. *SNCC Newsletter*, June–July 1967.
14. In point of fact, there were only three sub-Saharan nations in the United Nations at the time: South Africa, Liberia and Ethiopia. White-supremacist South Africa voted with the majority, as did Liberia. Ethiopia abstained. SNCC's contention was that the

Liberian vote for partition was controlled by the United States. According to SNCC, "Uncle Sam" also determined the Filipino vote in favor of the United States resolution.

15. One could argue that in view of its tiny following, the anti-Zionist American Council for Judaism received more space in the supposedly pro-Israeli *New York Times* than its membership merited. In a 1968 publication, the council, which consisted of highly assimilated Reform Jews, demanded of their co-religionists that "they devote at the very least the same energy and finances which they raise on behalf of Israel in assisting the Negro community to attain its full rights." Michael Selzer, *Israel as a Factor in Jewish-Gentile Relations in America: Observations in the Aftermath of the June 1967 War* (New York: American Council for Judaism, 1968), p. 26. Paradoxically, at the other end of the Jewish religious spectrum, there is also vocal oppostion to Zionism. It stems from a few ultra-orthodox Hasidic sects, for example that led by the Satmar Rebbe, that regard political Zionism as tantamount to blasphemy, secular tampering with divine matters.

16. *SNCC Newsletter*, September–October 1967. See also Cleveland Sellers and Robert Terrell, *The River of No Return—The Autobiography of a Black Militant and the Life and Death of SNCC* (New York: William Morrow, 1973), p. 202.

17. *SNCC Papers*, Martin Luther King, Jr. Library and Archives, Box 24, Series 4.

18. *SNCC Newsletter*, September–October 1967.

19. *New York Times*, 23 October 1967; and Jerome Bakst, "Negro Radicalism Turns Antisemitic—SNCC's Volte Face," *Wiener Library Bulletin* (Winter 1967–1968): 20–22.

20. *New York Times*, 15 August 1967. Featherstone, who had been an organizer in the voter registration campaigns in the South and for a time SNCC's program director, was killed in Maryland in March 1970 when an explosion destroyed the car he was driving.

21. Ibid., 19 August 1967.

22. Ibid., 16 August 1967.

23. Ibid.

24. *SNCC Newsletter*, September–October 1967.

25. Ibid.

26. James Forman, *The Making of Black Revolutionaries* (New York: The Macmillan Company, 1972), pp. 492–496. See also Fred Meeley, "The Chicken or the Egg of the Middle East," *AfroAmerican News for You* (July 1967): 1, 4; and Clayborne Carson, *In Struggle: SNCC and the Black Awakening of the 1960's* (Cambridge, Mass.: Harvard University Press, 1981), p. 267.

27. Clayborne Carson, "Blacks And Jews in the Civil Rights Movement." (Unpublished paper presented at the spring symposium of the Afro-American Studies Program at the University of Pennsylvania, 25–27 March 1982).

28. Forman, *Black Revolutionaries*, pp. 492–497.

29. *New York Herald Tribune* (Paris), 22 September 1967; *National Guardian*, 16 September 1967; *Ann Arbor News*, 27 August 1968.

30. Stokely Carmichael, *Stokely Speaks—Black Power Back to Pan-Africanism* (New York: Vintage Books, 1971), p. 138.

31. Ibid., p. 141. In the years that followed, Carmichael, who resided in Guinea, continued to attack Israel. He did so on occasional American television appearances. When he assailed Zionism on WABC-TV's "Like It Is" television interview program in June 1976, he was taken to task by the American Jewish Congress, the American Jewish Committee and the Anti-Defamation League of B'nai B'rith, all of which issued

strongly worded press releases. Carmichael had called Zionism "the major enemy of Africa and the Arab people." "Like It Is" (Transcript, 20 June 1976), p. 7.

32. J. A. Rogers, *100 Amazing Facts About the Negro with Complete Proof* (New York: Futuro Press, 1957), p. 21.

33. Shirley Graham Du Bois, "Egypt Is Africa," *The Black Scholar* (September 1970): 33.

34. Ibid.; and "The Liberation Of Africa: Power, Peace And Justice," *The Black Scholar* (February 1971): 35.

35. Sid Lens, "The New Politics Convention: Confusion and Promise," *New Politics*, VI, 1 (1967): 9.

36. Walter Goodman, "When Black Power Runs the New Left," *New York Times Magazine*, 24 September 1967, p. 124. See also Abdeen Jabara, "The American Left and the June Conflict," *The Arab World*, 14, nos. 10–11 (Special Issue, n.d.): 76.

37. *New York Times*, 18 September 1967.

38. Telegram, Morris B. Abram to Martin Luther King, Jr. (undated), provided courtesy of the American Jewish Committee.

39. Martin Luther King, Jr., "Of Rights and Wrongs Against Jews," *S.C.L.C. Newsletter*, 2, July–August 1964, 11.

40. Martin Luther King, Jr., statement of 11 December 1966, provided courtesy of the Martin Luther King, Jr. Library and Archives.

41. *Pittsburgh Courier*, 3 June 1967.

42. Letter from Martin Luther King, Jr., to Morris B. Abram (undated), provided courtesy of the American Jewish Committee.

43. Ibid. So solid was Dr. King's philo-Zionism that James Forman, then SNCC's director of international affairs, was absolutely convinced that "Martin King has cooked his goose with the African countries." See Forman, *Black Revolutionaries*, p. 495.

44. John A. Williams, *The King God Didn't Save—Reflections on the Life and Death of Dr. Martin Luther King, Jr.* (New York: Coward-McCann, 1970), p. 141.

45. Seymour Martin Lipset, "The Socialism of Fools—The Left, the Jews and Israel," *Encounter* (December 1969): 24.

46. Quoted in "Conversation with Martin Luther King," *Conservative Judaism*, XXII, no. 3 (Spring 1968): 12. This statement was quoted by Black Congressional leaders speaking about Israel and the United Nations, 1 August 1975.

47. *New York Amsterdam News*, 3 June 1967.

48. *Portland Observer*, 10 March 1977. Most of those persons designated as "righteous Gentiles" risked their lives to protect persecuted European Jews during the dark days of the Holocaust.

49. Dr. King's parents, the Reverend Martin Luther King, Sr., and his wife, did visit Israel in 1974. During the course of his visit, the senior Reverend King voiced his gratitude for the Jewish contributions to the civil rights struggle. See the *Los Angeles Sentinel*, 12 August 1976.

50. *New York Times*, 28 June 1970.

51. Ibid., 1 September 1970.

52. Quoted in Imamu Amiri Baraka (LeRoi Jones), ed., *African Congress—A Documentary of the First Modern Pan-African Congress* (New York: William Morrow and Co., 1972), p. 59. Black ambivalence about Israel was underscored at the same conclave by speakers such as Imamu Amiri Baraka, who saw Israel as oppressive but wanted Black

politicians to endorse Pan-Africanism in much the same way Senator Jacob Javits and other Jewish legislators defended Israel (p. 101).

53. *Manhattan Tribune*, 19 September 1970.

54. Ibid. In this connection it is noteworthy that at that time several Arab states, Jordan and Saudi Arabia to mention but two, flatly refused to admit Jews regardless of political persuasion.

55. See Roy Wilkins, "Israel's Time of Trial Also America's," *Afro-American*, 24 June 1967. He stated that "peace with justice and honor will come only with the recognition of the fact of Israel as a nation." See also Roy Wilkins, "The State of Israel," *New York Post*, 18 March 1972.

56. Examples of his approval of Zionism and his support for Israel may be found in Whitney Young "Israel and Equality," *New America* VIII, no. 18 (25 October 1969) and in many of his "To Be Equal" syndicated columns. See also Whitney Young "A Black American Looks at Israel, the 'Arab Revolution,' Racism, Palestinians and Peace." An American Jewish Congress Report, 7 October 1970.

57. American Jewish Committee (AJC), "The Black Panther Party—The Anti-Semitic and Anti-Israel Component," (Unpublished report 23 January 1970): 3. The poem originally appeared in the June 1967 issue of *Black Power*.

58. AJC, "The Black Panther Party," p. 5. This originally appeared in *The Black Panther*, 4 January 1969.

59. Ibid., pp. 4–5. This originally appeared in *The Black Panther*, 16 November 1968.

60. Ibid., p. 6. This originally appeared in *The Black Panther*, 30 August 1969.

61. Ibid. This originally appeared in *The Black Panther*, 13 September 1969.

62. Ibid. See *The Black Panther*, 15 August 1969.

63. *The Black Panther*, 31 May 1969.

64. Tom Milstein, "A Perspective on the Panthers," *Commentary*, 50, no. 3 (September 1970): 36. Quoted from *The Black Panther*, 19 May 1970.

65. *The Black Panther*, 25 April 1970. See Norman Hill, *The Black Panther Menace—America's Neo-Nazis* (New York: Popular Library, 1971), pp. 209–216; and Rabbi Albert S. Axelrad; Rabbi Robert E. Goldburg; Huey Newton; Morris U. Schappes; George Wald, eds., *The Black Panthers, Jews and Israel*, A Jewish Currents Reprint, no. 9 (New York: 1971)

66. In the early 1960's the Black sociologist C. Eric Lincoln called the *Los Angeles Herald-Dispatch* "the official Muslim organ." C. Eric Lincoln, *The Black Muslims in America* (Boston: Beacon Press, 1963), p. 129.

67. Ibid., p. 166.

68. George Breitman, ed., *Malcolm X Speaks* (New York: Grove Press, 1965), pp. 126–127.

69. Ibid., p. 123.

70. Ibid., p. 83.

71. Lincoln, *The Black Muslims*, p. 166.

72. Ibid.

73. Paul Jacobs, "Watts vs. Israel," *Commonweal* (1 March 1968): 649.

74. Malcolm X, *The Autobiography of Malcolm X* (New York: Grove Press, 1966), p. 283.

75. American Jewish Committee, "Currents—Fringe Movements and What They're Up To," no. 2 (February 1972): 1.

76. Ibid.

77. Ibid., p. 2.

78. Ibid, p. 3. Quoted from *Muhammad Speaks*, 22 October 1971.

79. *Jewish Telegraphic Association Daily News Bulletin*, 8 March 1974.

80. *Rhode Island Herald*, 28 February 1980. Ali's statement was originally quoted in the biweekly, *India Today*, 1 February–15 February 1980.

81. *"Playboy* Interview: Muhammad Ali,'' (December 1975): 71.

82. *New York Times*, 25 March 1978.

83. Zoë Marsh and G. W. Kingsnorth, *An Introduction to the History of East Africa* (Cambridge, Eng.: Cambridge University Press, 1965), p. 33.

84. *Ebony*, November 1968, 16.

85. *"Playboy* Interview: Malcolm X,'' *Playboy* (May 1963): 58.

86. Ibid.

87. *Muhammad Speaks*, 23 June 1967.

88. Resolution in memo of Arnold Aronson, National Jewish Community Relations Advisory Couuncil (NJCRAC), 21 March 1972.

89. See Le Roi Jones, "Black Art,'' in Le Roi Jones and Larry Neal, eds., *Black Fire, An Anthology of Afro-American Writing* (New York: Morrow & Co., 1966), p. 302.

90. *New York Times*, 23 March 1972.

91. NJCRAC Memo, 21 March 1972.

92. *New York Amsterdam News*, 25 March 1972.

93. Rep. William Clay (D, Mo.), statement of Congressional Black Caucus, released to the press, 20 March 1972.

94. Ibid. Jewish spokesmen who had been dismayed by the Gary resolution were greatly pleased by the repudiation by Black legislators. B'nai B'rith's Anti-Defamation League called the resolution "a totally baseless and one-sided statement aimed at dismemberment of the State of Israel.'' Seymour Graubard, ADL national chairman, statement, ADL press release, 28 March 1972.

95. See chapters 17, 18 and 19 in Marvin Kalb and Bernard Kalb, *Kissinger* (Boston: Little, Brown and Co., 1974).

96. American Jewish Congress press release, 18 January 1974.

97. *New York Amsterdam News*, 20 October 1973.

98. *Afro-American*, 16 October–20 October 1973.

99. James S. Tinney, "Will Black Troops Have to Fight Africans In Mid-East War,'' *Afro-American*, 3 November 1973.

100. American Jewish Congres press release, 18 January 1974.

101. Yankelovich, Skelly and White, Inc., "A Study Of The Attitudes Of Grass Roots Black Leaders Toward The Mideast Situation, Israel, The Arab Nations and American Jews'' (May 1975), Table 27.

102. Ibid., Table 28.

103. Ibid., Table 30.

104. Ibid., Table 31.

105. Ibid., Table 22.

106. Ibid., Table 23.

107. Ibid., Table 29.

108. American Jewish Committee, "The Yankelovich Interviews With Black Grass-

Roots Leaders And Trade Association Professionals'' (Unpublished report, August 1975), 6.

109. Reprinted in the *Congress Monthly*, October 1975, 5.

110. Black Congressional Leaders, statement on Israel and the United Nations, 1 August 1974.

111. Vernon E. Jordan, Jr., statement, 1 August 1975.

112. *Philadelphia Tribune*, 22 July 1975.

113. *Chicago Defender*, 22 July 1975.

114. *Kansas City Call*, 22 August–28 August 1975.

115. Ibid., 9 August 1976.

116. Ibid., 14 November–20 November 1975.

117. Ibid., 23 January 1976.

118. Ibid., 21 November–27 November, 1975; and *Los Angeles Sentinel*, 20 November 1975.

119. *Los Angeles Sentinel*, 29 January 1976.

120. Ibid.

121. Ibid.; and *Voice News and Viewpoint* (San Diego), 11 February 1976.

122. *The Black Panther*, 31 January 1976.

123. *New York Times*, 23 July 1969.

124. *The Black Panther*, 22 November 1975.

125. Ibid., 6 December 1975.

IV

Black Hebrew Israelites and Other Non-Whites in Israel

Adding to the jaundiced view that some Black Americans have of Israel is the predicament of the Black Hebrew Israelites, a group of Black nationalists who have resided in the Jewish state for almost a decade and a half. Their journey from urban America to the "Promised Land" was a troubled and tortuous one.

In the early winter of 1967, a year of racial turmoil and strife, approximately 175 Black Americans left the land of their birth and took up residence in the republic of Liberia. Back-to-Africa movements were nothing new in Black American history.[1] Liberia came into being as an independent nation in the pre-Civil War period as a result of the repatriation of "free" Negroes, a repatriation supported mainly by white racists. Until the military coup in 1980 the country was ruled continuously by Americo-Liberians and has been the locus of most Afro-American repatriation projects, Black-sponsored and white-sponsored, ever since.

What was novel about the 1967 Black Americans' relocation was that the new arrivals in Liberia described themselves as "Hebrew Israelites." Outsiders frequently referred to them as "Black Hebrews" or "Black Jews." They hailed from various states. Many were from Illinois, and they had been organized as the Abeta Israel Hebrew Center on the south side of Chicago whence they began their trek to Africa.[2] Most of the emigrants were young, in their twenties and thirties, but the contingent included one eighty-two year old woman. Some had Hebraized their names. One explained, "American names were given to slaves by their masters. I am no longer a slave, and my only master is the God of Israel." A spokesman for the Black Hebrews said it was their intention to surrender their United States citizenship, "if you can call it that—they really don't have a citizenship to give up."[3] Bitterness over racial oppression in America was apparent in their statements. "We'd rather live in the jungles of Africa than in a house in Cicero [Illinois]," exclaimed one.[4] Another, an ex-paratrooper, later explained, "I left the United States with my wife and daughter to escape economic slavery, hatred and murder."[5]

The Liberians were initially confused by the identity of the Black Hebrews. That confusion persisted until their departure. The *Liberian Star*, which had reported the presence of Black Muslim priests in the body of Afro-Americans that had arrived in September 1967, still depicted the Hebrew Israelites as Black Muslims a few years later.[6] Perhaps when they first settled in Liberia, which restricts its citizenship to Black persons, the Abeta Blacks accentuated their racial solidarity with the West Africans rather than their Jewishness. Yet, a correspondent who visited the Hebrew Israelites in Liberia said that their motivation in leaving the United States was "more religious than racial." They saw their emigration as a fulfillment of divine prophecy.[7]

Within months a small number of these pioneers returned to the United States. A few remained in Monrovia, the capital city. The majority established themselves on a three-hundred-acre site near Gbtallah in a snake-infested region, more than eighty miles from the capital. Bush was cleared, wells dug and dwellings constructed in short order. Work was begun on a house of worship for the migrants. Most tilled the soil though they were generally lacking in agricultural experience. To raise money the expatriate group resorted to sundry enterprises, such as operating a snack bar in Monrovia where the menu included "soul chicken" and an ice cream dish imaginatively advertised as "soul on ice." The real attitude of the Liberian government towards the Black Jews has been shrouded in mystery. Whereas the New York *Amsterdam News* stated that it had been informed by the government of President William V. S. Tubman that immigrants were still welcome,[8] the *New York Times* wrote that unidentified Liberian officials were fearful that these Blacks "could be the vanguard of large migrations from the United States that would upset the political balance here."[9] Life was difficult in the wilderness camp, but a report published in November 1968 indicated that the doughty band was content in Liberia. About the same time they vowed to an *Ebony* correspondent, "We are here to stay."[10] A year later James A. A. Pierre, Liberian attorney general, expressed displeasure with the immigrants. He faulted them for not assimilating into Liberian society.

The Liberian government usually scatters newcomers among the general population. It is reluctant to permit recent immigrants to congregate in one place, as the Hebrew Israelites did in Gbatallah. Attorney General Pierre further charged that the American Blacks had no apparent intentions of working or becoming useful citizens.[11] A deportation order for seventy-five of the Black Hebrews was issued in November 1969 but subsequently rescinded.[12] It was the late President Tubman himself who countermanded the deportation order. Taking issue with Attorney General Pierre, President Tubman said that the government was not coercing the immigrants to become naturalized Liberian citizens as some people mistakenly believed.

Especially remarkable were the unverified reports about the Hebrew Israelites which President Tubman refuted. False and conflicting gossip had been circulated that the Black Americans were in contact with unnamed outside reactionaries, that they had adorned their synagogue with pictures of Mao Tze Tung and that visitors to their bailiwick were restricted in their movements. These allegations had been investigated and found to be without any basis in fact, President Tubman emphasized.[13]

In retrospect the Hebrew Israelites argued that when he castigated the Afro-Americans, Attorney General Pierre spoke for himself and not for the government of Liberia. They perceived Pierre as their nemesis and President Tubman as their champion. Nasi Ahsiel Ben Israel, a high-ranking Hebrew Israelite, asserted in 1972 that President Tubman actually earmarked $40,000 for the immigrants but "thieves in the government" stole it.[14]

A little more than two years after they fled the United States seeking freedom in Africa, a second exodus was undertaken by about seventy of these Black Hebrews. Their new destination was the State of Israel. "Permanent" residence in West Africa had turned out to be a rather temporary settlement. Chicago-born Ben-Ammi, formerly Ben Carter, a one-time bus driver and now the all-powerful spiritual leader of the Black Hebrews, has insisted that Liberia was never regarded as their ultimate destination. From the start it was intended to prepare them for their return to Israel.[15] He and his followers had travelled to the wilderness of Liberia as their Hebrew forefathers had wandered in the wilderness after their ordeal in Egypt. The specific purpose of the Liberian sojourn was to enable the Black Hebrews to cleanse themselves after their period of bondage in the United States. In Liberia they could throw off the shackles of "niggertism," Ben-Ammi stated at a public forum in Jerusalem in May 1972.

Would the Hebrew Israelites have remained in Liberia had circumstances been different there?[16] No definite answer can be given to this hypothetical question. Their difficulties notwithstanding, they were still legally allowed to live in Liberia. Most chose to leave. To be sure they were not urged to migrate to Israel by Israeli diplomats in Monrovia, as has been suggested. Ben-Ammi has said publicly that his "nation" did not just descend upon Israel. The Black Hebrews were in touch with Israeli embassy personnel in Liberia, but he admits that they never received a definite authorization from the embassy. They decided to go anyway. It is conceivable that a handful of Israelis, private citizens who were working in Liberia, did encourage the Blacks to go to Israel by giving rosy descriptions of their country. At least one private citizen helped them to learn Hebrew.

In any event late in 1969 the first contingents of Black Hebrews landed at Lod's Ben-Gurion Airport. Ben-Ammi informed the Israeli officials that they were authentic Jews and were therefore entitled to Israeli citizenship under the Law of the Return.[17] That law passed in 1950 confers upon Diasporan Jews an automatic right to return to Zion. Exceptions are limited to cases of individuals who are deemed to be security risks and those who jeopardize the public health.

Because their religious credentials were unclear, the first two batches of Black Hebrew Israelites were not immediately recognized as Jews. At the same time

their entitlement to entry into Israel under the Law of the Return was not categorically rejected. Final decision about their status was deferred, pending investigation of their genealogical claims. They were dispatched to Dimona and
Arad, two Negev communities, and were accorded special privileges ordinarily
reserved for immigrants. Dimona, with a population of about 27,000 including
olim (new immigrants) from North Africa, India and Georgia in the Soviet Union,
drew the bulk of the Blacks. Subsequent platoons of Hebrew Israelites were also
sent to the Negev, some to Mitzpeh Ramon and a few were directed to Jericho
on the West Bank.

Non-white Jews were not complete strangers to the Israeli populace, a slight
majority of whom are Oriental in origin and swarthy in appearance. Indian Jews,
and some Falashas from Ethiopia, were among the exiles who had been ingathered
since the founding of the Jewish state. In addition, there are a few Black Americans living in Israel whose conversion to Judaism is beyond question and who
are accepted as bona fide Jews under *Halacha* (Jewish religious law). They have
no tie to Carter's sect. But the Hebrew Israelites who adamantly refused to
undergo conversion, which they deemed completely unnecessary, are *sui generis*
among would-be immigrants to Israel. As such they further complicated the
already seemingly insoluble problem of determining who is a Jew. In the process
they have stimulated the curiosity of countless Israelis and Americans alike about
Blacks who are adherents of Judaism.

Relatively little has been written about the origins, characteristics and tenets
of Black Jewish sects.[18] Actually not much is known about their genesis. The
Black Jews themselves are not very helpful in this regard. When asked how long
their families have been Jews or Israelites, they are apt to answer that they've
always been Israelites but didn't always know it.

Hebrew sects were clearly part of the Black urban landscape in New York,
Philadelphia, Chicago, Washington, D.C., and elsewhere by the time of World
War I. At least one and very possibly more of these sects antedated the turn of
the century. Some of the sects were communitarian and were led by self-styled
"prophets." Ideology and ritual varied somewhat from congregation to congregation. Christian beliefs were often merged with those of Judaism to form a new
syncretic faith usually with Black nationalist overtones.

How and why did Black Americans come to identify themselves as Jews or
Israelites? It is probable that such identification was based largely on the fact
that Negroes, like the Hebrews of antiquity, had experienced the brutality and
indignity of slavery. During the antebellum era many Black bondsmen drew an
analogy between their own plight and that of the Israelites as described in the
Old Testament. Plantation spirituals were replete with scriptural names and
places. References to Moses, Egypt, Jerusalem and the Jordan River in spirituals
have been adduced by Ben-Ammi as proof of early awareness by Blacks of their
Israelite heritage.

Moreover, the same rejection of Christianity, washed white as the religion of
the Caucasian oppressor, which helps to explain the Black nationalist/Black

Muslim movement, may have predisposed some Blacks to adopt Judaism. James Landing, a scholar who has studied Black Jews in the Chicago area, is convinced that the Black Jewish movement represents the first sectarian-based brand of Black nationalism in the United States which was not explicitly Christian. Not only did it predate the Muslims but it even anticipated the Muslims' immediate predecessor, the Moorish-Americans.

The Hebrew Israelites in Israel have repeatedly said that the ancient Hebrews were Black, not white. This notion has been shared by virtually all Black Jewish sects. Initially, however, its greatest appeal was to Black nationalist clerics who felt that it was self-deprecating for Black people to portray deities and holy personalities as Caucasians. For example, Bishop Henry McNeal Turner of the independent Black African Methodist Episcopal Church and the leading apostle of back-to-Africanism from the 1880's until his death in 1915, proclaimed that Christ in human form was Black. A thoroughgoing Black nationalist, Turner also declared that Adam, the first of the species, had himself been Black. For that matter Turner in the pages of his journal, the *Voice of Missions*, claimed that "God is a Negro."[19] James Morris Webb, another Black minister, wrote unequivocally that Mary, the mother of Christ, "was born out of the tribe of Judah, a black tribe." Consequently, the blood of the Negro flowed through the veins of Jesus. David too had Negro ancestors, and Daniel was described by Webb as "the black prophet."[20] John E. Bruce, a devotee of Black nationalist Marcus Garvey and his UNIA wrote that Solomon, the wisest of men, was Black.[21] George Alexander McGuire, chaplain general of the UNIA as well as founder, first bishop and patriarch of the Black independent African Orthodox Church, also propagated the belief that the Madonna and Christ were Black. Today, Reverend Albert B. Cleage, Jr., of the Shrine of the Black Madonna in Detroit is consistent with this religious tradition in insisting that Americans of African descent are actually God's chosen people in the Old Testament sense of that term. Cleage, also a Black nationalist, has denied that the nation of Israel whose history is chronicled in the Bible was ever a white nation. In enunciating his Black power theology, Cleage has described Jesus as "a revolutionary black leader. . . seeking to lead a black nation to freedom." Mary was a Black woman, he has written, and Moses was non-white, too.[22]

Essentially, Black Jews have belonged to this same school of religious thought. Rabbi Wentworth A. Matthew, founder and spiritual head of a sizeable Harlem congregation, the Commandment Keepers, commented in an interview published several years ago in an Afro-American newspaper: "The black man is a Jew because he is a direct lineal descendant of Abraham."[23] The patriarchs, in his judgment, were undoubtedly Black, and Rabbi Matthew said flatly that all genuine Jews are Black men. Prophet F. S. Cherry, who established the Church of God in Philadelphia, told his Black followers that they were the Jews discussed in the Scriptures. Black people, he taught, were descended from Jacob, himself a Black man. Because Jacob was known as Israel after he had wrestled with the angel, Blacks ought to be referred to as Israelites.[24]

Prophet William S. Crowdy, a chef on the Sante Fe Railroad who started another Black Jewish sect in Kansas in 1896, revealed to his worshipful disciples that the Lost Tribes of Israel were the forbears of American Negroes. At first the ancient Hebrews were Black but through miscegenation had become white. This group celebrated Passover and utilized a Jewish calendar with Hebrew names for the months.[25] However, many of its precepts and practices were essentially Christian. It is significant that Crowdy's sect was officially called the Church of God and Saints of Christ. National headquarters were established in Philadelphia in 1900. Seventeen years later "international" headquarters were set up in Virginia; and by the depression-ridden 1930's, it could boast of having seven thousand members. The Hebrew Israelites in Dimona frequently allude to Crowdy, who may have been the intellectual father to their movement.

Abundant evidence can be cited by Black Jews to buttress their contention that Judaism and the Hebrew culture have deep roots in Black Africa. In a short work written by Steven Jacobs and Rudolph Windsor, the authors aver that the biblical, anthropological and archaeological sources all indicate that "from the time of Abraham, onward, Black civilization and Hebrew civilization were synonymous."[26] Windsor is president of the Association of Black Israelites. According to the Jacob-Windsor interpretation, the ancient Hebrews who migrated to Africa before 1650 B.C. were the ancestors of Afro-Americans in terms of both blood and culture. Abraham and his brethren were Black in appearance. On the other hand, the white Jews of Europe and the United States today bear little physical resemblance to the original Israelites from whom they do not descend biologically.

Black Hebrews, wherever they are found, subscribe more or less to this version of their past. After the destruction of the Second Temple (A.D. 70) the Israelites fled to North Africa and to West Africa, Ben-Ammi has said. Centuries later they were victims of the nefarious Atlantic slave trade and for more than four hundred years resided in the United States, which Ben-Ammi has labelled the "House of Captivity." During the epoch of slavery the displaced Africans were constantly reminded that they were Israelites.[27] Another spokesman for the Hebrew Israelites in Israel has reported that in 1895, when Theodor Herzl launched the modern political Zionist movement, Black Americans were raised from their graves to preach that they were the real descendants of the ancient Israelites.[28]

The Black Hebrews in Israel call themselves a "nation." They eschew the word "sect" and take umbrage at those who apply it to them. Believing themselves to be the descendants of all twelve tribes, they reject the term Jew as inappropriate because the tribe of Judah for which the Jews are named is just one of the twelve. In their view all twelve tribes were Black. On a number of occasions they have denied that most Israelis, Ashkenazim and Sephardim, can trace their family trees to Abraham, Isaac and Jacob. Revealing woeful ignorance of modern Jewish history, Ben-Ammi has declared that Caucasian Jews cannot trace their lineage to Israel prior to Herzl's time.[29]

Suggestions that the Jewish inhabitants of Israel are not the true seed of

Abraham, that they are imposters, that they are not the rightful inheritors of the land of Israel have earned the Blacks considerable enmity. To the beleaguered Israelis it is irksome enough to be continuously accused of being usurpers by the Arabs. To be told the same thing, in effect, by transplanted Black Americans, erstwhile denizens of Chicago and other cities in the United States, is intolerable. Many of the troubles that have beset the Black Hebrews in Israel are attributable to this simple fact: their genealogical beliefs or pretensions are directly in conflict with the historical concepts that undergird modern Zionism and the very existence of Israel as a Jewish state.

At the outset very few Israelis knew of the Blacks' preemptive claim to their country. Consequently, the Blacks were initially more of a curiosity than a problem. Virtually all of the Blacks in Dimona lived in one compound, a few families occupying each apartment because the government was loath to allot additional living space. There was also a meeting room and a small library in the cramped quarters of the Hebrew Israelites. Mainly because work permits were frequently withheld, employment was difficult to procure. A few of the Blacks worked in textiles or in construction. Some were self-employed, making jewelry and leather goods. They also formed a musical band which entertained throughout the country. Family and friends were another source of funds. Although the Blacks said that money was a problem for them, they did have sufficient money to charter buses for periodic trips to Tel Aviv and Jerusalem.

Garbed in floor-length robes, the Black Hebrews, male and female, were a colorful sight. Both sexes wore head coverings because "when they speak they are doing so before the Creator." Even the young children who seemed to abound wore distinctive dress. A number of the men, especially elderly ones, carried staffs. When greeting each other it was common for the men to kiss on both cheeks. Puritanical in many respects, the Blacks abstained from smoking. They fasted on the Sabbath, i.e., Saturday. Worship on Sunday, Carter taught, is the mark of the beast. Many of the Blacks were reputed to be vegetarians. How strictly they adhered to the dietary laws of Kashruth is debatable. They circumcized their male offspring but did not have the Bar Mitzvah rite of passage.[30]

In their way they were exceedingly devout. Gatherings, even parties, often began with a prayer. But they deviated from Judaism in that they accepted only the Torah, not the Talmud or Mishnah. They had no rabbis. Their leaders were often addressed as Nasi or prince.

Elements of Christianity were occasionally insinuated in their faith. When Ben-Ammi Carter wrote to the Ugandan strongman Idi Amin in 1978, he spoke of the Hebrew Israelites' faith in the "God of Jacob, Noah, David, *Paul and John the Baptist*" [emphais added]. By the mid-1970's some of the sect referred to Carter as "the Prince of Peace" or the "Son of God."[31] And when a Black American Jew unaffiliated with the sect visited Arad, he asked one of the Hebrew Israelites if he had a sacred Torah. "Yes" was the immediate reply, and he pulled out a St. James Bible.[32] Given the Christian background and upbringing of most of the Hebrew Israelite nation, the foregoing is not surprising.

Polygamy is permitted. If he can support them, a Hebrew Israelite may have seven wives. Clearly, women's liberation has made no inroads among the Hebrew Israelites. It is abundantly plain that the place of a Black Israelite woman is in the home. The two sexes congregate separately. Men usually do not shake hands with women. One man will not enter a second's apartment if only the latter's wife is at home. In some of these prudish respects, Hebrew Israelite practices resemble those of the Black Muslims. Another Black Hebrew custom is worthy of note. When a woman is having her menstrual period a red string is attached to her door and her husband is forbidden to touch her.[33]

The Hebrew Israelites converse in both English and Hebrew. Fluency in the latter tongue varies greatly from person to person. Some knew Hebrew in America and added to their mastery of the language in Israel. In the early 1970's the Blacks had their own classes in Hebrew at the Dimona Cultural Center. Interestingly, they also wanted to study Arabic at the center, but their request to do so was rejected.

The United States may be out of sight, but it has not been completely out of the Hebrew Israelite mind. When this author visited the Dimona complex inhabited by the Blacks, he found approximately twenty of the male members of the "nation" crowded into the corner of one apartment listening to a tape recording of the Muhammad Ali-Floyd Patterson heavyweight championship fight!

At first, despite overcrowded accommodations and a paucity of jobs, the Blacks appeared to be faring well. Their children attended local schools, and their Israeli neighbors accorded them a cordial welcome. Gabriel Katan, a Hebrew Israelite notable, once tearfully proclaimed, "It is wonderful to be in a free country and be among one's own brothers who behave so kindly to you."[34]

But the honeymoon was short-lived. After the arrival of a third wave of Blacks, circumstances changed for the worse. In August 1971 Ben-Ammi held a news conference at which he found fault with the job and housing situations and decried the "Jim Crow policies similar to what we left behind." A press release the following month enumerated the manifold grievances of the Blacks. They had been "refused Medical Care, Equal Housing, Schooling and Birth Certificates for some 30 babies born in Israel." "Why," asked the press counselor for the Black Hebrews "are others given apartments, and furnishings on their arrival, but Israelites are denied them?" Others were given land and financial assistance to become self-reliant. Why, he inquired further, were these refused to the Hebrew Israelites? In short, why were they not granted the benefits of the Law of the Return? Why indeed?[35]

Israeli skepticism about the Blacks' religious identity and the doubts which Blacks voiced about the heritage and ethnic pedigree of most Israelis had fostered disharmony. In addition, a number of specific incidents had a decidedly chilling effect on Israeli-Black Hebrew relations. For example, a Hebrew Israelite protest demonstration in a Dimona supermarket in October 1971 triggered a loud outcry. On that occasion the Blacks entered the supermarket, proceeded to fill their shopping baskets with goods and then adamantly refused to pay. After the police arrived, the Blacks left the premises quietly without the items that they had removed from the shelves.[36] To this day they contend that they merely wanted to dramatically protest their plight in Dimona. The fact that the Blacks had invited the press and a television camera team to witness their actions lends credence to their contentions. Nonetheless among the Israeli populace and perhaps in government circles also, the brief episode probably conjured up visions of racial friction and lawlessness, American-style. Relations between the Hebrew Israelites and their Israeli neighbors were soured further when some of the Blacks illegally entered five vacant apartments reserved for new immigrants and, in effect, carried out a "sit-in," the avowed purpose of which was to underscore their shortage of living space. Again, they left only after the police appeared.

Contributing more to the deepening troubles of the Hebrew Israelites than any other single incident was a bloody confrontation which took place on the streets of Dimona. Involved were members of the Hebrew Israelite community and dissident Blacks who had been expelled from their midst for wrongdoing. The clash resulted in the death of twenty-six year old Cornell Kirkpatrick, originally of Chicago. Supposedly the deceased had previously been ejected from the community for having publicly beaten his spouse. A second Black had been banished because of a series of thefts which he had committed. A third man, reputed to be a homosexual, had also been barred from Dimona. In January 1972 there occurred a pitched battle between these three and a group of Hebrew Israelites, members in good standing. Weapons included rocks, axes and wooden staves. In connection with Kirkpatrick's death, five Hebrew Israelites were charged with manslaughter in a Beersheba courtroom. They were convicted and sentenced to prison terms ranging from six months to two years. In one respect it is ironic that the homicide and subsequent trial and convictions should have led to so much adverse publicity for the Hebrew Israelites. The banishment of the three "troublemakers" had been prompted in large measure by the desire to improve the badly eroded public image of the Hebrew Israelites by purging the community of "thieves, wife-beaters and perverted people."[37]

Racial strife in the United States in the 1960's had been given extensive coverage in the Israeli press, Pictures of defiant Black Americans participating in civil disobedience campaigns and pictures of angry Blacks looting during urban riots were fixed in the minds of many Israelis. These helped to shape the reactions, official and unofficial, to the killing of Cornell Kirkpatrick and other isolated cases of Hebrew Israelite lawbreaking, including the protest demonstrations. Fears of racially motivated bloodshed were inevitably instilled in the Israeli consciousness. It is also possible that public opinion was molded to some degree by the prominence given to Black anti-Semitism, real and imagined, in 1968–1969 during the New York City teachers' strike and its aftermath.

Stories were widely circulated that rowdy Black Hebrews were disturbing their neighbors by playing musical instruments into the early morning hours. In October 1971 the chairman of the regional council in Mitzpeh Ramon, where there

were approximately twenty Black families living, said that their children were
a constant source of difficulty in school there. He threatened to expel some fifteen
youngsters.[38]

Hostility to the Hebrew Israelites was simultaneously exploited and incited
by Rabbi Meir Kahane, head of the Jewish Defense League (JDL) who had
settled in Israel. In the fall of 1971 Rabbi Kahane addressed seven hundred
persons in a Dimona cinema. He told his receptive audience that the Blacks
were not Jews. They were instead racists and anti-Semites who wished to bury
Israel. Kahane wanted them deported from the country forthwith.[39] As a result
of his appearance a number of Dimona's residents enrolled in the Jewish Defense
League. Almost a year later, speaking in the ramshackle Hotel Zion in downtown
Jerusalem, which served as headquarters for the JDL in Israel, Kahane reiterated
his strong opposition to the Black Hebrews. He was convinced that they were
"con men," "frauds," "vicious Jew haters, psychopaths and dangerous people"
who had migrated to Israel because they believed that Jews could be relied upon
to help poor Blacks. He thought it possible that they would cause trouble for
Israel by linking up with dissatisfied Oriental immigrants, the so-called Israeli
Black Panthers and with local leftists.[40]

Hebrew Israelite leaders were adding incalculably to their own difficulties by
broadcasting wildly extravagant figures of the numbers of Black "Jews" in the
United States. Ben-Ammi, in a nationwide television interview, said that there
were between two and fifteen million Black Hebrews. One million of them were
preparing to return home to Israel in the near future.[41] Precise census data on
Black "Jews" in the United States do not exist, but estimates of 25,000[42] to
40,000[43] would certainly be closer to reality. The *Negro Almanac* published in
1971 put the figure at 44,000.[44] Although Black Jewish sects proliferated in the
1950's and 1960's, they still represent an infinitesimal segment of the total Black
American population. As recently as July 1973, a Black rabbi, Abel Respes,
spiritual head of Temple Adet Beyt Mosheh in Elmwood, New Jersey, stated
that he had just about relinquished the hope of persuading Blacks to accept
Judaism after a quarter of a century of proselytizing.[45]

Israeli authorities must have recognized Ben-Ammi's figures on his Black co-
religionists for what they are: nonsensical hyperbole. Still, they may have suspected that there existed a substantial reservoir of Hebrew Israelites in the United
States ready and waiting to immigrate to the promised land. Already upset by
the presence of a small body of Blacks who regarded lighter-skinned Jews as
mountebanks, the Israeli government would have viewed with dismay the possibility of a mass Black Hebrew aliyah. Even individual immigration of Black
Hebrews was frowned upon.

By 1972 relations between the Hebrew Israelites and officials in Dimona were
strained to the breaking point. Local Histadrut functionaries were at odds with
the Afro-Americans. The Blacks were supposed to take part in the annual Independence Day ceremonies, but the mayor refused to appear on the same
platform with them. In his antipathy to the Blacks the mayor seemed to reflect

the sentiments of his constituents. Words of sympathy and/or support for the Hebrew Israelites in Dimona were only expressed by a couple of social workers. One believed that American Jewish fears of Blacks had been transferred to Israel. It was also his opinion that there was a serious problem of communication. For example, the Blacks, who often speak symbolically and figuratively, had told a former mayor that his time would come. He construed the remark as a threat on his life. However, it was the judgment of another social worker that the Soviet Georgian immigrants caused him more headaches than the Blacks. And this was his feeling months before about two thousand disgruntled Georgians laid siege to Ashdod and virtually paralyzed that port city in July 1973.[46] Few Israelis shared the social workers' generally positive attitude toward the Hebrew Israelites. Nationwide public opinion was decidedly unfavorable to them. Seventy-eight percent of Israelis polled by a Hebrew-language paper wanted them deported from the country.[47]

Early in 1972 a member of the opposition Gahal bloc, Menachem Yedid, told the Knesset of the woes of the residents of Dimona, woes ascribable to the Hebrew Israelites. People who dwelled in that Negev town did so in fear and suffering. Murder had occurred there once, and it might occur again. The Blacks were challenging the rights of the Jewish people to the land of Israel. He called for an investigation to determine if foreign, anti-Israeli elements were backing or exploiting the Hebrew Israelites.[48] A few months earlier government sources had revealed that a probe was already underway to ascertain if forces hostile to Israel had fostered the movement of Black Hebrews to Israel.[49] No proof that Black Hebrew actions had been instigated by the enemies of Israel has ever been disclosed. There was one half-hearted Arab attempt to take advantage of Israel's discomfit in grappling with the dilemma of the Blacks. The head of a delegation of Egyptian socialists who attended a convention in Rome said that Black Hebrews who were ousted from their ''abode'' in the Jewish state would be welcome in Egypt.[50]

It has been alleged that in 1971, if not before, the government of Israel decided to solve the problem of the Hebrew Israelites by ridding itself of them. The decision, which has never been implemented, was supposedly made at the highest government level, i.e., by Prime Minister Golda Meir herself. There were some in the Interior Ministry who favored a wholesale expulsion of the Hebrew Israelites. They had wished to cut the Gordian knot in this fashion from the day the Blacks first set foot on Israeli soil. However, largely for reasons of public relations, the government opted for Fabian tactics of attrition. The problem would be attacked piecemeal. No new Hebrew Israelites would be admitted to the country. Those who left for any reason whatsoever would not be allowed to reenter, and those whose visas expired would be required to leave. Additional pressure was to be exerted on the Blacks by not making work permits and apartments available. When twenty-one Afro-Americans flew into Israel in October 1971 to join the Negev Blacks, they were turned out of the country. In the first six or seven months of 1972 approximately sixty-five Hebrew Israelites were repatriated to the United States, a small percentage at United States government expense. Some left Israel reluctantly. Others informed the American embassy that they had been kept in the Black community by force. They alleged that they had been beaten and had had their heads shaved for wanting to leave. In November 1972 a spokesman for the ministry of the interior said that there were about two hundred Hebrew Israelites in the whole country, which was probably an understatement.[51] In any event, in the ensuing years the ranks of the sect were swollen by a high birthrate and clandestine infiltration of new arrivals.

At the beginning of 1973 the Israeli High Court of Justice handed down a decision very harmful to the Hebrew Israelite cause. The petitioners in the case were an eight-member family belonging to the sect. They had gone to Israel in September 1971 and had been granted three-month tourist visas. When the visas expired, a request for renewal was denied, and their expulsion was ordered. They appealed to the minister of the interior who ruled that as tourists they had no vested right to remain in Israel. The Law of the Return did not apply to them. The petitioners then carried their appeal to the High Court of Justice. Simply stated, their position was that they were scions of Abraham and they were faithful to the Laws of Moses and of Israel as set forth in the Torah. Although their counsel conceded that his clients were not Jewish in the usual sense of the term, they were Jewish enough to quality for entry under the Law of the Return.

Justice Berinson, speaking for the Court, rejected this argument. Tourists, unlike Israeli citizens and immigrants under the Law of the Return, are not entitled to permanent residence in the country. All countries, he observed, exercise the right to bar foreigners or to expel non-citizens whose presence is not desirable, and some nations do not even give reasons for their verdicts regarding entry and residence.

As far as the petitioners' entitlement to the benefits of the Law of the Return was concerned, Justice Berinson indicated that a Jew was legislatively defined (1970) as a "person who was born of a Jewish mother or has become converted to Judaism and who is not a member of another religion." Although the Hebrew Israelites follow the laws of the Torah, they do not accept the other books of the Bible. Therefore it could not be said that they believed in the Jewish religion as it had evolved over generations. Justice Berinson stated that no legal conclusions could be reached about their Hebrew roots. In addition, he discountenanced the idea that members of the Hebrew Israelite nation had mothers who would qualify as Jews. He concluded that the Hebrew Israelites had always been isolated from the traditions, culture and heritage of Judaism and did not fall within the definition of Jew as far as the Law of the Return is concerned. However, it is interesting that he did recommend that the respondent, the minister of the interior, might reconsider the possibility of permitting the petitioners to stay in Israel with the other Black Hebrews as they were already in the country.[52]

The Hebrew Israelites are convinced that their presence in Israel is an integral part of a divine plan. They say that Israel, unlike other countries, is holy land, which will "spit out unrighteous governments." They believe that they are the vanguard of the coming messianic age. In a press conference held on Mt. Zion, the Blacks spoke of plagues that would befall Israel and the western world and prophesied that Israeli planes would fall from the skies. In May 1972 Ben-Ammi predicted that there would be a war in the Middle East and that blood would flow. He talked about a takeover of the government and the establishment of a new kingdom. Ben-Ammi employed many parables in his remarks, but it is likely that he was taken literally by his audience. In the opinion of the Hebrew Israelites the final cataclysm was to have come in 1977. That year, they believed, would mark the millennium. Thereafter, the Hebrew Israelites in conjunction with all men of righteousness, white and Black alike, would control the world's spiritual powers.

Feeling more and more isolated, the Hebrew Israelites in 1972 hoped to broaden their base of support. To that end they planned a Jersualem summit to which Black Americans and Black Africans were invited. In their invitation to Kenyon C. Burke, a Black who then served as an urban affairs consultant to the Anti-Defamation League of B'nai B'rith, the Hebrew Israelites likened themselves to the David of ancient Israel in challenging the world's Goliath. They charged that during "the past several decades prophets, scholars, archaeologists, anthropologists and many renown [sic] historians have labored to cover up an international, diabolical plot to deceive the world. The greatest conspiracy ever conceived in the minds of men was the creation of a National Homeland for Jewish People."[53] The Jerusalem summit, a quixotic scheme to begin with, was abortive.

As discord between themselves and the government deepened, the Blacks became progressively vitriolic in their statements about Zionism and about the State of Israel. Their press counselor inveighed against "the great international religious conspiracy against the Hebrew Israelites and the black people in America,"[54] a comment that could easily be construed as anti-Jewish.

A flyer printed by the Blacks reflected their burgeoning indignation and frustration. It accused the "Israel Racist Government" of refusing reentry to a Black American, Gavriel Ben Israel on April 18, 1973. The flyer, which was distributed in the United States called for a boycott of all "Jewish Businesses that support Israel, until Black Americans—Hebrew Israelites—are permitted Free Entry like all other people into the Holy Land."

Written in the same mood of irritation was a public letter dated May 4, 1973. In it the Hebrew Israelites claimed that the human rights of Black Americans living in Israel had been violated. They declared that Gavriel Ben Israel had returned to the United States in January 1973 for business reasons and to visit his family in Chicago. When he tried to reenter Israel, he was prohibited from doing so without cause or reason; although, it was contended, he had been granted immigrant status under the Law of the Return upon his initial arrival in the country. He was jailed and supposedly denied permission to communicate with his wife and children in Arad. His son and daughter, both born in Israel, had never been issued birth certificates, which constitutes a breach of international law. In addition, they were not allowed to register for school. Other putative violations of human rights were the revocations of visas, the denial of work permits and the crowding of families into apartments with sixteen to twenty people. Not only were the Hebrew Israelites living under the "most deplorable and inhuman conditions ever," but they were "isolated from the outside world and living in a state of terror and siege." Israel was, in fact, "the most racist place in the world for black Americans."

In November 1972 Ben-Ammi Carter wrote to the then United Nations sec-retary-general Kurt Waldheim, contending that European Jews were not the authentic Hebrews to whom the Land of Israel had been promised by "prophetic vision." On the contrary, Black Hebrews were the rightful owners of the territory which had been expropriated by the Zionists. He called upon the world body to recognize the national rights of Black Hebrews as a people in their own land.[55] The sect also sent a petition to the Pan-African Congress asserting that the original inhabitants of Palestine were the forbears of the Hebrew Israelites and not the ancestors of the Jews of Israel.[56]

In the spring of 1973 representatives of the Hebrew Israelites approached the NAACP and asked for assistance. Loath to act on its own, the NAACP referred the Hebrew Israelites to the International League for the Rights of Man, of which it is an affiliate. The League is an international non-governmental organization enjoying consultative status with the United Nations in the human rights field. After examining the Hebrew Israelites' claim that they had been denied Israeli citizenship on racial grounds, the League tentatively concluded in July 1973 that there was no evidence the Black Americans had made any efforts to comply with the citizenship laws of Israel.[57]

In the years that followed, Black Hebrews, some of whom had been deported from Israel and others who had been unsuccessful in their bid for admittance to Israel, sought aid from a wide variety of groups. These included the Organization of African Unity, the Arab League and the Southern Christian Leadership Con-ference—in each instance to no avail.[58] In October 1977 a boycott of Israel, its products and its tourist attractions was called for by a minister of the Black Hebrew nation in an interview with the widely read Black weekly, the New York *Amsterdam News*.[59] This, too, failed to materialize.

Perhaps criticism of the sect's leadership by former members had hurt the Hebrew Israelite cause in Black America. Dissidence has long been a chronic problem for the Black Hebrew community as it has been for most Black na-tionalist movements. As many as twenty-five defectors, disillusioned with their Dimona "utopia," fled to Eilat. After one loyal Hebrew Israelite appeared on a Chicago radio program and simply accused the government of Israel of racism, three Hebrew Israelite women who had returned from Israel gave the *Chicago Defender*, a popular Black newspaper, a somewhat different version of their tribulations in the Jewish state. They pointed to power struggles among Black

Hebrew leaders, to the polygamy which was forced upon females in the sect and to the "fact" that most of the males were averse to work. Furthermore, they disclosed that on several occasions beatings had been inflicted on them and their children for failing to comply with the wishes of the Hebrew Israelite leaders. Those leaders, the interviewer from the *Defender* was told, styled themselves "gods" and "princes."[60]

Other defectors have told of the enormous control which Ben-Ammi Carter exercised over their lives. There are persistent rumors to the effect that Carter, who is commonly referred to as the "messiah," confiscates the passports of his disciples to deter defection. There have been complaints from sect members who were allegedly subjected to physical punishment and humiliation. For example, some said their heads had been shaven for an infraction of Hebrew Israelite rules.

Tom Whitfield, a charter member of the sect who had sought a life of dignity and self-esteem in Israel, subsequently became disenchanted and left. He has charged that two of his children died of malnutrition in the Black Hebrew community. In Whitfield's view they were the victims of neglect and died needlessly. Whitfield's harrowing experiences have been chronicled in grisly detail in his autobiography entitled *From Night to Sunlight.*[61] He has also recounted his dream-turned-nightmare in a one-hour documentary made for American television. Its theme was underscored in its title: *A Return to Freedom.*

Whitfield, an accomplished guitarist, served as musical director for the Hebrew Israelites. Initially, at least, he and his wife had so abiding a faith in Ben-Ammi Carter that they actually believed that he possessed the power to raise their infant son from the dead. Whitfield's commitment to the "nation" may explain his involvement in the 1972 killing of dissident Cornell Kirkpatrick. Later he was convicted and imprisoned for fraud. At one point the Whitfields' marriage was arbitrarily annulled because of his wife's insubordination to her husband and her use of foul language on a holy day.[62]

The Whitfields eventual defection was facilitated by a group of white Southern Baptist missionaries residing in Israel. Is the option to break with the Dimona cult a viable one for others? A reborn Tom Whitfield has written that Hebrew Israelite women in particular have a difficult time defecting because they must leave their children behind.[63] Prior to 1971 there was also the problem of where to go, for Carter had predicted that in September of that fateful year the United States would be destroyed. If Whitfield's account of life in the Hebrew Israelite community is accurate, discontent and fear must be rife for those who live under Carter's "dictatorial" rule.

Discontent and fear notwithstanding, the Hebrew Israelite community grew substantially throughout the 1970's due to a very high birthrate and to clandestine immigration. Over the years many Black Hebrews entered Israel under false pretenses. With every intention of taking up residence in Dimona, Arad or Mitzpeh Ramon, they deplaned at Ben-Gurion Airport or crossed the Allenby

Bridge from Jordan and described themselves as tourists or Christian pilgrims. Once safely in the country, they gravitated towards the Negev communities of the Hebrew Israelites and vanished.

Because Israeli immigration authorities found it next to impossible to distinguish bona fide Black tourists and pilgrims from apostles of Ben-Ammi Carter, they began to routinely subject Black visitors to intensive interrogation. There were many cases of harassment. Actor Lou Gossett, perhaps best known for his role in *Roots*, has alleged that he was taken out of passport control no fewer than six times and had a gun held to his head.[64] When Michael Hooks, a Democratic city councillor from Memphis, Tennessee, and a Black, arrived by air in February 1981, he too was mistreated.[65] There is no gainsaying the fact that Black passengers at Ben-Gurion Airport were more closely scrutinized than white arrivals, Christian or Jewish. Kenyon Burke, the former staff member of the Anti-Defamation League of B'nai B'rith, was questioned at length by Israeli immigration authorities. Even Bayard Rustin, the venerable civil rights and labor activist and Israel's most loyal booster in Black America, had a bad experience. An overzealous and insensitive official carried out his duties in a most unpleasant way before Rustin was recognized.[66]

According to United States Embassy officials in Tel Aviv, during the years 1979, 1980 and 1981, twenty-four, twenty-five and thirty-one Blacks were denied admission into the country by the Israelis who suspected them of membership in the Hebrew Israelite denomination.[67] There were many other instances in which Afro-American visitors were intensively interrogated before being given tourist visas. Those forbidden to enter the country usually lacked identification other than passports, carried a great deal of cash rather than credit cards or travellers checks, had excessive luggage for a short sojourn, had vague itineraries and/or lacked reservations or even knowledge of available accommodations in Israel. The names of some who were rejected for admission by airport personnel corresponded to those on Israeli lists of Hebrew Israelite sect adherents.

The Embassy received numerous complaints from Afro-Americans who said they had received discourteous treatment. None of the complainants cited physical abuse, but several stated that they had suffered emotional stress when they were denied entry.[68] Complaints of human rights violations have also been lodged at the United Nations. Among the complainants to the world body were two educators, Robbo Torrence and Yvonne Madison, who flew to Israel accompanied by a six-year-old child. All three were suspected of being Black Hebrews and were not allowed to enter the country. They alleged that their money was confiscated by Israeli officials. After being interrogated at length and subjected to strip searches they were roughly hustled aboard a Paris-bound Air France jet. According to a front-page account in the *New York Voice*, which bills itself as "New York's fastest growing interracial newspaper," the office of the Israeli Consulate-General conceded that an error had been made in this case.[69]

Publicity given to allegations of mistreatment at Ben-Gurion Airport unquestionably and understandably irritated Black Americans, but the dilemma of Israeli immigration officers who cannot differentiate between authentic tourists and pilgrims on the one hand and covert Hebrew Israelites on the other hand was real. It was underscored by a 1980 incident. A party of Black Americans, which included the Reverend Charles Kenyatta of New York, told of having their passports seized, of being strip searched and of being detained at the airport through the night until 7 A.M. the following day when they were summarily placed on board a plane for London. William Raspberry, a Black syndicated columnist, devoted an entire column to this incident, which he found most objectionable.[70] However, Raspberry discovered afterwards that a few members of the Kenyatta group had not been entirely candid when they insisted that they had no connection whatsoever with the Hebrew Israelites.[71]

Still, the fact that immigration authorities have sometimes been deceived by bogus pilgrims and fraudulent tourists is no excuse for the heavy-handed, rude reception which was frequently accorded Afro-Americans because of the color of their skin. Those Afro-Americans certainly attributed their cool "welcome" to racial discrimination, and they were not wrong. It is not difficult to imagine the furor that would ensue if Jewish travellers were, as a matter of course, subjected to comparable humiliation because of their Jewishness.[72]

How much the image of Israel among Afro-Americans has been tarnished by the evolution of the Hebrew Israelite drama cannot be calculated with precision. Also unclear is the extent to which the perennially delicate Black-Jewish equilibrium in the United States has been further strained. With its long history of undisguised animosity to Jews, the *Los Angeles Herald-Dispatch* is hardly typical of Black periodicals. It ostensibly endorsed the ideas expressed by "Asiel Israel" [sic] when that Black Hebrew Israelite visited the United States. He said that the exploitation of Blacks in the United States enabled Jews to aid their white Israeli brethren while at the same time the Jewish state withheld immigrant rights from the Black Hebrews.[73]

Much space has been devoted to the plight of the Hebrew Israelites by the *Amsterdam News*. In 1977 it repeated the Hebrew Israelite accusation that Israel was guilty of "outright racism" and linked that indictment to Ashkenazi prejudice against "non-white" Jews in Israel, meaning the so-called Oriental Jews. If Hebrew Israelite charges of racism were found to be valid, the *Amsterdam News* editorialized, "we would expect President Carter to take as hard position [sic] on this human rights issue as he has taken on human rights violations elsewhere in the world."[74] A few months later the same newspaper publicized the thirty-page report of a contingent of religious leaders who journeyed to Israel and who found much to criticize in the conditions under which many of the Black Hebrews were compelled to live.[75]

According to Joan Borsten, writing in the *Jerusalem Post*, the Israeli consul-general in Atlanta bemoaned the fact that repercussions of the Black Hebrews' case had damaged Israel's standing among Blacks in the American South and had injured the "good relations which exist between Jews and Blacks in the South."[76] A 1980 article in the *Pittsburgh Courier* commented that Dimona was quickly becoming the center of the Middle East's "hotbed of racial and religious intolerance."[77]

Because they were deeply worried about the thorny problem of the Black Hebrew community, which they said had serious human rights implications which aggravated Afro-American and Jewish American tensions and adversely affected "Israel's well-deserved reputation as a freedom-loving democracy," BASIC sponsored a fact-finding mission to Israel in January 1981. The six-person delegation, five men and a woman, was led by Bayard Rustin.

While in Israel they consulted government officials, United States Embassy officials, Histadrut personnel, American Jewish Agency staff people, the mayors of Dimona and Arad, Black Hebrews dwelling in both towns (including Ben-Ammi Carter), and other Black residents of Israel who were not affiliated with the Hebrew Israelite "nation." The delegation avoided involvement in the prickly "Who is a Jew" issue and deftly sidestepped the question of altering Israel's immigration laws; instead they focused on human rights.

After eleven days in the country, the group concluded that there was no official racism involved in the Hebrew Israelite dilemma.[78] Paradoxically, however, they did find that at Ben-Gurion Airport "black Americans are often singled out for discriminatory treatment and delayed on entering Israel." White visitors who were suspect were interrogated by immigration officers on an individual basis; but Black Americans, solely on the basis of pigmentation, were taken out of the passport control line at an earlier stage by the police. The delegation suggested a review of objectionable immigration procedures and accentuated the need for "great care and impeccable courtesy in this area."[79]

Mission members also concluded that as long as the Black Hebrews remained on Israeli soil it was the obligation of the Israeli government to safeguard their fundamental rights: the right to adequate health care, the right to adequate housing, the right to education for their children, and the right to earn a living.[80]

While the short report compiled by the delegation reflected the thinking of the entire group, individuals were free to express their own views. It is especially noteworthy that the report did not address the most basic question of all: "Should the Hebrew Israelites be permitted to remain in Israel or should they be expelled?" On that the report was conspicuously silent, but Bayard Rustin on his own opined that Israel had the right, both legally and morally, to oust the sect. "If a group of Nigerians had entered the U.S. illegally, refused to obey our immigration laws and practiced polygamy, I don't believe a single civil rights leader would question America's right to deport them," he said.[81] While he did not advocate expulsion—in fact he declared that he would grant Black Hebrews already there the legal right to reside anywhere in the country on condition that they did not violate the law[82]—Rustin believed that the sect as such was not digestible by Israel.[83] As for Ben-Ammi Carter, Rustin minced no words: "Carter is a dictator and dictators don't have the same moral standards as democratic leaders."[84] Within days of the publication of Rustin's views in the *Jerusalem Post*, the members of the commission, except for Rustin, dissociated themselves from the characterization of the Black Hebrew messiah as a dictator. While endorsing the report and its recommendations, the *entire* commission (including Rustin) repudiated "any commitment, real or hypothetical, to support Israel in a plan to deport the Black Hebrew Community" and reiterated that such a crucial policy decision was not theirs to make.[85] Unfortunately the government of Israel was still not prepared to make a decision on the Hebrew Israelites that would break the impasse.

When Prime Minister Begin conferred with more than twenty-five Black American leaders at New York's Waldorf Towers in September 1981, the encounter generated questions about Israeli attitudes towards South Africa's apartheid regime, Israeli policy on the West Bank and in Lebanon and what was perceived as Jewish American opposition to affirmative action. Some Blacks expressed interest in the Hebrew Israelite controversy. Indeed, Mrs. Marion Logan, a special assistant to the New York State commissioner of transportation, flatly declared that the problem of the Hebrew Israelites in Dimona constituted her "prime concern." Begin, for his part, solicited Black America's help in getting Ben-Ammi Carter to stop issuing anti-Israeli statements and to drop his claims that the Black Hebrews were the original owners of the land of Israel.[86] There is good reason to believe that Begin's government had no policy to resolve the vexing enigma of the Black Hebrews. If anything, the Israeli government was probably further from a solution than it had been almost a decade earlier when Prime Minister Golda Meir had virtually decided to repatriate the cult.

Back in 1972 and 1973 it appeared that the unhappy saga of the Black Hebrews' odyssey was drawing to a close. It seemed that their days in Israel were numbered. There was good reason to believe that almost all would be back in the United States in a year or two. Yet they were not expelled. They were not repatriated to the United States. Why? In all likelihood the major deterrent was the fear that large scale deportation could alienate Black American support for Israel and jeopardize the fragile and often uneasy relations between the Black American and Jewish American communities. It could conceivably impair Israel's badly eroded image in sub-Saharan Africa. A complicating factor was that many Hebrew Israelites had already surrendered their United States citizenship or were disposed to do so. It was presumed that such stateless persons could no longer be accepted by the United States.

Known for its bold and decisive strokes in other spheres (e.g., the capture of Eichmann in Argentina, the Entebbe Airport rescue, the bombing of the Iraqui nuclear facility), the government of Israel was paralyzed in its dealings with this Black nationalist sect in its midst. Faced with a deteriorating situation in the Negev, it resorted to a time-honored and dilatory tactic. It appointed a committee. The Interior and Environment Committee of the Knesset had recommended to Interior Minister Dr. Yosef Burg that he appoint a body to examine the problem of the Black Hebrew cult. In August 1978 a committee was duly appointed with David Glass, a Knesset member and a National Religious party luminary, as chairman.

The long-delayed report of the Glass committee, which was finally submitted in June 1980, chastised the Israeli government for its mishandling of the Hebrew Israelite dilemma. It ascribed the failure to block the initial entry of the Hebrew Israelites to the fear that Israel would be accused of racism. Glass concluded that Israel would have been perfectly justified in denying the Black Hebrews, who were not refugees without a homeland, the right to immigrate. The failure to do so was mistake number one. As soon as the cult's nature and ideology were understood, the members should have been dispatched to the United States with no more than two hundred expelled at one time.[87] Failure to do so was mistake number two. Instead, Glass declared, the Israeli authorities, in ostrich-like fashion, tolerated the growth of the movement to the point where it consisted of fifteen hundred souls, all technically criminals because they resided illegally in Israel. Some actual felons from the United States had infiltrated the community, which Glass asserted was so overcrowded as to constitute "a disgrace to the State of Israel."[88]

After setting forth the various possible solutions available to the government, Glass recommended that the Hebrew Israelites be granted legal status and be permitted to remain in Israel.[89] Exceptions would be made with individuals who had acted against the Jewish people or who were likely to threaten the security of the state or the public health.

Furthermore, it was recommended that the sect be relocated in a special village community, modeled on the controversial settlements which had been established by Jews on the disputed West Bank. An area south of Beersheva, the gateway to the Negev, was mentioned as a suitable site. In exchange the Hebrew Israelites would promise not to try to enlarge the community by adding new immigrants from overseas, a condition that Ben-Ammi Carter had previously agreed to in a letter sent to Interior Minister Burg on January 14, 1979.[90] Glass pronounced his recommendations "moral, humane and Jewish" and called for their speedy implementation.[91]

But there was to be no speedy implementation as Israeli public opinion, hostile to the Hebrew Israelites, hardened; and demands for their deportation were often voiced. Burg stalled for time. After five months of sitting on the fence and on his hands, in November 1980 the minister of interior rejected Glass' recommendations. He informed the Knesset that he was not willing to legalize the cult's presence in Israel, nor was he inclined to relocate them in a special village community as Glass proposed. Burg's own solution was to repatriate them either by persuasion or, if necessary, by force.[92]

Governmental indecisiveness and confusion were dramatized when Prime Minister Begin spoke to the board of governors of the American Jewish Committee on February 11, 1980, about various issues. During the question and answer period the prime minister was asked about the fate of the Hebrew Israelites, and he replied as follows: "This is a complex question and we will do our best to deal with it seriously so that the people will feel equal. . . . They'll be citizens of this country."[93] But within hours one adviser to Begin retracted the prime minister's utterance calling it a "slip of the tongue." There was no intention to alter policy and grant them Israeli citizenship, he explained.[94]

From all available evidence one may justifiably infer that Black Hebrew-Israeli frictions were further exacerbated during 1980 and 1981. In Dimona Israelis forcibly prevented several Blacks from occupying an apartment they had rented. Dimona's mayor, Jacques Amir, wired Interior Minister Burg imploring him to intervene as the matter of the Hebrew Israelite sect was reaching "dangerous dimensions."[95] But angered residents did not wait for governmental intervention. Instead they took the law into their own hands and constructed an iron gate to impede Hebrew Israelite entry into the rented flat. Their extralegal tactic was successful. In addition, when the Dimona municipality agreed to lease to the Blacks a building previously used as an absorption center, students in the adjacent junior high school organized a protest strike.[96] Disgruntled Israelis in Arad formed a Committee to Expel the Black Hebrews from Israel. In November 1980 hundreds demonstrated to press their demand that the cult be deported.[97] When the Hebrew Israelites in Arad were able to purchase a flat, the opposition decided to copy the direct action technique of the Dimona Jews and threatened to erect an iron gate to prevent cult members from entering. However, the "lock-out" never materialized as community pressure discouraged the owner of the apartment from completing the sale.[98]

In both Negev development towns embittered Israelis conceded that their conduct was illegal but necessary nonetheless. Black Hebrews were supposedly guilty of racism, anti-Semitism and anti-Zionism. Furthermore, they insisted that Black overcrowding had led to deplorable conditions, hazardous to community health. Their demeanor was often noisy, sometimes immoral. Moreover, it was prophesied that property values would plummet, a prophecy all too familiar to students of race relations in American history.[99]

The sore that was the Hebrew Israelite quandary continued to fester to the point that a scheduled basketball game between the Hebrew Israelites and an Israeli Air Force team had to be cancelled. Opponents of the match contended that Israeli defense forces personnel ought not fraternize with adherents of the Black sect, several of whom allegedly were in Israel illegally.[100]

Thus, both the Hebrew Israelites and the Israeli government find themselves mired in a morass with poor prospects of extricating themselves. While Israeli racism per se cannot adequately explain the inability of Israeli society to absorb the Black Hebrews—Irish, Finnish or any other white cultists who had acted as Ben-Ammi Carter and his disciples had acted would probably have had the same difficulties—color may well have made their absorption more problematic. But the Hebrew Israelites, by challenging the very legitimacy of Jewish ownership to the land of Israel, immeasurably damaged their chances of acceptance there. At heart the problem is not that the Black Hebrews are the "con men" or "frauds" that Rabbi Kahane believed them to be. It is not that they are dangerous subversives. It is that the Hebrew Israelites are Black nationalist religious zealots who have been victimized by their own zealotry which has rendered them unassimilable and unacceptable in a Jewish state. That zealotry plus the abrasiveness of the Black Hebrew leadership probably have made the ordeal of the sect an unreliable test of Israeli racial attitudes. Therefore, it would be instructive to look at the experiences of the other non-whites, Jewish and Gentile, in the Jewish state.

At the present time the fastest growing group of Israelis of African background is the Ethiopian Jews. In the dim, distant past they were dubbed "Falashas," which means "stranger" or "exile" or "immigrant," by their neighbors in the highlands of Ethiopia near Lake Tana. They referred to themselves as Beta-Israel, the House of Israel; and for many centuries, perhaps for more than two millennia, they thought they were the only Jewish community extant. Once they were a few hundred thousand strong, but today the tragic remnant of Ethiopian Jewry comprises approximately twenty-eight thousand souls.

What was their provenance? How and when did they arrive in the Horn of Africa? There are, of course, numerous theories as to their origins. Perhaps after the destruction of the First Temple in antiquity they migrated southward from Egypt or the Holy Land. Perhaps they departed Jerusalem as members of the retinue of Menelik, the misbegotten son of Sheba and Solomon. Maybe they are descendants of Jews who emigrated from Palestine after the Romans destroyed Jerusalem. To this day their origins are a riddle, enveloped by folklore and encased in historical conjecture.

Falasha interest in Palestine and in their fellow Jews was stimulated when they were "discovered" by Professor Joseph Halevy, a French Jewish scholar, in the nineteenth century. But very few trekked to Zion, and over the decades oppression and assimilation appreciably thinned their ranks. Even after Israel was reborn in 1948, the Falashas were not ingathered as were hundreds of thousands of their co-religionists in the Diaspora.

At long last, in 1972–1973 in the face of considerable rabbinical reluctance, the Sephardic Chief Rabbi, Ovadia Yosef, ruled that the Beta-Israel were Jews of the tribe of Dan. He further declared that he felt obligated to redeem them from assimilation, to speedily bring them to Israel and to educate them in the Holy Torah.[101]

Interior Minister Yosef Burg, for one, dissented. For two decades no Falasha had received an immigrant visa from his ministry, but in 1975 an interministerial committee officially recognized the Beta-Israel as bona fide Jews entitled under the 1950 Law of Return to automatic Israeli citizenship.[102] Having been granted the government's *heksher*, the secular imprimatur of Jewish authenticity, they could now enter Israel without restriction. Or could they? There were still obstacles, it seems. In the first place, the government, a Labor government, was slow to implement the ministerial decision, probably in part because some in the country's power structure were not eager to see a wave of *"shvartzers"* (Blacks) become citizens. It was rumored that Yitzhak Rafael, then minister for religious affairs, said as much.[103] And Ashkenazi Chief Rabbi Shlomo Goren, while he finally recognized the Falashas' Jewish identity, was a less than enthusiastic supporter, perhaps because their cause had been taken up first by his rival, Chief Rabbi Yosef, or perhaps because he regarded the ministerial decision as an unwarranted secular encroachment into the rabbinical sphere. He believed determining "who is a Jew" to be the prerogative of the religious establishment. Ostensibly, Goren also entertained some nagging doubts about whether the Falashas were really Jews.

In the second place, in 1974 after almost five decades on the Ethiopian throne, Emperor Haile Selassie was overthrown in a coup conducted by Marxist-inspired military officers. After the revolution civil strife and dislocation occurred in politically and geographically fragmented Ethiopia. In the chaos that followed Selassie's ouster, persecution of the "Zionist" Falashas was intensified both by pro-government officials and by anti-government forces. Arrest and torture were not uncommon. Some Falashas lost their land; others, their lives. Apparently reliable sources told of Falashas being sold into slavery. Hunger, malnutrition, dehydration and disease resulted in countless deaths, especially among Falasha children. Some of the Beta-Israel sought sanctuary outside the country; there they languished in refugee camps.

Officially the xenophobic Derg, the military regime, was opposed to the emigration of its citizens, particularly Falashas whose ultimate destination was the Zionist state. In 1977 the newly elected Begin government quietly inaugurated a rescue program, but the following year Foreign Minister Moshe Dayan inadvertently revealed that Israel was covertly arming the revolutionary rulers in Addis Ababa. Dayan's "slip of the tongue" temporarily impaired the exodus program and unleashed gory *pogroms* carried out against the Falashas by conservative elements, infuriated by Zionist collusion with the central government.[104]

By 1982 in excess of two thousand Falashas were residing in Israel, adding to that nation's fascinating mosaic of ethnicity. Why, one may justifiably ask, had not more been rescued over the years? Recalcitrance on the part of both the imperial Selassie government, with which Israel had good relations, and its military successor was certainly a factor. In key Israeli religious and secular circles apathy fueled by racial prejudice was a second important factor. No *shaliach* (emigration emissary) had ever been dispatched to Ethiopia. No "Operation Magic Carpet," which extricated nearly fifty thousand Jews (virtually the entire community) from Yemen in 1949–1950, had been contemplated. It would probably be an unwarranted disparagement to simply accuse successive Israeli governments of bigotry, but it is inconceivable that a desperate community of white Jews in danger of extinction would have been ignored so long.[105] Also noteworthy is the fact that some communities in Israel have been less than enthusiastic about the prospects of having Falashas settled in their midst.

In addition to the Falashas, a sizeable segment of Oriental Jewry, i.e., Jews from predominantly Muslim lands, are sufficiently dark-skinned to have qualified for the rear of buses in Alabama or Mississippi a few decades ago. Included in this segment are Kurdistani Jews, who hail from a mountainous area that overlaps the boundaries of Iran, Iraq and Turkey. Almost all of the Jews of Kurdistan were repatriated within a few years of Israel's birth. Dark-complected Jews from Yemen, who had lived under degrading conditions for centuries, left for Israel in a wholesale exodus. Still larger was the mass departure of more than a quarter of a million Jews from Morocco.

Another dark-skinned Jewish community is the Bene Israel from India, whose true origins are as murky as those of the Falashas. Most legends date their ancestral migration from the Holy Land to the west coast of India in pre-Christian times. Geographical isolation from other Jews over the centuries caused them to forsake the Hebrew tongue and to adopt the Marathi language as well as many of the traditions of the Hindus, among whom they dwelled as members of lower castes. Yet, they retained Jewish prayers and festivals, Sabbath observance, dietary regulations and the rite of circumcision. Most lived in Bombay whence approximately twelve thousand immigrated to Israel. The majority of them gravitated to settlements in the Negev desert.[106] Questions posed by an ultra-orthodox minority about the authenticity of their Judaism were resolved by the passage of a Knesset resolution declaring the Bene Israel "Jews in all respects, without qualification, and with the same rights as all other Jews."[107]

Several thousand other "Black" Jews from the Malabar coast in southwest India relocated in Israel. They were the product of intermarriage between lighter-skinned Jews and local Blacks on the Indian subcontinent. Raphael Patai has speculated that the community also grew as converts were made among the servants and slaves of Malabar.

A third group, the Meshuararim, emerged among the Jews of Cochin in India. All of these immigrated to Israel by the 1960's. As of 1968, according to Patai, the Indian Jewish population of Israel was twenty-three thousand.[108]

Ashkenazim (European Jews) often entertain cultural and racial prejudices toward their brethren from Asia and Africa. However, charges that the Orientals do not enjoy as high a living standard as European Jews in Israel are often simplistic. They ignore the higher educational achievements of the Ashkenazim, the smaller families and the fact that the Orientals were, in the main, later arrivals. Moreover, they fail to differentiate between and among the widely varying non-western Jewish communities and simply attribute Ashkenazi dominance to racial bigotry. In point of fact, the Yemenites though darker have fared better than the Moroccans for several reasons. The former have a culture which is generally admired by the Israeli populace. The Yemenites possessed a religious mentality and a Zionist ideology which facilitated their adaptation to life in Zion, and they carried with them more marketable skills than their North African counterparts whose father-centered traditional family has not proven very durable in Israel.

*   *   *

Perhaps another means of gauging racial attitudes in Israel is provided by sporadic contacts with Black Americans. Since the 1950's goodwill trips to Israel for Black American politicians, labor leaders and journalists have been sponsored by the government of Israel and by American Zionists. Early visitors were in awe of the young nation's near miraculous accomplishments. Hubert T. Delany, a retired justice of the Domestic Relations Court in New York City, travelled to Israel as a consultant on questions relating to juvenile delinquency. He reported on his journey in the pages of the *Crisis*, the organ of the NAACP. Delany's piece talked of the Israeli struggle as an "anticolonial movement" and described the Jewish state as a country of hope and fulfillment. A civil rights activist himself, Delany found no evidence in Israel of a "concept of inferior races."[109]

One little-known link between Black Americans and Israel was established in the 1960's. Leaders of Black cooperative development programs in the South thought they might learn something useful from the *kibbutz* and *moshav* movements. Only a fraction of the land in Israel is privately owned. Most agricultural production is carried out on *kibbutzim*, collective enterprises in which members toil and live together and share the fruits of their labors equally. On *moshavim* individual families work their own plots of land but purchase equipment and supplies jointly while marketing their produce cooperatively. Community services are also shared.

Could these highly successful Israeli models benefit Southern Black farmers, many of whom were migrating to the cities in desperation? Administrators of low-income rural collectives in Alabama, Georgia, Mississippi and elsewhere thought so; and several journeyed to Israel under the auspices of the Histadrut, the Israeli Federation of Labor. They studied innovative irrigation systems, aquaculture, consumer cooperatives, flower-growing and marketing techniques. Israeli agricultural expertise, which was then being dispensed in Asia and Africa, was thus made available to the Afro-American community. Among the beneficiaries were the Acadian Delight Bakery, a Louisiana-based cooperative, the Southwest Alabama Farmers Cooperative Association and the Northern Bolivar Farm Cooperative, a project stimulated by a number of Mississippi Delta Blacks who were sent to Israel by the Histadrut. Reverend Charles Sherrard returned to the American South from Israel, having seen a miracle—"people having put together nothing into something. This is what we knew we'd have to do in our country."[110] Georgia's New Communities, Inc., which envisioned "rural new towns" inhabited by impoverished landless Blacks was the tangible result of Reverend Sherrard's determination. Although these Black experiments with cooperatives have not been resounding successes in recent years, the inspiration and technical assistance provided by the Israelis should not be forgotten. Motives are often impossible to pinoint, but it may be surmised that Histadrut was actuated at least as much by Labor Zionist idealism as by the desire to win the goodwill of Black Americans who were then flexing long-atrophied political muscles during the civil rights revolution.

Over the decades a small number of individual "New World" Americans have taken up residence in Israel. For example, a Caribbean-born Black mannequin and entertainer named Lois Chezik was described some years ago by the

Los Angeles Sentinel as "Israel's top fashion model." She reportedly married an Israeli and settled contentedly in the country.[111]

From time to time one encounters Black converts to Judaism who have become inhabitants and citizens of Israel. One such was Larry Lewis, a graduate of Talladega College, who joined a kibbutz and served in the Israeli army.[112]

A handful of Black American athletes have played in Israel's "amateur" basketball league and have managed to achieve stardom there. A case in point is Aulcie Perry, a 6 foot, 10 inch native of New Jersey, who sought and found in Israel the recognition which had eluded him in America's professional ranks. As a non-Israeli—each team is permitted one "designated" foreign player— Perry played for the Tel Aviv Maccabi club and quickly established a reputation for athletic excellence. In 1978 Perry announced his intention to convert to Judaism and to become an Israeli citizen. True to his word, Perry formally converted; but the legitimacy of the conversion was challenged by certain orthodox religious authorities and by the Tel Aviv Hapoel sports club, Maccabi Tel Aviv's archrival, which feared that Perry's conversion would entitle his team to recruit another blue-chip foreign player. The controversy over the conversion was short-lived; and Perry, despite very occasional racial epithets, has become a national hero. On more than one occasion, he has expressed his love for Israel and its people.[113]

A second Black American sports hero, Earl Williams, embraced Judaism during 1982. Williams was also one of the superstars of the Tel Aviv Maccabi basketball team, perennially besieged by fans and well-wishers.[114]

It is difficult to generalize about the Israeli reaction to persons of African background. Some Blacks in Israel have complained about racial catcalls, usually from the lips of children. "Kushi" is a favorite epithet. To defend this mindlessness by explaining that "Kushi" translates simply as "Black" just will not do. If Jews in countries where they are minorities were greeted in the streets with cries of "Jew," they would hardly be appreciative. Undoubtedly they would describe such experiences as anti-Semitic.

Of course, there are so few persons of Black African descent in Israel that institutionalized racism does not exist. On the other hand, one may assume that people of European background, wherever they are in the world, share a condescending attitude toward those of African lineage. Indeed, this might well be a reasonable assumption when one considers the outlook of people other than Europeans. Feelings of superiority are rooted not just in exaggerted, perverted ethno-centrism but in racial mythology spawned centuries ago to justify and rationalize the slave trade. Israeli attitudes toward Blacks are no more racist than those found elsewhere. They are not more racist than those harbored by Arabs. Why should the Arabs, who engaged in slave trading in East Africa for centuries and who sent their Black cargo by the hundreds of thousands to the Persian Gulf, be immune to the bacillus of racism?

Except for the tribulations of the Black Hebrew Israelites on the edge of the Negev, the position of darker-skinned people in Israel has been given short shrift by the Black American media. It is probably fair to say that most Afro-Americans know little and care less about the subject. Burgeoning Black interest in Zionism and the Middle East is attributable to several other factors which are examined in this volume.

NOTES

1. For a survey of such movements in the nineteenth and twentieth centuries, see Robert G. Weisbord, *Ebony Kinship: Africa, Africans and the Afro-American* (Westport, Conn.: Greenwood Press, 1973).

2. In the late 1960's and early 1970's there were approximately a dozen Black Jewish groups in Chicago, not including the Abeta congregation. Two sects, the House of Israel Hebrew Culture Center and the B'nai Zaken, are also believed to have supplied a few of the migrants. According to the Chicago Board of Rabbis, the Abeta congregation of Hebrew Israelites had little contact with the Jewish community in Chicago.

3. *New York Times*, 20 September 1967.

4. Ibid., 18 January 1968.

5. Larry Price, "Black Jews in the Promised Land," *Chicago Today Magazine*, 8 November 1970, 8ff.

6. *Liberian Star*, 18 September 1967 and 4 November 1969.

7. Era Bell Thompson, "Are Black Americans Welcome in Africa," *Ebony* (January 1969): 44–46.

8. *New York Amsterdam News*, 23 December 1967.

9. *New York Times*, 18 January 1968.

10. Thompson, "Black Americans Welcome," p. 46.

11. *Liberian Star*, 4 November 1969.

12. An article published in New York in a Black nationalist periodical was sharply critical of the actions of the Liberian government. External pressures were suspected. See *African Opinion*, March–April 1970.

13. *Liberian Star*, 14 November 1969.

14. Nasi Ahsiel Ben Israel, Personal interview, 15 November 1972.

15. *Jerusalem Post*, 10 February 1971.

16. In a 1981 interview Ben-Ammi Carter insisted that it was a lie that his group had been "kicked out" of Liberia. In point of fact there were still perhaps 150 Hebrew Israelites in Liberia who survived the coup there in April 1980. They seem to have had government support.

17. *New York Times*, 23 November 1969.

18. The best known work on the subject is Howard Brotz, *The Black Jews of Harlem— Negro Nationalism and the Dilemmas of Negro Leadership* (New York: Schocken Books, 1970). In Morris Lounds, Jr., *Israel's Black Hebrews: Black Americans in Search of Identity* (Washington, D.C.: University Press of America, Inc., 1981), he makes a distinction between Hebrew Israelites and Black Jews.

19. Edwin S. Redkey, ed., *Respect Black: The Writings and Speeches of Henry McNeal Turner* (New York: Arno Press, 1971), pp. 176–177; and Edwin S. Redkey, *Black Exodus—Black Nationalist and Back-to-Africa Movements, 1890–1910* (New Haven and London: Yale University Press, 1969), p. 182.

20. James Morris Webb, *The Black Man—The Father of Civilization* (Seattle: Acme

Press, 1910), pp. 6–13; and James Morris Webb, *The Black Man Will Be The Coming Universal King Proven By Biblical History* (Chicago: n.p., 1919), pp. 10–13.

21. John E. Bruce, *Tracts for the People*, no. 14 (n.d.): 2.

22. Albert B. Cleage, Jr., *The Black Messiah* (New York: Sheed and Ward, 1968), pp. 4, 40–41.

23. Quoted in Roi Ottley, *"New World A-Coming"—Inside Black America* (Boston: Houghton Mifflin Co., 1943), p. 144.

24. Arthur Huff Fauset, *Black Gods of the Metropolis—Negro Religious Cults of the Urban North* (Philadelphia: University of Pennsylvania Press, 1944), pp. 34–35.

25. Elmer J. Clark, *The Small Sects In America* (Nashville: Cokesbury Press, 1937), pp. 188–190.

26. Steven Jacobs and Rudolph Windsor, *The Hebrew Heritage of Our West African Ancestors* (Wilmington, Del.: Rose-Lee Inc., 1971), p. 2. The authors draw most of their information from an earlier book, Joseph J. Williams, *Hebrewisms of West Africa: From Nile to Niger with the Jews* (New York: The Dial Press, 1930). For additional information see Rudolph R. Windsor, *From Babylon to Timbuctoo—A History of the Ancient Black Races Including the Black Hebrews* (New York: Exposition Press, 1973).

27. Ben-Ammi Carter, tape recording of remarks at a public forum, Jerusalem, 10 May 1972.

28. Nasi Ahsiel Ben Israel, Personal interview, 15 November 1972.

29. Ben-Ammi Carter, Tape, 10 May 1972.

30. Lounds, *Israel's Black Hebrews*, pp. 60–61.

31. Thomas Whitfield, *From Night to Sunlight* (Nashville, Tenn.: Breadman Press, 1980), p. 75. See also "The Black Hebrews" (Jerusalem: American Jewish Committee and American Jewish Congress, 1980), p. 5. This is known as the "Glass Report."

32. Rabbi Abel Respes, Telephone interview, 20 March 1982. Respes visited the Dimona community and recounted this incident to the author.

33. Traditional Jewish practice demands total avoidance of sexual contact of any kind during the wife's menstrual period and for seven days thereafter. However, in contrast to Hebrew Israelite practice, in traditional Judaism there are no visible indicators that a woman is undergoing menstruation, as this is supposed to be the intimate information of husband and wife. See Lev. 15:19–32 and Lev. 18:19.

34. Shulamit Korn, "Dimona—A Black Misunderstanding," *Jerusalem Post*, 15 October 1971.

35. Press release, September 1971.

36. Korn, "Dimona."

37. Aron Manheimer, "The Black Israelites of Dimona," Part II, *Davka*, vol. II, no. 3 (May–June 1972): 48–53.

38. *Jerusalem Post*, 19 October 1971.

39. Ibid.

40. Meir Kahane, Personal interview, 20 November 1972.

41. Korn, "Dimona."

42. This is the estimate of James Landing, an associate professor of geography at the University of Illinois (Chicago Circle). He has been studying the Black Jews of Chicago.

43. This is the estimate of Robert T. Coleman, director of the Department of Social Justice of the Synagogue Coucil of America.

44. Harry A. Ploski and Ernest Kaiser, eds., *The Negro Almanac* (New York: The Bellweather Co., 1971), p. 908.

45. *Afro-American*, 21 July 1973.

46. An interesting coincidence is that seven of the Georgians, a people who require strictly decorous behavior on the part of their women, killed a youthful Arab male in Nazareth. He had been found in a parked car in the company of a Georgian woman. As a punishment she was forced to shave her head. The incident did not cause a furor comparable to that evoked by the killing of Cornell Kirkpatrick in Dimona.

47. Clark Kent, "Dashikis in the Promised Land," *Israel Horizons* (May–June 1972): 11.

48. *Jerusalem Post*, 27 January 1972. The mayor of Dimona told a writer for *Ma'ariv* that 150 French-speaking Jewish families didn't want to settle in Dimona because of the Blacks. Some people had allegedly left Dimona because of distress engendered by the Blacks. One woman is supposed to have had two miscarriages because she was so upset by the Blacks. See Eli Ayal, "Dynamite in Dimona," *Ma'ariv* (6 April 1973).

49. *Jerusalem Post*, 8 October 1971. Concern about an international conspiracy has been nurtured by the allegation that the Blacks correspond with China and have Chinese books.

50. Ruth Cale, "Israel Grapples with a 'Black Hebrew' Problem," *Baltimore Sun*, 6 November 1971.

51. Yitzhak Agassi, Personal interview, 20 November 1972. A few days earlier Nasi Ahsiel Ben Israel said that there were about 550 Black Hebrews in Israel, 250 in Dimona alone.

52. For further details of the decision, see Doris Lankin, "Law Report—Leonia Clark and others v. Minister of the Interior," *Jerusalem Post*, 9 January 1973.

53. Letter from Shaleak Ben Yehuda to Kenyon C. Burke, 31 July 1972.

54. Letter from Ashkeazehr Ben Yisrael to Arnold Forster, 22 March 1973.

55. "The Black Hebrews," p. 21.

56. St. Clair Drake, "The Black Diaspora in Pan-African Perspective," *The Black Scholar* (September 1975): 6.

57. Letter from Roberta Cohen, executive director of the International League for the Rights of Man, to Ambassador Jacob Doron of the permanent mission of Israel to the United Nations, 19 July 1973. Additional information about the status of the Hebrew Israelites was requested from the minister of the interior.

58. *Jerusalem Post*, 28 January, 3 February 1979, International edition.

59. *New York Amsterdam News*, 15 October 1977.

60. Tony Griggs, "Angry Black Jews Return Here," *Chicago Daily Defender*, 27 September 1972. It should be noted that one of the three women interviewed was Mrs. Renee Kirkpatrick, the widow of Cornell Kirkpatrick, who was beaten to death in Dimona.

61. Whitfield, *From Night to Sunlight*.

62. Ibid., p. 80.

63. Ibid., pp. 67–68.

64. *Jerusalem Post*, 28 January–3 February 1979, International edition.

65. *Jerusalem Post*, 24 February 1981 and 6 March 1982.

66. Bayard Rustin, Personal interview with the author, 16 June 1983.

67. James F. Hughes III, counselor for consular affairs, United States Embassy, Tel Aviv, letter to the author, 31 March 1982.

68. Ibid.

69. *New York Voice*, 7 March 1981. See also the *New York Amsterdam News*, 28 March 1981.

70. William Raspberry, "Unholy Time in Holy Land," *Jerusalem Post*, 7 November 1980.

71. William Raspberry, "More to the Story," *Washington Post*, 19 November 1980.

72. At long last in February 1981 the prime minister's office issued what was described as a "top priority order" designed to avert the harassment of Black visitors arriving at Ben-Gurion Airport. See *Jerusalem Post*, 25 February 1981.

73. *Los Angeles Herald-Dispatch*, 7 September 1972.

74. *New York Amsterdam News*, 15 October 1977.

75. Ibid., 28 January 1978. The Reverend Robert M. Kinlock, who led the delegation, explained that he had initially been concerned because Black Hebrew youth had been barred from schools and excluded from unions. However, he felt that the situation had improved greatly. On a subsequent trip to Israel, Rev. Kinlock said he had been given red carpet treatment. Telephone interview with the author, 22 March 1982.

76. *Jerusalem Post*, 28 January – 3 February 1979, International edition.

77. *Pittsburgh Courier*, 6 December 1980.

78. Unpublished Report of the First Findings Of The Delegation To Israel Of BASIC and the A. Philip Randolph Educational Fund Regarding Human Rights As They Pertain To The Orginal Hebrew Israelite Nation (17–28 January 1981), 3.

79. Ibid., p. 5.

80. Ibid., pp. 6–9.

81. *Jerusalem Post*, 28 January 1981.

82. Ibid.

83. Rustin confirmed this view in a telephone interview with the author, 1 June 1982.

84. Ibid. Ben-Ammi Carter was deeply pained by Rustin's derogatory remark and asserted that Rustin was not knowledgeable about "Jewish history, the God of Israel or the plan of the God of Israel." Carter denied that he was a dictator in the mold of Nicaragua's Somoza or the Shah of Iran. *Jerusalem Post*, 21 May 1981.

85. Letter from BASIC to *Jerusalem Post*, 2 February 1981.

86. *New York Voice*, 19 September 1981 and the *Jerusalem Post*, 15 September 1981.

87. "The Black Hebrews," p. 29.

88. Ibid., pp. 30–31.

89. Ibid., p. 38.

90. Ibid., pp. 43–44.

91. Ibid., p. 45.

92. *Jerusalem Post*, 14 July 1980. Interviewed in May 1981 Ben-Ammi Carter said, "At this point, I feel the Glass report is either dead or dying." See the *Jerusalem Post*, 21 May 1981.

93. *Jerusalem Post*, 17 February–23 February 1980, International edition.

94. *New York Times*, 12 February 1980.

95. *Jerusalem Post*, 15 August 1980.

96. Ibid., 9 October 1980.

97. Ibid., 17 November 1980.

98. Ibid., 5 December 1980.

99. Ibid., 13 October 1980 and 5 December 1980.

100. Ibid., 23 March 1981.

101. Howard Lenhoff, "You are our brothers; you are our blood and flesh," *Present Tense*, 9, no. 4 (Summer 1982): 40.

102. Ibid., p. 41.

103. Louis Rapoport, *The Lost Jews—Last of the Ethiopian Falashas* (New York: Stein and Day, Publishers, 1980), p. 207.

104. Ibid., p. 9.

105. Judgments about the willingness of the Israeli government and the Israeli populace to treat the Falasha immigrants in an unprejudiced manner are premature. However, one ominous development was the charge made in October 1983 by the director general of the Absorption Ministry. He accused the mayors of three Israeli communities, Upper Nazareth, Tiberias and Eilat, of opposing Falasha settlement in their cities. The officials allegedly obstructed the suppy of water to apartments earmarked for the Ethiopians. See the *Jerusalem Post*, 23 October – 29 October 1983, International edition.

106. Raphael Patai, *The Vanished Worlds of Jewry* (New York: The Macmillan Company, 1980), pp. 174–182.

107. Norman L. Zucker, *The Coming Crisis in Israel—Private Faith and Public Policy* (Cambridge, Mass.: The M.I.T. Press, 1973), p. 120.

108. Patai, *Vanished Worlds*, pp. 183–184.

109. Hubert T. Delany, "Hubert T. Delany Reports on Israel," *Crisis* 63, no. 9 (November 1956).

110. See Nora Levin, "The Southern Cooperatives—Working to Save Rural America," *Tuesday Magazine* (June 1971): 1–6; Also see Nora Levin, "Israeli Models for Black Co-ops," *The Progressive* (June 1972): 23–26; Dick Edwards, "The Kibbutz—A Model For Black Collectives," *National Council of Jewish Women* (October–December 1970): 8–10; and Father A. J. McNight and John Zippert, Memo on Study Opportunities in Israel for Persons From the Cooperative Movement in the South to Organizers and Staff of Southern Cooperative Development Program (n.d.).

111. *Los Angeles Sentinel*, 26 May 1977.

112. Larry Lewis, "Black American Soldier in the Israeli Army," *Sepia* (October 1975): 18–24.

113. *Atlanta Daily World*, 28 September 1980; and *Jerusalem Post*, 14 July 1978, 7 and 28 November 1978, and 16 – 22 December 1979, International edition.

114. Ibid., 29 August – 4 September 1982 and 7 January – 15 January 1983.

V

Israel, South Africa and Black America

No Israeli policy, foreign or domestic, has so rankled Black Americans as the much publicized "normalization" of relations between the Jewish state and South Africa, a country which is perceived by most people of African descent in much the same way world Jewry perceived Nazi Germany in the 1930's. Elombe Brath, who describes himself as a veteran Pan-African activist and lecturer and co-chairman of the Patrice Lumumba Coalition, was deeply upset by Israel's "cynical" relationship with South Africa, where he opined, Blacks were subjugated to a greater degree than Jews whether in Nazi Germany or currently in the Soviet Union.[1] During a June 1976 television interview on the WABC-TV (New York) "Like It Is" show, Stokely Carmichael, erstwhile SNCC chairman and Black Panther prime minister, lambasted Zionists for remaining the "primary supporters of the repressive South African regime."

But it is abundantly clear that this view is not limited to Afro-Americans with Pan-African, Black nationalist, revolutionary or radical opinions—which should be of concern to Israeli policymakers. In the fall of 1979 some two hundred Black leaders insisted that American Jews exert pressure on the Israelis to terminate their "support of these repressive regimes" in South Africa and Rhodesia.[2] At approximately the same time, TransAfrica, a Black lobbying group based in Washington, D.C., which claims broad support among Black Americans, issued a statement critical of the "growing intimacy between Israel and the state of South Africa."[3] TransAfrica, which was formed explicitly to cement bonds between American Blacks and Blacks in Africa and to influence United States foreign policy on behalf of the latter, noted that respect for and acceptance of Israel had been eroded and it endorsed the idea of a Palestinian state. Benjamin L. Hooks, Roy Wilkins' successor as executive director of the NAACP, the oldest and largest civil rights organization in the United States, announced at a news conference in September 1981 that he was "very alarmed by the closeness of the relationship between Israel and South Africa."[4] It is by no means inconceivable that Hooks' failure to attend a breakfast meeting that Prime Minister Begin held with twenty prominent Afro-American leaders was at least partly attributable to that alarm. Essentially the same position has been taken by Professor John Hendrik Clarke;[5] by Donald McHenry, Andrew Young's successor as United States ambassador to the United Nations;[6] by columnist William Raspberry, who saw the warming trend between Pretoria and Tel Aviv as inevitably exacerbating relations between American Jews and Black Americans;[7] by Reverend Joseph Lowery, president of SCLC; and by the Reverend Jesse Jackson, who went so far as to interpret Israel's growing trade with South Africa as a "declaration of war on the blacks."[8] Even Bayard Rustin, Israel's most reliable ally in Black America, initially expressed his "deep sense of concern and disturbance" about the 1976 visit of South Africa's Prime Minister John Vorster to Israel and the subsequent jointly announced plans to expand commercial and other relations between the two nations.[9]

Only by surveying the nexus between South Africa and Israel and the bonds between Israel and Black Africa can we determine if the profound concern expressed by Black Americans is justified. One of the first acts of the nationalist government elected in South Africa in 1948 was to accord *de jure* recognition to the fledgling Jewish state, which had previously been recognized *de facto*. Prime Minister Daniel Malan, who had made no secret of his hope that Hitler would win World War II and in 1940 had alleged that South Africa had been transformed into a Jewish imperialist war machine,[10] later described the revival of Israel as "the greatest event in modern history."[11] It has been suggested that some Afrikaners, being devout Calvinists, saw the fulfillment of Old Testament prophecies in the new state. Others admired what they chose to regard as the Jews' maintenance of their racial identity for a few thousand years. Malan felt that a "race-conscious nation like the Jews, proud of their identity," will more easily understand and respect the sentiments of the Afrikaners.[12]

Edwin S. Munger, long a perceptive observer of the South African scene, has pointed out that Afrikaners found it easy to sympathize with the plight of Israel, which many saw as a small, struggling nation adrift in a sea of millions of Arabs.[13] The parallel with Afrikaners, struggling for survival against millions of Blacks, was an appealing one to many Afrikaners. In this view Israel and South Africa, two white nations bombarded with charges of imperialism, were natural allies, which actuated the Pretoria government to extend the hand of friendship to Israel.

Beleaguered by hostile neighbors bent on her destruction, Israel eagerly sought allies in the world; but to many idealists in the ruling Labor party, South Africa's policy of apartheid was repugnant. Moreover, Israel hoped to establish a strong economic and political posture vis-à-vis Black Africa. Less than a decade after Israel won the bloody War of Independence (1948), she launched a far-flung program of international cooperation with Third World countries, many of which had just achieved independence themselves as a result of anti-colonial conflicts. Africa was the major focus of the program whose principal architect and driving force was Golda Meir, first as foreign minister and subsequently as prime minister. In Mrs. Meir's autobiography she explained in some detail her country's development cooperation with Africa. She claimed that the main reason for the "African adventure" was humanitarian. "We had something we wanted to pass on to nations that were even younger and less experienced than ourselves."[14] Israeli assistance to struggling developing countries was an expression of both Labor Zionism and Judaism, she insisted. Jews and Africans shared a legacy of oppression and degradation; and their common fate had prompted Theodor Herzl, the founder of modern political Zionism, to write in his novel, *Altneuland* (Old-New Land), "Once I have witnessed the redemption of the Jews, my people, I wish also to assist in the redemption of the Africans."[15]

Golda Meir admitted that her policy with regard to Africa was also shaped by more practical considerations. In the words of Abba Eban, when he was minister of foreign affairs, development cooperation with emerging nations in Africa and elsewhere was a "political necessity as well as a moral imperative."[16] With less generosity anti-Zionists have interpreted Israel's involvement in Africa as a "Trojan horse of imperialism."[17]

Israel had been excluded from the 1955 Afro-Asian Conference, held in Bandung, Indonesia, where a resolution upholding the rights of the Palestinians was passed. Israel feared that African nations, many of whom had sizeable Muslim populations and therefore a natural affinity for the Arab cause, would give Israel the diplomatic "cold shoulder" at a time when she desperately wanted votes at the United Nations. Economic aspirations, e.g., the desire for markets for her industrial products, were probably much less significant in Israeli thinking.

Israel posted an ambassador to Ghana shortly after that one-time British colony achieved independence in 1957. On the occasion of the first anniversary of Ghanaian independence, Golda Meir undertook a sojourn to several West African states. She met many African leaders, and their dialogues paved the way for Israel's multifaceted development aid programs in sub-Saharan Africa which reached some thirty-one countries. Thousands of Jewish technicians and teachers were dispatched to Africa to help the Africans improve their health and well-being. Projects ran the gamut from irrigation and water resource management and eradication of serious eye ailments and tuberculosis to hotel construction. Africans, also by the thousands, visited Israel to attend short-term institutes or to study for longer periods at Israel's major universities.[18]

Some Afro-Americans have duly noted Israeli largess. They include the editors of the *Chicago Daily Defender*, Roy Wilkins, Whitney M. Young, Jr., and several members of the Black Caucus, such as Ralph H. Metcalfe, then a congressman from Illinois. One Black has written appreciatively that a single "tiny nation has contributed more in foreign technical aid to Black Africa than all of the oil-rich Arab bloc. That nation is Israel."[19]

Throughout the 1960's Israel continued to court the newly emergent Black African states. Simultaneously she maintained relations with the Republic of South Africa that were at best correct but uneasy and at worst strained. There was only a modicum of trade between the two countries. South Africa would have preferred more cordial relations, but Israel was fearful that overt friendship with Pretoria would alienate new-found friends in Black Africa where the apartheid regime was anathema.

Israel frequently took a stronger stand in opposition to apartheid than that taken by the principal western democracies. A few incidents will serve to illustrate this little-appreciated and rarely mentioned point. In the summer of 1961 Maurice Yameogo, the first president of the Francophone West African nation of Upper Volta, paid a visit to the Jewish state. A joint communiqué issued by Yameogo and by David Ben-Gurion, then Israel's prime minister, denounced expressions of racial discrimination and declared that South African apartheid was detrimental to the interests of the African majority in that country.[20] Israel was roundly condemned by the South African newspaper *Die Transvaler* for interfering in South Africa's domestic affairs and the issuance of the joint communiqué was labelled "an unfriendly act."[21]

Later the same year in the General Assembly, Israel voted to censure South Africa's minister of foreign affairs, Eric Louw, who had presented a spirited defense of his government. Louw, a long-time Jew-baiter, was censured for his "offensive, fictitious and erroneous statements." Most of the western world abstained, but Israel and Holland felt the need to underline their abhorrence of apartheid and accordingly voted "aye."[22] In both this matter and the Upper Volta episode, South Africans called upon their Jewish countrymen to repudiate the stand taken by their brothers in Israel.

Matters worsened in November when the Israeli delegate to the United Nations supported an Afro-Asian motion which recommended that all states impose economic sanctions on South Africa and break off diplomatic relations with Pretoria. This motion, which came to a vote in the Political Committee, was opposed by Britain, the United States and many other nations in the "free world."[23] Israel's vote shocked and upset the powerful South African Zionist movement, which was held accountable for the Israeli vote. Furthermore, the vote was costly to Israel as the South African government, angered by the Israeli action, temporarily discontinued the transfer of gift funds and goods from South African Jews to the Jewish Agency.[24]

Relations between Israel and South Africa deteriorated still further in 1962 when the former once again aligned itself with the Afro-Asian bloc in voting for strong sanctions against Pretoria, an action which predictably angered Prime Minister Hendrik Verwoerd and the Afrikaans-language press which pointed an accusing and threatening finger at South African Jewry.[25] Foreign Minister Golda Meir explained that Israel had no alternative but to support sub-Saharan African countries which "have the right...to expect Israel's support in their fight for liberty and freedom."[26] The following year Israel voted for an oil embargo against Pretoria in the General Assembly's Trusteeship Committee, expressed its backing for the Security Council's ban on the sale of weapons to South Africa and also reduced its diplomatic representation in South Africa to the level of a chargé d'affaires.[27]

It was apparent that the Israeli government, a Labor-dominated coalition, had decided to cater to Third World, especially African, sentiment on the emotional South African question in the hope that the non-aligned countries would press for direct negotiations between the Arabs and the Israelis. Golda Meir in particular believed that ethical imperatives as well as the Israeli initiative in Black Africa required a tough line on South Africa. She was heard to say that as long as apartheid existed she would refuse to set foot in South Africa. She toyed with the idea of not allowing El Al, the national airline of Israel, to fly to South Africa. According to a former director of the Tel Aviv office of the South African Zionist Federation, it was South African Zionists in Israel who dissuaded her from imposing this sanction, at least until other national airlines indicated their willingness to adopt a similar policy.[28] Another source attributes Golda Meir's failure to terminate El Al flights to Johannesburg to objections from Kenya, which enjoyed transit rights.[29] By contrast, Menachem Begin's opposition Herut party had serious doubts about the wisdom of supporting sanctions against South Africa, a nation which had been favorably disposed to Israel since its founding in 1948 and a nation in which there resided a sizeable and ardently Zionist Jewish population.

In point of fact, the early 1960's were marked by an increase in anti-Semitic activities and incidents in South Africa. Disproportionate Jewish involvement in anit-apartheid movements in South Africa and the pro-Black African thrust of Israeli foreign policy undoubtedly contributed to the climate of anti-Semitism. In addition, questions of Jewish loyalty to South Africa were raised with increasing frequency; and Jews in South Africa were reminded, in effect, that their acceptance was conditioned upon their unconditional acceptance of Afrikanerdom.

For example, in October 1965 an article entitled "Where Does the Jew Stand in the White Man's Struggle for Existence?" appeared in *Dagbreek*, an Afrikaans Sunday newspaper. The author of the article, *Dagbreek*'s editor, Dirk Richard, was expressing the doubts of many in the ruling Nationalist party about the loyalty of South Africa's Jews. Richard was greatly distressed by the frequency with which he encountered Jewish names among the forces of liberalism and by the failure of the South African Jewish community to protest against the anti-apartheid position taken by Israel in the United Nations. Essentially he was reflecting the suspicion of the nationalists that in a showdown, "when the country has to be defended to the last ditch," the South African government would not be able to rely on the Jews. If the Jews as a group wished to protect their identity, if they hoped to maintain their institutions, and if they desired to live as Jews, Richard argued, they must collectively adopt more positive attitudes. This position was strongly rejected by the South African Jewish Board of Deputies; however, the thinly veiled threat in the article could not be ignored, particularly in light of the fact that the chairman of the board of *Dagbreek* was Dr. Verwoerd.[30]

Israel's overwhelming victory in the Six Day War of 1967 paved the way for her estrangement from Black Africa and the concomitant rapprochement with South Africa. Forcible acquisition of territory was an accursed practice to Black African states, which jealously guarded their own boundaries, especially when some of the conquered land, the Sinai peninsula, was on the African continent and belonged to Egypt, a bona fide and influential member of the Organization of African Unity (OAU). President Leopold Sedar Senghor of Senegal expressed his annoyance this way: "Because we share our continent with Arab-Africans, and because we feel that Africa ends at the Sinai, we have been deeply disturbed by the fact that since 1967, a part of Africa has been occupied by an outside power."[31] And, it must be understood that Senghor, a revered poet, is clearly sympathetic to Jews, whom he classifies with Arabs and Africans as a trio of suffering people.

Still Israel's carefully cultivated relations in sub-Saharan Africa were not ruptured immediately except by Guinea, whose president, Sekou Toure, had a long pro-Arab and Marxist orientation. In fact, Israeli technical assistance to Africa expanded for some years after the Six Day War. Some African states, including Idi Amin's Uganda, broke relations with Israel in 1972; but 1973, the year of the Yom Kippur War when the Arabs first used their oil as a weapon in international diplomacy, was the watershed in Black Africa-Israeli diplomatic affairs. Twenty-five African states severed diplomatic ties with Israel from January to November 1973. By then several countries in Africa had been radicalized, and Islam was already on the way to becoming a more potent political force in the international arena. It is noteworthy that although Israel and South Africa were enjoying somewhat better relations in the post–Six Day War era, especially by 1972 and 1973, this friendship was seemingly not the main reason for Black Africa's disenchantment with its former friend and benefactor, the State of Israel. More important, taking an anti-Israeli stance was one way an African nation could dramatize the fact that it was not a lackey of western imperialism. At the same time an anti-Israeli stance could yield substantial dividends in the form of more reasonable oil prices and Arab development aid, or so Black Africa hoped.

As late as 1971 Israel was still attempting to woo Black African support, although the effort jeopardized the warming trend in South African-Israeli relations. In June, almost certainly at Golda Meir's behest, the Israeli ambassador to the United Nations, Joseph Tekoah, announced that his country would contribute ten thousand Israeli pounds (two thousand South African rand) to African liberation movements.[32] The OAU would serve as a conduit for the contributions. South African reaction, Jewish and non-Jewish alike, was swift in coming. To many segments of South African opinion, the Israeli gesture was the height of ingratitude for the republic had backed Israel in the Six Day War. Even Christians had donated to the Zionist cause in June 1967, and the South African treasury had subsequently enabled sympathetic South Africans to invest in the Jewish state. Moreover, it has been suggested that for many South Africans the timing of the proffered Israeli gift was most unfortunate as it came shortly after two

South African policemen were killed by a land mine laid by Black guerrillas on the border.[33] Prime Minister Vorster could not comprehend how Israel with its own terrorist problem could channel money to other terrorist organizations and prophesied, correctly in this instance, that Israel would fail to buy an advantage for itself.

In this atmosphere of shock and anger, the Israeli consulate in Johannesburg received a bomb threat. Many South African Jews, including the South African Zionist Federation and the Board of Deputies, were dismayed by the news of the Israeli donation to "terrorism." One Jew wrote that the Israeli gift actually endangered the lives of young Jews in the South African military who were defending their country's frontiers against terrorists. There were many threats to protest by holding back planned contributions to Zionist fund-raising campaigns.

The Israeli response was cautious. Yitzhak Unna, the Israeli consul-general in South Africa, initially observed that western support for the OAU reduced the effect of Communist penetration into Africa,[34] so dreaded by white South Africans. Later on he said that his government would not be giving cash but rather would supply blankets, foodstuffs and medicines.[35] Back home in Israel the donation found little favor with the Hebrew press. A cartoon in the widely read daily, Ma'ariv, showed Israel contributing a boot to African liberation movements which then use it to kick Israel in the derrière.[36] The OAU was portrayed as an anti-Israeli enterprise. Under the barrage of criticism, internal and external, it was announced that the donation would go to the United Nations High Commission for Refugees and would be utilized for educational purposes.[37]

Why had Israel originally offered to make the donation? For senior diplomat Gershon Avner, who was in South Africa on a United Jewish Appeal speaking tour at the height of the controversy over the offer, Arab political attacks required Israel to find friends across the world, including Black African states.[38] Those states cast votes at the United Nations and could help bring about the direct negotiations between Israel and the Arabs, which the former wanted desperately and the latter resisted. Ironically, the Israeli offer did nothing to recoup the goodwill which had been eroding in Black Africa since 1967. A few Africans in the OAU were insulted, not placated. In exile in the Tanzanian capital of Dar es Salaam, the Pan-African Congress, which had been outlawed by the Pretoria regime for years, asserted that it would ask the OAU to reject the Israeli donation. It also branded Israel as "a colonial and racist country" which enjoyed cordial political, military and economic ties with South Africa.[39]

Other Black South Africans, for example, some officials of the rival African National Congress, ridiculed the proposed donation as "paltry." Thus, the Israeli move pleased nobody—not the banned Black South African liberation organizations, probably not the independent Black African countries and certainly not the South African government, which promptly suspended the transfer of substantial funds from the republic to Israel.[40] Even Rhodesia and Portugal, allies of South Africa, declared that they would henceforth forbid the transfer of money to Israel because of the Israeli donation to the OAU.[41]

Over the next few years, between 1971 and 1973, a change in Israeli behavior at the United Nations can be easily discerned. No longer would Israel be so conspicuous by its anti-South African voting patterns. In the fall of 1971 Israel voted to condemn the policy of apartheid as a crime against the conscience and dignity of mankind and expressed its indignation and concern over the maltreatment and torture of opponents of apartheid.[42] Israel voted in favor of a General Assembly resolution declaring an arms embargo against the republic, a resolution which made no distinction between arms for external defense and arms for internal repression.[43] Also in 1971, which was the International Year for Action to Combat Racism and Racial Discrimination, Israel supported a series of resolutions to condemn the establishment of Bantustans and to aid trade union activities against apartheid.[44] Israel voted to terminate South Africa's mandate over Namibia (Southwest Africa) and supported a resolution chastizing "those countries which by their political, economic and military collaboration with the Government of South Africa encourage and invite that government to persist in its social policy."[45]

In November 1972 Israel still voted for a resolution criticizing the torture of prisoners and detainees in South Africa and several other anti-South African measures.[46] However, it did abstain on one very stong, comprehensive resolution which not only condemned the racist government of South Africa, but also called for a boycott of South Africa in sports and cultural activities and asked for the cessation of all activities by foreign economic interests which encourage the Pretoria regime in its imposition of apartheid. The same motion discouraged immigration to South Africa and asked for the discontinuance of all military, political and economic collaboration with South Africa. It should be noted that both the United States and Britain voted against this omnibus resolution. Ever since December 1973, except on very rare occasions, Israel has either abstained or voted against a series of anti-South African resolutions, some of which were strikingly similar to motions which the Israelis had favored in previous years, e.g., motions on arms embargoes of South Africa on Namibia and Bantustans.[47]

Despite the change in voting patterns, Israel has not hesitated to lambast South Africa's white supremacist policies in the United Nations. Typical was the speech to the General Assembly given on October 7, 1976, by the late Yigal Allon, the deputy prime minister and foreign minister. Allon said, "Racism and racial discrimination, in any guise, including apartheid, are abhorrent to my country and my people. The basic tenets of Judaism are irreconcilable with any form of racism and racial discrimination,"[48]

But by that juncture the Republic of South Africa and the State of Israel had already become the two major pariahs on the international scene. Not only has each been ostracized and stridently criticized by a majority of United Nations members, but also the two have often been paired as racist powers, two peas in the same imperialist pod. In a resolution adopted on December 14, 1973, the General Assembly denounced *inter alia*, "the unholy alliance" between South African racism, Zionism and Israeli imperialism.[49] Twelve months later the

General Assembly condemned the strengthening of political, economic, military and other relations between Israel and South Africa.[50] This occurred a year and a half before Prime Minister Vorster's journey to Jerusalem. A resolution specifically denouncing Israeli collaboration with South Africa has since become an annual ritual in the General Assembly.

By the mid-1970's it was commonplace in the global community to discuss Zionism and apartheid in the same breath. In the new political lexicon authored by the Arabs, abetted by their Third World allies and the Soviet bloc, Zionism had been defined as just another expression of racial bigotry. The International Women's Year Conference held in Mexico City in June and July 1975 called for the elimination of "Zionism, apartheid and racial discrimination in all its forms."[51] A resolution adopted by the OAU in July 1975 stated "that the racist regime in occupied Palestine and racist regimes in Rhodesia and South Africa have a common imperialist origin... the same racist structure... aimed at the repression of the dignity and integrity of the human being."[52] All of these sentiments were incorporated in the highly controversial resolution equating Zionism with racism,[53] which was adopted by the General Assembly in November 1975.

As a conciliatory gesture to Black Africa, Israeli diplomatic representation in Pretoria had been kept at the level of chargé d'affaires. In March 1974 the representation was upgraded with the appointment of an ambassador, thereby signalling a new era in Israeli-South African relations. Less than two years later, on January 13, 1976, Dr. Charles B. H. Fincham, South Africa's first ambassador to Israel, presented his credentials to the president of Israel in Jerusalem. An embassy was opened in Tel Aviv, although some wags circulated the joke that a slightly uncomfortable Israeli government would have preferred the South African embassy be located in Metulla, a tiny town on the remote Lebanese border. But it was no joke when in April 1976 Prime Minister Vorster travelled to Israel. To some extent the groundwork for Vorster's visit had been laid a few years earlier by his brother, a dour, unsmiling activist in the Dutch Reformed Church. The latter had made a four-day trip to the Holy Land, which had been organized by the South African Zionist Federation. He had been so moved by his experience that he expressed a desire to have the prime minister follow in his footsteps. For many Afrikaners, Israel, the land of the Bible, has long had magnetic appeal, and it is no coincidence that South Africa is dotted with place-names drawn from Scripture. Beyond that, among white South Africans there was tremendous admiration for Israelis after their smashing victory in the Six Day War. Of course, *realpolitik* rather than fundamentalist affinity for the people of the Book, explains Vorster's eagerness to establish closer ties with Israel, a fellow outcast from the global community. South Africa has also strengthened ties with Taiwan whose status as a pariah has also been underscored in recent years.

For Israel the decision to invite Vorster was not an easy one. Debate in the Labor party's inner circles was emotional, partly because apartheid was truly odious to many. There was also an awareness of the virulent anti-Semitism which had been so widespread in South Africa, especially among Afrikaners, during the period 1933–1945. Israeli government officials were also acutely aware of the fact that John Vorster himself had been interned during World War II because of his pro-Nazi sympathies and activities. Lastly, the government knew that openly flirting with the Pretoria regime could provide grist for anti-Zionist propaganda mills and eventuate in further international isolation for Israel. But a new set of international circumstances existed by the middle of the decade. Relations between Black Africa and Israel had soured. Since the dark days of the Yom Kippur War, only three sub-Saharan Black African nations, Lesotho and Swaziland (both politically independent enclaves within the Republic of South Africa) and Malawi, had retained formal diplomatic links with Israel. Policymakers in Jerusalem were keenly disappointed that virtually all of Black Africa was playing footsie with the oil-rich Arab world.

Ostensibly, Golda Meir's initiative in Black Africa had failed. A fresh assessment of Israeli interests on the African continent was in order. It was reasoned that normalizing relations with South Africa could bring certain benefits. A shaky Israeli economy could profit from widening trade opportunities. Liberalized currency transfers from South Africa, South African investment in Israel, the extension of credit by South Africa and the unfettered sale of Israeli bonds in South Africa could all help to shore up the sagging economy in Israel.

And so the prime minister arrived. Accompanied by Foreign Minister Hilgard Muller, a dozen aides, fourteen journalists and his wife Balthazar, Johannes Vorster landed at Ben-Gurion Airport on an El Al jetliner. He and his party were guests of Prime Minister Yitzhak Rabin who, flanked by Foreign Minister Allon, greeted Vorster and his entourage. While in the country Vorster was escorted to an Air Force base and to Israeli Aircraft Industries. He went to various holy sites, to Masada and to the Holocaust memorial at Yad Vashem, where we can only wonder about his innermost thoughts in light of his earlier Nazi sympathies.[54] At a gala dinner held at a Jerusalem hotel and attended by civilian and military dignitaries, Rabin and Vorster emphasized the goodwill that prevailed between Israel and South Africa.[55]

At the conclusion of Vorster's four-day stay, it was announced that economic, scientific and industrial pacts between South Africa and Israel had been signed. Vorster stated that among the areas in which the two countries hoped to broaden contacts were investments, trade and scientific and technical cooperation. He also hoped for shared utilization of South African raw materials and Israeli know-how and manpower. No arms supply deal had been arranged, he asserted.[56] A first in South African history was recorded when a joint South African-Israeli ministerial committee was created to foster economic cooperation.

South African editorial opinion was jubilant. In the opinion of the *Pretoria News*, what had begun as a "surprise...low key 'pilgrimage' to the Holy Land...was now only to be seen as a major international diplomatic coup."[57] South African Jewish agencies were also delighted, while Israeli newspaper opinion was favorable, if not ecstatic. Even the liberal *Jerusalem Post* observed that for Israel, "Mr. Vorster's visit constitutes a long overdue coming to grips with political reality, not a change in political ethics."[58]

But, as is usually the case in Israel, there was vocal dissent. During the visit demonstrators armed with placards calling Vorster a Nazi and a racist marched outside the South African Embassy in Tel Aviv. A telegram was sent to Prime Minister Rabin by concentration camp survivors who excoriated the one-time Hitler fan. His trip, they said, "defiles the memory of the victims of nazism."[59] But it seems that for Rabin, et al., the lesson of Auschwitz was that Israel's survival had to be insured, and South Africa, they believed, could contribute to that survival.

America's Black press did not look at all kindly on Vorster's "tour of Occupied Palestine" as the *Bilalian News* termed it under the headline "Israel and South Africa intensify unholy alliance." Vorster's photograph was also published with the caption "a proven enemy of both Palestine and Africans."[60]

The *Bilalian News* and a column in the *Pittsburgh Courier* each saw the Vorster visit as confirmation of the United Nations condemnation of Zionism as racism. "With South Africa...representing the epitome of racism and fascist-like oppression...and with the Israeli government's relations to Vorster and his ilk, is this not racism?" the *Courier* writer asked rhetorically and then urged his readers to protest "Israel's relations and collaboration with the racist government of South Africa."[61]

While visiting Sharm el-Sheik at the southern tip of the Sinai Desert, Prime Minister Vorster told journalists that "relations between South Africa and Israel have never been so good."[62] They were to get even better. In the wake of the Vorster visit, a milestone in South African-Israeli relations, contacts between the two "outlaw states" were intensified, and relations improved further. Since 1976 there have been many cultural, sports and scientific exchanges. Tourism between South Africa and Israel has risen markedly. Passenger traffic moving in both directions between Johannesburg and Tel Aviv has increased significantly—much to the delight of South African Airways and El Al. An Israel-South Africa Chamber of Commerce with headquarters in Tel Aviv has held symposia to encourage private investment and trade. Economic achievements and prospects have been chronicled in the *Israel-South Africa Trade Review* which is published monthly in Israel. One consequence of a December 1980 meeting of the finance ministers of the two countries was an agreement to allow Israel Bonds up to twenty-five million dollars to be sold in South Africa. The ceiling on South African investment in Israel was raised at the same parley.[63]

South African exports to Israel have included steel, raw diamonds, timber, sugar and processed foods. Israel also imports coal, which it uses to fuel the large Hadera power station near Tel Aviv.[64] Among the Israeli exports have been electronic equipment, tools and dies and fashion goods.[65] Between 1970 and 1979 South African exports to Israel increased fifteenfold, and by the end of the decade Israeli exports were five times what they had been in 1970. But withal the total volume of South African-Israeli trade is not significant.[66] Israeli Ambassador Chaim Herzog reminded the General Assembly on November 9, 1976, that his country's trade with South Africa represented just two-fifths of one percent of South Africa's overall trade. United Nations members, many of whom deride Israel for her commercial ties to South Africa, were responsible for the remaining ninety-nine and three-fifths percent of South Africa's trade.[67] Four years later South Africa still absorbed barely 1 percent of all Israeli exports, and the south African economy provided Israel with roughly 2 percent of its imports. And in 1982 Israeli trade with Black Africa continued to exceed her trade with the white redoubt in southern Africa.

Israel is not alone in trading with South Africa. Although the OAU wants an effective economic boycott of South Africa, commerce is lively between the republic and the rest of the continent. Much of that commerce is covert with goods relabelled to disguise the fact that they originated south of the Limpopo River. Not uncommonly, South African products are shipped through third parties. At the request of Black African states which would be embarrassed by the disclosure, South Africa does not disclose country by country statistics, but the republic claims that it trades with virtually the entire continent—fifty-nine independent states. Agriculture and mining machinery, clothing, canned fish, corn, wheat, fruits and medicines are all exported to Black Africa with annual exports exceeding one billion dollars.[68]

Despite the foregoing, critics of Israel have taken a dim view of South African-Israeli trade, which is cited to demonstrate the existence of a "Tel Aviv-Pretoria axis." They have flayed the Jewish state for being a trading partner of South Africa while that white supremacist regime subjugates its non-white population. Israel's defenders contend that criticism is hypocritical and unfair, that it takes Israel to task for conduct vis-à-vis South Africa which is no different from that of countless other states. They argue that a double standard has prevailed; one for Israel, which is to serve as an international whipping boy, and one for the rest of the world.

It is clear that, in some respects, Israel and her defenders are right. South African heads of government have received Black African dignitaries from abroad, and they have visited Black African nations; so the Vorster visit to Jerusalem was not without precedent. As early as September 1968 Dr. Hendrik Verwoerd, the prime minister of South Africa, met in Pretoria with Chief L. Jonathan, the prime minister designate for Lesotho, formerly Basutoland. In August 1971 President Kamuzu Banda of Malawi paid a state visit to South Africa, four years after the two countries had established diplomatic relations. In September 1974 Vorster met President Felix Houphouet-Boigny of the Ivory Coast in Abidjan, the capital of that Francophone West African nation. On February 12, 1975, Vorster conferred with President William Tolbert of Liberia in Monrovia, and six months later he engaged in a dialogue with President Kenneth Kaunda of Zambia, a front-line confrontational state. That meeting took place in Livingston,

Zambia, on a bridge spanning the Zambezi River near the awe-inspiring Victoria Falls. In a sense the location of the Vorster-Kaunda encounter was symbolic of the Zambian president's position—precariously perched between Black Africa and the white fortress in southern Africa. It is no exaggeration to say that by 1975 there was a lucrative trade by air, sea and road between the Lusaka and Pretoria regimes. At Kaunda's initiative Kaunda and P. W. Botha, Vorster's successor, met in April 1980 despite the outcry from much of sub-Saharan Africa, which regards the prime minister of South Africa, whoever occupies that post, as the devil incarnate. With its chronically fragile economy worsened by protracted drought, Zambia has been dependent on other countries, including South Africa, for substantial quantities of corn. It is a dependence which Pretoria relishes and therefore cultivates by subsidizing sales of the staple.[69]

Several Black African countries adjacent to or near South Africa are also reliant on the Afrikaner regime, which they detest. Lesotho, previously a British high commission territory, and South Africa share a highly expensive hydroelectric system involving four dams—a system financed by affluent South Africa. Lesotho's participation was arranged at a 1980 summit meeting between Prime Minister Botha and Prime Minister Jonathan. Remittances from Basuto workers in South Africa serve to augment Lesotho's anemic economy.

The same is true for another one-time British high commission territory, Botswana, which receives nine-tenths of its imports from South Africa and sells virtually all of its exports to or through South Africa. Without employment opportunities in South Africa, especially in the mines, Botswana's jobless rolls would swell to dangerous proportions. Samora Machel's Mozambique is also dependent upon the wages of its citizens who toil in the bowels of the earth in South Africa. A fixed percentage of the miners' earnings are transferred in the form of gold bullion to the Mozambique government, which then pays the workers in local currency. Several African states have their nationals laboring in South African mines, usually under deplorable conditions. Mozambique, along with Botswana, Lesotho, Swaziland, Malawi, Angola and Zimbabwe, collaborate with South Africa in a system that can best be described as indentured servitude in exchange for desperately needed hard currency. Its loathing of South Africa's racial policies notwithstanding, the Maputu regime utilizes the skills of South African technicians and regularly imports consumer goods and spare parts from the "enemy" in Pretoria. Expediency has obviously triumphed, at least for the time being, over anti-apartheid rhetoric in shaping Mozambique's policy. "South Africa is real, its power is real," asserted a planning official in the ex-Portuguese colony, "no one expects us to precipitate suicidal confrontations."[70]

If Israel is assailed for its cooperation with South Africa, why should Black African states not be similarly assailed? "If it is wrong for Israel to have any relations with South Africa," Rabbi Arthur Hertzberg of the American Jewish Congress asked Bayard Rustin, "why is it not also wrong for Black African states to have such relations? And if it is right for Black Africans, why is it not right for Israel?"[71] Rustin replied that he is "deeply troubled by the double standard and hypocrisy that excuses or ignores black Africa's trade with South Africa while blaming Israel for a far less volume of trade with South Africa."[72]

But a few years afterwards, when Yehuda Blum, Israel's permanent representative at the United Nations, suggested at a meeting with a deputation from the SCLC that the Black African trade with South Africa surpassed that of Israel, he failed to change the thinking of Joseph Lowery. At a press conference held after the session with Blum, Lowery said that it was irrelevant what Black African countries did regarding South Africa because their very survival depended on their economic ties with the republic, but Israel's survival did not.[73] Lowery's contention is not accurate as far as most of Africa is concerned. For the front-line states a complete economic break with South Africa would entail great suffering, but for the rest of the continent, as for Israel, the benefits of doing business with South Africa are really quite marginal. Their survival does not really hang in the balance. Of course, unlike Black African nations, Israel is surrounded by foes aiming at its destruction. Its economy is feeble, and its friends are few. Consequently it reaches out to South Africa not merely for the minimal economic gains it can make but to forestall isolation in an increasingly terrifying world.

What is the excuse for oil-rich Arab states, whose very existence is not in jeopardy, doing business with South Africa? Despite an oil embargo of petroleum-poor South Africa, there is very good reason to believe that Arab countries are among the leading suppliers of oil to Afrikanerdom. Not until 1973, at a time when Israeli-Black African relations were in the doldrums, did the Arab League accede to the request of the OAU to impose an oil embargo on South Africa. Prior to that time Arab oil producers had openly supplied South Africa. Since 1973 they have furnished petroleum but in a stealthy manner.[74]

In July of 1977 the *Daily Times* of Nigeria reported that "Arab oil still finds its way to South Africa." A correspondent in the *Sunday Times*, published in the same country, Africa's most populous, complained, "It is disgusting to see that we are prepared to go to any length with the Arabs even when they supply oil to South Africa. Or do we pretend not to know that the Arabs still sell oil to the apartheid administration in Pretoria?"[75]

An analysis by the Shipping Research Bureau based in Amsterdam of oil tankers calling at South African ports concluded that of the twenty-three tankers most likely to have delivered crude oil during 1979 and the first quarter of 1980 five sailed from Oman, two each from Saudi Arabia and Kuwait and one each from Iraq, Qatar and the United Arab Emirates. Many others, including a pair from Colonel Qaddafi's hard-line regime in Libya, docked at South African ports and may have delivered oil there.[76] It is possible to argue that the Arab exporters did not know of the ships' actual destinations. Skeptics would counterargue that they really did not want to know.

Clandestine trade has long existed between South Africa and several Arab countries, i.e., Jordan, Lebanon, Dubai, Abu Dhabi, Morocco and Saudi Arabia.

Kuwait's royal family was a major investor in Lonro, the London Rhodesia Company, a multinational corporation with extensive holdings in South Africa. The hush-hush nexus between Arab states, especially Saudi Arabia and Persian Gulf sheikdoms, and South Africa also encompasses the purchase of huge quantities of South African gold with petro-dollars.[77] What all of this adds up to is a partnership, albeit a silent, covert partnership, between Arab states and South Africa, in which the former simultaneously denounce and trade with the latter. Black African countries have good reason to be vexed about this. So do Joseph Lowery and other Black Americans involved in the crusade against apartheid.

One of the other actions for which Israel has been taken to task by the United Nations has been military collaboration with South Africa. Under this rubric, many and varied sins have been alleged. Some are grave indeed. Others appear to be frivolous, such as the oft-repeated charge that "Several hundred South African volunteers fought with the Zionists after 1947" and "the first pilot to fall in battle in the Israeli Air Force was a South African volunteer." In this same general indictment, the Special Committee Against Apartheid cited the unremarkable fact that "Jewish volunteers from South Africa served in Israel during the 1967 war, officially in non-military posts, replacing Israelis who had been called up for combat duty."[78] Identical statements could be made about other countries in the Diaspora where there are substantial Jewish populations. For decades South African Jews have boasted of one of the most ardent Zionist communities in the world. When they have extended help to Israel, they have done so as fellow Jews and Zionists and not really as South Africans. Nor has the South African government been deeply involved in efforts to enhance Israel's military might. Special regulations designed to facilitate the transfer of funds collected by the Zionist Federation of South Africa were primarily concessions to influential Jewish citizens of the republic.

It is true that the South African government and most of its white population has sided with Israel rather than its Arab neighbors, but their tangible contribution to Israeli security has been quite minimal. As to judging a nation by its supporters and allies, it is worth remembering that Franco's Spain was solidly pro-Arab. So is the Soviet Union, hardly a model of democracy; and Yasir Arafat, chairman of the PLO, freely admitted that his "liberation" organization was supporting Idi Amin who, in point of fact, was responsible for the murder of tens of thousands of his Black countrymen. Yet Arafat once told CBS' Mike Wallace that he was proud of his relationship with the anti-Zionist Amin.[79]

More deserving of serious discussion is Israeli military aid to South Africa, particularly since 1976. There is little doubt that Israel's armaments industry has grown by leaps and bounds since the Yom Kippur War of 1973, to the point that one British publication ranked Israel seventh among the nations of the world exporting weapons.[80] However, because relevant data are highly classified in security conscious Israel, it is not possible to confirm the British assessment. Still, it is virtually certain that the Israelis have provided the South Africans with Gabriel ship-to-ship missiles and Reshef-class fast patrol boats.[81]

Is there anything unique about this military link to the republic? Arms traffic is usually clouded in secrecy. This is especially true where South Africa is concerned because of the United Nations' embargo. Consequently, information about weapons exported to South Africa is sometimes fragmentary and frequently uncorroborated. Because many of those making accusations of military assistance to Pretoria have a political axe to grind, extreme caution is a necessity for the scholar.

Of those monitoring world armaments, the Stockholm International Peace Research Institute appears to be the most thorough and perhaps the most objective. It has called Israel the leading exporter of weapons in the Third World[82] but has ranked it behind France and Italy, which it calls the two major suppliers of arms to South Africa.[83] Britain, West Germany, the United States and possibly even the Soviet Union have furnished weapons for the South African military arsenal in the past. In the case of the Communist nations, verification is difficult.[84]

A list of countries which have exported arms to South Africa in the recent past should raise eyebrows. Conspicuous by its presence is Jordan. In 1974, using a private South African firm located in Liechtenstein as an intermediary, the Hashemite Kingdom "sold its entire Tigercat air defense system with all support equipment and over fifty missiles as well as forty-one Centurian tanks"[85] to South Africa. Only the personal intervention of President Sadat prevented the additional sale of sixty Hawker Hunter fighter planes from King Hussein's government, which was receiving modern fighter planes and a new air defense system from the United States. It is possible, according to the Stockholm group, that the final destination of the older weapons was Ian Smith's Rhodesia, a white minority regime.[86] Naturally, the Jordanian government has categorically rejected the foregoing and insists that it has no dealings in armaments or non-military goods with South Africa.[87]

Spain and India are two other unlikely trading partners in armaments with South Africa. Spain has broadened its industrial base in recent years and has entered the lucrative international arms market. They have sold submarines to bellicose Libya; and in 1979 the post-Franco regime refurbished some sixty antiquated Centurion tanks which India, a leading non-aligned critic of South Africa, had placed at its disposal for sale to the Pretoria government.[88]

While it is true that Israel's military links with South Africa are not *sui generis* and that much vilification of Israel supposedly based on these links is hypocritical and politically motivated, ill-considered statements by a few Israeli officials have served to blacken the reputation of the Jewish state. For instance, in the fall of 1977 Moshe Dayan, who was foreign minister at the time, imprudently told a group of academics from the United States that his country "will not abandon South Africa because of President Carter's position" in support of the arrms embargo. "It is not the business of the President of the United States whom we have for friends so long as we are within the limits of the law," Dayan declared.[89] In short order a statement of clarification was issued in Jerusalem reasserting Israel's intention to adhere to the resolution of the United Nations Security

Council calling for a weapons boycott of Pretoria. "Israel conducts its relations with South Africa on a legal basis and if there is a Security Council resolution Israel will not violate it," a government spokesman promised.[90]

Three years later Ariel Sharon, Israel's defense minister who also suffers from "foot in mouth disease," that common malady of politicians, especially those in the Middle East, announced that South Africa required additional modern arms to enable it to repel Soviet-supplied fighters. Sharon had visited South African forces in Namibia and remarked that the republic was one of a small number of nations in Africa or the Middle East that was standing firm against Soviet penetration in those regions.[91]

Remarks of this kind raise doubts about Israel's willingness to comply with the United Nations' arms embargo of South Africa and are bound to spawn more jaundiced views of Israel. Sharon's cold war rhetoric in particular implies that the South African-Israeli connection is more than a marriage of convenience. Israel's detractors will likely cite Sharon's comment to prove that the tie is a love match and that it is indeed, without parrallel. After all, defense ministers of other nations do not ordinarily make statements portraying South Africa as a bastion of anti-communism, deserving of appreciation and military succor.

Countries seeking loopholes in the embargo can easily find them. It is possible to follow the letter of the "law" but not its spirit. For example, raw materials that are essential for manufacturing weapons may be sold. Electronic equipment which is not inherently military but may be put to military use is not prohibited. Technical services and consultants' advice may also be provided.[92] Thoughtless assertions by Dayan and Sharon hint that Israel is not above circumventing the embargo and would if it could.

Also hurtful to Israel's moral standing is the charge made in 1976 by Marcia Freedman, an American-born Knesset member, that hundreds of Israeli Defense Forces personnel were serving as instructors in the South African military.[93] The charge, which had been made previously, was denied in the Parliament by the defense minister.[94] Quoting Meir Amit, former Israeli chief of intelligence, the *Guardian* reported that high-ranking Israeli officers were advising South African soldiers in counterinsurgency, a field in which the Israelis have considerable expertise. The Pan-African Congress, Black freedom fighters with headquarters in London, said that such Israeli involvement was "bound to lead to a wider escalation of the fighting between the African people and the white minority regime."[95] Because the sympathies of Black Americans are with the dehumanized Blacks in South Africa, if the Israelis are assisting in their repression (and that is a large *if*), their popularity among Black Americans will inevitably decline.

Most sinister and most alarming of all allegations about Israel and South Africa are those regarding nuclear weapons. Rumors have long circulated about nuclear collusion between Israel and South Africa, which boasts the western world's largest reserves of uranium. Barbara Rogers, a former British Foreign Office employee and now a freelance journalist, has written that "hundreds of Israelis are working on secret projects in South Africa, some of them scientists with military background, working in South Africa's most sensitive nuclear programs."[96] Before the Camp David rapprochement Egypt's Foreign Minister Mohammed Ibrahim Kamel stated that Israel and South Africa were guilty of a nuclear conspiracy which threatened the peace both in the Middle East and Africa.[97] In 1980 at a conference convened to review the 1968 Treaty on Non-Proliferation of Nuclear Weapons, the so-called Group of 77, consisting of developing Third World countries, declared that South Africa and Israel had been implicated in "oblique proliferation." That term referred to assistance given for civilian nuclear energy 'hat could be put to military use. The Group of 77 demanded that nations exporting nuclear materials end all cooperation with Tel Aviv and Pretoria.[98]

United Nations' agencies have specifically charged that the two international "black sheep" are cooperating secretly in the nuclear field. A 1977 report of the Special Committee Against Apartheid noted ominously that agreements concluded by these governments in 1976 may have involved the exchange of nuclear information.[99] The hypothesis that South Africa might be bartering uranium for Israeli weaponry can be found in an earlier report.[100] There has also been conjecture that the Israelis may be aiding South Africa in evolving its delivery capability for nuclear weapons.[101]

Both countries have emphatically and repeatedly denied the charges of nuclear cooperation. Speaking on November 30, 1981, Yehuda Z. Blum found the allegations of nuclear collusion "substantiated" only by journalistic speculation.[102] Abraham J. Roux, chairman of South Africa's Atomic Energy Board, categorically denied that any Israeli scientists were working on his nuclear projects. "It's the biggest nonsense I've ever heard in my life," he said.[103]

Despite vehement denials, rumors persist. Precisely what Israel, with its large reservoir of scientific talent, has accomplished at its atomic research center in Dimona is unknown, although it is believed in American military circles that Israel probably already possesses a number of nuclear bombs and the capacity to deliver them. For her part South Africa can justly claim not only uranium in abundance but a clandestine uranium enrichment plant at Valindaba, near Pretoria.

Speculation was rife on September 22, 1979, when an unexplained flash of bright light was detected in the South Atlantic. In the absence of hard evidence, some concluded that the flash, which had been detected by an American Vela reconnaissance satellite, was a South African atomic explosion. Others believed that the Israelis had detonated a nuclear device either on their own or in conjunction with the South Africans.

These included CBS News, whose Tel Aviv stringer, Dan Raviv, had his accreditation cancelled because he attributed the mysterious flash to Israeli efforts.[104] When CBS reported that the flash of bright light was, in fact, an atomic bomb detonated by the Israelis with South African cooperation, Defense Minister Ezer Weizmann categorically rejected the report. In Britain, Independent Television's *World in Action* program also jointly credited Israel and South Africa.[105]

A panel of non-governmental scientific experts was convened at the behest of the White House to investigate the puzzling event of September 22. It was headed by Dr. Frank Press, scientific adviser to the president and director of the Office of Science and Technology Policy. The panel concluded that "there is no persuasive evidence to corroborate the occurrence of a nuclear explosion" and one had probably not taken place. It was more likely that the phenomenon was a "zoo event," i.e., a signal of unknown origin, possibly a consequence of the impact of a small meteoroid on the satellite.[106]

These findings were probably contradicted by an independent study done for the Defense Intelligence Agency. That study is entitled "The South Atlantic Mystery Flash—Nuclear or Not?"[107] Unfortunately, the most crucial portions of the document are "currently classified in the interest of national defense and are not releasable."[108] Nevertheless, a *New York Times* story suggested that the Pentagon study had reached the conclusion that the flash was produced by a small nuclear device which had been covertly detonated.[109] Failure to make the findings of the Pentagon report public can only serve to heighten conjecture about Israeli and/or South African nuclear potential. For the time being the truth remains elusive.

Contacts between countries have an intangible texture that often defines their real relationship. At least when viewed from the South African perspective, the connection with Israel is special if not unique. South African diplomats who have served their country in Israel, but prefer to remain anonymous, are not reluctant to admit as much to foreign interviewers. Israel's great popularity among the South African white population is readily apparent to visitors from overseas.

Undermining Israel's argument that its behavior via-à-vis South Africa is no different from that of countless other nations in their dealings with the republic are gestures of amity and goodwill, some of which receive no attention in the United States. Symbolic of the spirit of deepening friendship between Israel and South Africa was the 1975 proclamation of Haifa and Cape Town as twin cities. It was a gesture which Cape Town's Jewish mayor, David Bloomberg, hoped would promote tourism and trade and foster cultural, athletic and educational exchange.[110] Yosef Almogi, mayor of Haifa, a city with a strong socialist tradition, observed that by fostering sisterhood between cities, they were promoting harmony between human beings. Although the twin city declaration went virtually unnoticed by Afro-Americans, their reaction would be obvious. It is the reaction that Jewish Americans would have had during the 1930's to the news that a city in the United States, Britain or elsewhere had been twinned with Berlin, Munich or Frankfort.

In his country's defense Israel's ambassador to South Africa, Yitzhak D. Unna, took every opportunity to make plain his dislike of South Africa's racial policies. Given its objectives, Israel's choice of Unna, a distinguished career diplomat, was a most felicitous one. He had served for several years, beginning in 1968, as Israel's consul-general in South Africa and in 1974 was elevated to the position of ambassador. Unna quickly achieved great popularity in government circles and among white South Africans. Unlike most foreign diplomats, he took the

time and trouble to learn Afrikaans.[111] This gave him access to many Afrikaner
politicians and enabled him to establish close relations with the republic despite
the criticism of apartheid which was his leitmotif. On one occasion, during a
television interview, he denounced apartheid in the Afrikaans tongue. To his
surprise he was subsquently congratulated by several staunch defenders of white
supremacist policies in South Africa who were more impressed by his mastery
of their language than by his critical remarks.[112]

On another occasion, while speaking on "Cooperation Between South Africa
and Israel," Unna explained that Israel's friendship for the republic could not
be unqualified. Because Jews in their two millennia of exile had been victimized
by every form of discrimination, including "group area acts, job reservation and
every other repressive measure . . . it is impossible for us to be indifferent when
we see that other people in this country are subjected to measures which dis-
criminate [sic] or humiliate them."[113] He then informed the white South Africans
in his audience that to resist external pressures all South Africans had to unite.
This could only occur if all "social imbalances" vanished. Of course, what the
ambassador did not say was that there were external pressures precisely because
of those social imbalances, not to mention the gross political and economic
inequalities that existed between the races.

To dramatize his government's opposition to apartheid, in June 1978 Ambassador Unna refused an invitation to be the guest of honor at a gala premiere
of "Golda," a musical show based on the life of the Israeli prime minister. As
a matter of policy, Blacks were not admitted to the Breytenbach Theatre in
Pretoria, where the play was to be staged by a South African Jewish producer,
Leonard Schach, who actually resided half of the year in South Africa and half
of the year in Israel. More than once Golda Meir as prime minister had said that
she would not visit South Africa as long as racial separation was the law of the
land.[114] Unna asserted that he would not insult Golda Meir by attending a
performance at which non-whites were unwelcome. Moreover, he explained,
"as Ambassador of Israel, I have a responsibility not only to Israel but to the
legacy of Jewish ethics and morality. We as a people have a collective experience
of being the victims of discrimination and exclusion. And by officially visiting
a theatre which excludes segments of the population because of the color of their
skin I would commit an act of infidelity to our heritage."[115] Unna further explained that shortly after his arrival in South Africa he had been invited to
become an honorary member of a posh country club known to exclude Jews.
He had declined for the same reason: racial and religious discrimination were
loathsome to him. Unna has confided that he boycotted the Breytenbach Theatre
on his own initiative. He was not instructed to stay away by the Foreign Office
which, after the fact, did tell him that they were delighted that he had done
so.[116]

In general the response to Unna's stance was favorable. A dozen other foreign
ambassadors joined the boycott. Golda Meir herself applauded Unna's decision.
For the most part the South African press, including Afrikaans publications, also

lauded his action. Several Afrikaner playwrights and actors did likewise. Because of the furor sparked by Unna, petitions aimed at desegregating the theatre were widely circulated, and the Pretoria Women Zionists who had sponsored the premiere had to cancel it.[117] Unna's gesture of opposition to South African "Jim Crowism" was much appreciated by the racially mixed colored community. Unna has told an interviewer that coloreds approached him in the street to express their thanks for what he had done.[118] However, among Black Africans who constitute the large majority of the population of South Africa, Unna enjoyed little popularity during his tenure because he embodied the invigorated bond of friendship between Israel and the South African government which repressed them.[119]

Even an improvement in relations between Israel and Black Africa in the future is unlikely to impress Israel's detractors. In actuality, throughout the 1970's Israeli diplomats continued to serve in many sub-Saharan African capitals where they were inconspicuously attached to the embassies of friendly nations. Little publicity is given to this arrangement. Similarly, Israeli advisers who were once ubiquitous in Black Africa have by no means disappeared. They can still be found dispensing technical assistance in at least twenty African countries, although they now operate less openly and in a "private capacity."[120] Just about everywhere the Israeli technicians, who are helping in agricultural and dairy projects, irrigation schemes, beekeeping undertakings, etc., keep a low profile. Africans, mostly middle-level personnel, still attend programs at the Mt. Carmel International Training Center in Haifa: programs mainly in early childhood education, the promotion of small crafts and industries and rural community development.[121] Small numbers of African students continue to study at Israeli universities and African travellers and pilgrims may be seen at the myriad tourist attractions in Israel. Israeli exports to sub-Saharan Africa in 1979 were two and a half times what they were in 1973 and sales were close to one hundred million dollars in 1980.[122]

Ever since the Camp David peace process began, there has been talk about the possible reestablishment of diplomatic relations betweeen several African states and Israel. Many Black African states were disappointed over the amount of aid they had received from the Arabs, and talk of lower oil prices turned out to be wishful thinking. Israel's return of the Sinai to Egypt in 1981 removed an impediment to the restoration of formal ties with Israel. In May 1982 after an official hiatus of nine years, it was announced that Zaire, formerly the Belgian Congo, and Israel were resuming diplomatic links.[123] It is possible that the surprise Israeli annexation of the Golan Heights in December 1981 and the siege of Lebanon in the summer of 1982 caused a delay in the renewal of relations with other African countries.

Suddenly in the summer of 1983 there appeared to be a breakthrough. President Samuel Doe of Liberia, who had seized power in a military coup three years earlier, visited Israel—the first head of a Black African state to do so since the dark days of 1973. Would there be a domino effect? Israel, which had been assiduously courting sub-Saharan African countries for a few years, fervently hoped so. A delegation from the Central African Republic had travelled to Israel to explore the possibility of ending the rupture between the two nations.

For South Africa the deepening friendship between Israel and some nations in Black Africa could be construed as an ominous trend placing Jerusalem's association with Pretoria in jeopardy. Only time will tell. Even if other countries do follow the example of Zaire and Liberia, it is not likely that Blacks in South Africa or in the United States will be mollified as long as Israel appears to be giving aid and comfort to the brutal white minority government in Pretoria.

At the same time, even if other countries are also culpable, the friendly tone of the "normalized" relations between the Jewish state and South Africa will cause Israelis and Diaspora Jews of conscience to fret about the consequent diplomatic damage and the soiling of Israel's reputation. Just as importantly, they will agonize over the appearance that Israel's moral compass is in a state of disrepair.

Perhaps realists should expect amoral *realpolitik* of an embattled nation-state in today's imperfect world. Why should a Jewish state be any more principled than others?

In the first place, for some of Israel's founding fathers a higher morality was an integral element in their vision of Palestine's future. Six decades ago philosopher Martin Buber hoped that Palestine would evolve into a center for humanity, the salvation of the human race, rather than become a Jewish Albania, i.e., a plaything of the world's powers. David Ben-Gurion, Israel's first prime minister, envisioned the Jewish state as a light unto the nations of the earth, a model for the redemption of mankind.

A prayer book widely used by the Conservative branch of Judaism denies that the concept of the "Chosen People" implies a feeling of racial superiority on the part of the Jews. Rather the term suggests that a greater degree of morality is expected of Jews than non-Jews. Jewish conduct is to be judged by a more rigorous standard.[124] If such is the case, to be faithful to its ancient religious and ethical tradition, Israel ought to reassess its relationship with the Republic of South Africa. Israel can argue that at times, especially perilous times, a government must pursue a pragmatic course in its foreign policy, a course which compromises moral imperatives. But to be consistent, this means Jews in Israel and the Diaspora must stop bemoaning the indifference and silence of the "civilized" world during the Holocaust.

NOTES

1. *New York Amsterdam News*, 15 September 1979.
2. *Time* (3 September 1979).
3. *New York Times*, 28 August 1979.
4. Ibid., 15 September 1981.
5. *Black Books Bulletin* (Winter 1976).

6. *Jerusalem Post*, 5 December 1980.

7. William Raspberry, "Israel and South Africa: Toward U.S. Tensions," *Washington Post*, 21 April 1976.

8. *Jerusalem Post*, 9 October 1978. On "Sixty Minutes" Jackson bemoaned Israel's expanding relationship with South Africa, a state of "consummate terrorism." Transcript of broadcast of "Sixty Minutes," 16 September 1979.

9. Bayard Rustin, letter to Arthur Hertzberg, president of the American Jewish Congress, 27 August 1976.

10. Eric Robins, *This Man Malan* (Cape Town: South Africa Scientific Publishing Co., 1953), p. 29.

11. Ibid.

12. Israel Abrahams, *The Birth of a Community* (Cape Town: Hebrew Congregation, 1955), foreword.

13. Edwin S. Munger, *Jews and the National Party* (New York: American Universities Field Staff, 1956), p. 7.

14. Golda Meir, *My Life* (New York: Dell Publishing Co., 1975), p. 306.

15. Ibid., p. 309. See Theodor Herzl, *Old-New Land*, trans. Lotta Levensohn (New York: Bloch Publishing Co., 1941).

16. Shimeon Amir, *Israel's Development Cooperation with Africa, Asia, and Latin America* (New York: Praeger Publishers, 1974), foreword.

17. Leonid Teplinsky, *Tel Aviv Fails in Africa* (Moscow: Novosti Press Agency Publishing House, 1975). Chapter II, which deals with Israeli involvement in Africa, is entitled the "Trojan Horse of Imperialism."

18. See Amir, *Israel's Development Cooperation*; Moshe Decter, *"To Serve, To Teach, To Leave:" The Story of Israel's Development Assistance Program in Black Africa* (New York: American Jewish Congress, 1977); "Israel Programme for International Cooperation." (Unpublished report of the Division for International Cooperation of the Ministry of Foreign Affairs, undated); and *Israel's Program of International Cooperation* (Jerusalem: Ministry for Foreign Affairs, 1967).

19. See the *Chicago Daily Defender*, 5 August 1975; Roy Wilkins, "Life Goes On In Israel," *Afro-American*, 1 April 1972; Whitney M. Young, Jr., "A Black American Looks at Israel, the 'Arab Revolution,' Racism, Palestinians and Peace," (Letter, 7 October 1970; republished by the American Jewish Congress); and Charles Kenyatta, "Consistent Ties between Blacks and Jews," *New York Amsterdam News*, 20 October 1979.

20. *South African Jewish Times*, 21 July 1961; and the Associated Press Communiqué, 13 July 1961. See also Gideon Shimoni, *Jews and Zionism: The South African Experience 1910–1967* (Cape Town: Oxford University Press, 1980), p. 305.

21. *Die Transvaler*, 7 July 1961.

22. United Nations General Assembly, Official Records, Plenary Meetings 1033rd and 1034th Meeting, 16th sess., 11 October 1961. See also Shimoni, *Jews and Zionism*, p. 307.

23. United Nations General Assembly, Official Records Special Political Committee, 287th Meeting, 16th sess., 3 November 1961. In a highly controversial letter to a South African Jewish lawyer, Prime Minister Hendrik Verwoerd implied that his country would no longer support Israel, which was aligning itself with Black Africa for "selfish reasons." See the *Jerusalem Post*, 21–22 November 1961.

24. *Jerusalem Post*, 17 April and 20 April 1962.

25. Ibid., 9 November 1962.

26. Ibid., 11 November 1962.

27. Ibid., 25 September 1963 and 10 November 1963. Prime Minister Verwoerd labelled Israel's decision to lower its level of representation as a "slap in the face" for South African Jewry.

28. Leib Frank, Interview with author, 31 May 1981.

29. Ambassador Yitzhak Unna, Interview with the author, 18 December 1980.

30. See Henry Katzew, "How the Nationalists View the Jews," *Jewish Chronicle*, 15 October 1965.

31. "Africa, the Middle East and South Africa," *Africa Report* (September/October 1975): 18.

32. *Jerusalem Post*, 21–22 June 1971.

33. Edgar Bernstein, "Israel, the O.A.U. and South Africa," *Jewish Affairs*, 26, no. 7 (July 1971): 8.

34. *Jerusalem Post*, 4 June 1971.

35. Ibid., 6 June 1971.

36. Henry Katzew, "Israel's Reaction to the Contribution," *Jewish Affairs*, 26, no. 7 (July 1971): 12–14.

37. Bernstein, "Israel," p. 9.

38. Gershon Avner, Interview with the author, 6 July 1981.

39. *Jerusalem Post*, 8 June 1971.

40. Ibid., 15 June 1971.

41. Ibid., 16 June 1971.

42. United Nations General Assembly, Official Records Supplement no. 29 (A/8429), 26th Sess., 9 November 1971.

43. Ibid., 29 November 1971.

44. Ibid.

45. Ibid., 6 December and 20 December, 1971.

46. United Nations General Assembly, Official Records Supplement no. 30 (A/8730), 27th Sess., 15 November 1972.

47. Ibid., Supplement no. 30 (A/9030), 28th Sess., 14 December 1973; and Supplement no. 31 (A/9361), 29th Sess., 30 September 1974, 12 November 1974, and 16 December 1974.

48. Yigal Allon, statement, 31st General Assembly of the United Nations, 7 October 1976.

49. United Nations General Assembly, Official Records Supplement nos. 24–31, 28th Sess., 14 December 1973.

50. Ibid., 29th Sess., 16 December 1974.

51. Ibid., Supplement nos. 24–34, 30th Sess., 10 November 1975.

52. Ibid. The resolution was adopted by the Assembly of Heads of State and Government at an OAU meeting held in Kampala, Uganda, 28 July–1 August 1975.

53. Ibid.

54. *Rand Daily Mail*, 13 April 1976; and *Jerusalem Post*, 12 April 1976.

55. *The Star*, 12–13 April 1976; and *Jerusalem Post*, 13 April 1976.

56. *Jerusalem Post*, 13 April 1976.

57. *Pretoria News*, 13 April 1976. See also *Diamond Fields Advertiser* (Kimberley), 14 April 1976; and the *Rand Daily Mail*, 15 April 1976, which commented that "In a friendless world South Africa and Israel have at least one friend in each other."

58. *Jerusalem Post*, 11 April 1976.

59. A critical view of the visit and its implications may be found in Naomi Chazan, "Israel's Shortsighted Policy in South Africa," *Jerusalem Post*, 13 April 1976.

60. *Bilalian News*, 7 May 1976.

61. Ishmael Flory, "What I Think," *Pittsburgh Courier*, 1 May 1976.

62. *New York Times*, 11 April 1976.

63. *Jerusalem Post*, 14 December 1980.

64. *Rand Daily Mail*, 20 February 1978.

65. David Frank, editor of the *Israel-South Africa Trade Review*, interview with the author, 19 December 1980.

66. Apart from the moral trauma and diplomatic costs, the economic benefits of Israeli commercial collaboration have been called into question. In a penetrating analysis Israeli scholar Naomi Chazan has demonstrated that "during the past decade the Israeli economic position vis-à-vis South Africa has lapsed into. . . rank inequality and incipient dependency." See Naomi Chazan, "The Fallacies of Pragmatism—Israeli Foreign Policy Towards South Africa." (Paper prepared for the Eighth Annual Spring Symposium of the Afro-American Studies Program, University of Pennsylvania, on "Jews in the Afro-American Perspective: A Dialogue," Philadelphia, 25–27 March 1982), p. 17.

67. Chaim Herzog, permanent representative of Israel to the United Nations, statement to the General Assembly, 9 November 1976. This was Herzog's explanation of his vote prior to the vote on the apartheid resolution.

68. "South Africa: Good Neighbor in Africa," No. 10/81 (Washington, D.C.: Minister [Information], South African Embassy, 1981). See also Moshe Decter, "South Africa and Black Africa—a Report on Growing Trade Relations," (American Jewish Congress, 1976, unpublished). It documented a flourishing trade between nineteen sub-Saharan African nations and South Africa.

69. *New York Times*, 26 May 1982.

70. Ibid., 14 November 1977.

71. Arthur Hertzberg, letter to Bayard Rustin, 1 September 1976.

72. Bayard Rustin, letter to Arthur Hertzberg (undated). Republished in *Congress Monthly* (October 1976): 7.

73. *JTA* (Jewish Telegraph Agency) *Daily News Bulletin*, no. 162 (22 August 1979).

74. *Africa Report* (July–August 1975): 33.

75. *Congress Monthly*, (December 1977): 5–8. This information was taken from Chaim Herzog, speech delivered to the United Nations, 17 November 1977.

76. *Oil Tankers to South Africa* (Amsterdam: The Shipping Research Bureau, 1981), pp. 3–5.

77. Harris O. Schoenberg, "South Africa's Silent Partners: A Study In Trade and Hypocrisy" (August 1976, unpublished report).

78. United Nations General Assembly, Official Records, document A/31/22 Add. 2, 1976, in Second Special Report on Relations Between Israel and South Africa, 1977.

79. Transcript of broadcast of "Sixty Minutes," 18 March 1979.

80. *New York Times*, 24 August 1981. The publication in question was the *Defense Attaché*.

81. *World Armaments and Disarmament—Stockholm International Peace Research Institute (SIPRI) Yearbook* (London: Stockholm International Peace Research Institute, 1978), p. 236; 1980, p. 87; 1981, pp. 197, 239.

82. Ibid., 1981, p. 116.

83. Ibid., 1978, p. 236.

84. See Moshe Decter, "Arms Traffic With South Africa: Who Is Guilty?" (American Jewish Congress, 1976, unpublished report).

85. *SIPRI Yearbook*, 1975, p. 194.

86. Ibid.

87. Hazem Nuseibah, permanent representative of Jordan to the United Nations, letter to the *New York Times*, 21 December 1981.

88. *SIPRI Yearbook*, 1980, pp. 84–85.

89. *Jerusalem Post*, 8 November 1977.

90. *Washington Post*, 8 November 1977.

91. *New York Times*, 14 December 1981.

92. *International Herald Tribune* (Paris), 13 February 1978.

93. *Jerusalem Post*, 1 June 1976.

94. Ibid., 29 June 1976.

95. Ibid., 10 July 1975.

96. Barbara Rogers, "South Africa Gets Nuclear Weapons Thanks to the West," in *Dirty Work 2—The C.I.A. in Africa*, ed. Ellen Ray, William Schaap, Karl Van Meter, and Louis Wolf (Secaucus, N.J.: Lyle Stuart Inc., 1980), 279.

97. *Jerusalem Post*, 1 June 1978.

98. *SIPRI Yearbook*, 1981, pp. 297–299.

99. United Nations General Assembly, Official Records, Documents A/32/22/Add. 3 and S/12363/Add. 3, 32nd Sess., in *Relations Between Israel and South Africa—Special Report of the Special Committee Against Apartheid*.

100. Ibid. Supplement no. 22A (A31/22/Add. 1–3), 31st Sess. See document A/31/22 Add. 2, paragraph 52.

101. Ronald W. Walters, "South Africa's Nuclear Power Development: Political and Strategic Implications," Testimony before the Sub-Committee on Africa of the Committee on International Relations of the United States House of Representatives, 21 June 1977.

102. Yehuda Z. Blum, statement, In the Plenary On Policies of Apartheid Of The Government of South Africa, Item 32, 30 November 1981.

103. *New York Times*, 30 April 1977.

104. Ibid., 25 February 1980.

105. *Jerusalem Post*, 21 October 1980.

106. "Ad Hoc Panel Report on the September 22 Event." Unpublished report prepared by the Office of Science and Technology Policy of the Executive Office of the President of the United States, July 1980, p. 2.

107. "The South Atlantic Mystery Flash—Nuclear or Not?" DST–1510 D–934–80 Rpt. 5 Unpublished report prepared by the Defense Intelligence Agency, June 1980.

108. Brigadier General Donald W. Goodman, United States Air Force, Chief of Staff, letter to the author, 23 February 1982.

109. *New York Times*, 15 July 1980.

110. *Jerusalem Post*, 17 June 1975. Actually by 1979 three Israeli cities had been twinned with South African cities. In addition to the pairing of Haifa and Cape Town, there was the twinning of Eilat and Durban and that of Acre with Simonstown. It should be noted that the French Mediterranean port of Nice is also a sister city of Cape Town.

111. Marinus Naude, counsellor to the South African Embassy in Tel Aviv, Interview with the author, 25 June 1981.

112. Yitzhak D. Unna, Interview with the author, 18 December 1980.

113. *Co-operation Between South Africa and Israel*, information bulletin no. 384 (Pretoria: Department of Agricultural Technical Services, 1977): 8. This bulletin contains remarks made by Ambassador Unna on 26 August 1977.

114. This has been confirmed by Leib Frank, Personal interview with the author, 31 May 1981.

115. *Jerusalem Post*, 20 June 1978.

116. Yitzhak D. Unna, Personal interview with the author, 18 December 1980.

117. Thelma Ruby Frye, "Golda vs. Apartheid," *Present Tense*, 6, no. 3 (Spring 1979): 5–7.

118. Yitzhak D. Unna, Personal interview with the author, 18 December 1980.

119. Informed Black South African opinion may be represented by Dr. N. H. Montlana, chairman of the Council of 10 in the Black township of Soweto. Montlana has described the South African-Israeli relationship as a "love affair" which has caused disillusionment on the part of South African Blacks. Israel, while not alone in her dealings with Pretoria, is more open than other countries. Personal interview with the author, 23 August 1983.

120. Walter Eytan, one-time director general of the Foreign Office, wrote in April 1980 that there are as many as two thousand Israelis (experts and their dependents) in one African country, which he did not mention by name. According to Naftali Blumental, chairman of Kor Industries, an Israeli conglomerate, there were twice as many Israelis working in Africa in 1980 as in 1970. See Walter Eytan, "Will Africa Resume Relations with Israel? *Hadassah Magazine*, 61, no. 8 (April 1980): 4; and *Jerusalem Post*, 12 November 1980. Others believe that these figures are inflated.

121. Mina Ben Zvi, director, Mount Carmel International Training Center in Haifa, Personal interview with the author, 15 March 1981; and Betty Shiloah, Israeli Foreign Office, Personal interview with the author, 20 April 1981.

122. Yitzhak Shelef, head of the South African Desk—Israeli Foreign Office, Personal interview with the author, 19 April 1981; and *Jerusalem Post*, 12 November 1980.

123. *New York Times*, 16 and 18 May 1982.

124. Rabbi Morris Silverman, ed., *High Holiday Prayer Book* (Hartford, Conn.: Prayer Book Press, 1951), p. 308.

VI

A Confrontation Between Friends: The Andrew Young Affair

On August 15, 1979, the charismatic Andrew Young resigned as United States ambassador to the United Nations amidst furor over his unauthorized talks with the PLO. News of his resignation swept across the front pages of American newspapers, as did speculation over the reasons why President Jimmy Carter's appointee left his post. For the next several weeks controversy raged over Young's resignation, fueled by a series of dubious and incomplete explanations. All that seemed certain was that Young had violated the guidelines of his office by secretly meeting with a Palestinian representative. His independent action immediately raised questions about the direction of American foreign policy in the volatile Middle East, questions which the Carter administration had a difficult time answering.

The mystery surrounding Young's unexpected resignation soon turned into a full-fledged affair with serious implications for Black-Jewish relations. Almost immediately contradictory accounts emerged with regard to the sequence of events which brought the U.N. ambassador's clandestine activities into full public view. At the start Israeli and American Jewish leaders appeared to be the force behind Young's ouster. On August 10, 1979, *Newsweek* magazine's correspondent in Jerusalem, Milan J. Kubic, received a tip from Israeli intelligence agents who were apparently following the PLO observer at the U.N., Zehdi Labib Terzi.[1] On the next day a Washington correspondent for *Newsweek* asked the State Department about the reported meeting. C. William Maynes, assistant secretary of state for international organizations, phoned Young in New Orleans later that day to ask about it. Young confirmed that he had met with Terzi but said the meeting was "inadvertent" and that no substantive matters were discussed.[2] This "official" version was given to Secretary of State Cyrus R. Vance and to the Israeli Embassy in Washington, and a State Department spokesman passed it on to *Newsweek*. When *Newsweek* broke the story on August 13, it called the meeting "inadvertent" and limited to fifteen minutes of social amenities.[3]

On the same day that *Newsweek* first published an account of the Young-Terzi meeting, Young conferred with Yehuda Blum, the Israeli delegate to the U.N. There have been conflicting reports on who initiated the meeting, but it was clear that Israeli officials did not accept Young's "official" version of the encounter with Terzi. At 5 P.M. on August 13, Young met with Blum and gave him the full story that he had withheld from his own government. Young acknowledged that he had discussed Security Council business with Terzi and conceded that he had not told the State Department of this. Young and Blum apparently disagreed over whether discussing the Security Council meeting was substantive business, and on August 14 the Israeli government lodged a formal protest in Washington and Jerusalem over Young's apparent breach of a U.S. pledge to have no dealings with the PLO before the organization accepted Israel's right to exist. Acknowledging the breach and its own misleading statements on the incident, the State Department announced that Young had been reprimanded both for the meeting with the PLO observer and for giving the department a false version of what had happened. Young conceded that he had misled the department "because the less they know, the less they would be responsible." On the following day, August 15, Young submitted his resignation to President Jimmy Carter who accepted it "with deep regret" but without hesitation.[4]

Young said that it was concern about a political backlash that largely had prompted him to go to Yehuda Blum. He gave the Israeli delegate a full account of his July 26 meeting with Terzi whereas he had furnished only a partial account to the State Department, which he acknowledged was "not a lie but not the whole truth." In urging the Israelis not to make the matter public, he told them any "big uproar" was likely to create a Palestinian constituency, which did not then exist in the United States.[5] However, the Israeli delegate did not appear to take this threat seriously. At the time Young's suggestion that a pro-Palestinian backlash might develop, especially among Black Americans as a result of the affair, seemed unrealistic. But Young's threat would not remain idle for long. Blacks and Jews in this country were about to enter into an extended period of hostilities over the meaning of Young's resignation.

This was not the first time that Andrew Young found himself immersed in controversy. It was no secret in Washington that his freewheeling statements on a wide range of foreign policy issues had met with adverse, sometimes hostile reaction. Soon after he was sworn in as U.S. delegate to the U.N., Young provoked a storm by saying that the Cubans had brought a certain stability and order to Angola. His penchant for impulsive and provocative statements caused irritation and embarrassment for the administration and foreign allies during his two and one half year tenure. At the end of a trip to Africa in May 1977, Young managed to enrage the Soviet Union, Sweden, Great Britain, the New York borough of Queens and a host of State Department officials. In a conversation with a reporter on his plane, he called the Russians "the worst racists in the world," said the Swedes were "terrible racists who treated blacks as badly as they are treated in Queens" and asserted that Great Britain's "old colonial mentality" remained intact. On the same trip he vexed Black African revolutionaries by advocating a negotiated solution for the problems of Rhodesia and South-West Africa and had previously infuriated the white government in South Africa by urging the Black majority in that country to launch economic boycotts to protest the official policy of apartheid. Previously, in an interview with a Paris newspaper in July 1978, Young said in response to a question about political prisoners in the Soviet Union that there were "hundreds, perhaps thousands of political prisoners in the United States." This tendency to act impulsively led him into the greatest imbroglio of his tenure at the U.N.—when he decided to meet on his own with the PLO in order to find a peaceful solution to the war-ridden Middle East.[6]

Strongly criticized for his outspoken views and occasional indiscretions, Young was defended just as passionately by those who credited him with restoring an important negotiating role for the United States and constructive exchanges with the Third World. Young was most valued by the Carter administration because of his empathy with the aspirations of developing nations in Africa, Asia and Latin America. Unlike other foreign policymakers and spokesmen, he did not approach the problems of developing nations as matters to be decided exclusively by white diplomats. His personal reputation and public concerns lent credibility to American foreign policy, credibility which was sorely lacking in the Third World. In the view of a great many non-white nations, Andrew Young appeared as the "Prince of Peace" or, at least, a benevolent force.

The appointment of Young as U.S. ambassador was not only an encouraging sign for many developing nations, but Andrew Young also symbolized the aspirations of Black America. He clearly represented a new level of Black achievement in the federal government. His very presence at the U.N. raised the issue of Black American influence on U.S. foreign policy. The rapport that he so easily established with Third World leaders suggested that Black Americans approached foreign policy matters with a sensitivity and understanding that was theretofore lacking. It further implied that Black Americans could no longer be left out of foreign policy decisions and suggested the connection between domestic and foreign policy concerns for all poor people. Although Young's foreign policy approach was certainly not universally accepted by the Black community, it did present a rare instance in which one could perceive the influence of a Black American on global concerns.

Young brought a unique set of credentials to his office. He was in the forefront of most of the battles for racial equality in the late 1950's and early 1960's. A preacher turned politician, Young had started out as a Congregationalist minister in small-town southern Georgia before joining the Reverend Martin Luther King, Jr., in the work of the Southern Christian Leadership Conference. He was standing alongside King on a motel balcony in Memphis, Tennessee, when the civil rights leader was shot and killed by James Earl Ray in April 1968. In 1970 Young ran unsuccessfully for a seat in the U.S. House of Representatives. Two years later he won the state's Fifth District seat, becoming the first Black congressman from Georgia in 101 years. He was reelected twice and then gave up the seat in 1977 when Carter appointed him to the U.N.

Young was a symbol and a carryover of the idealism growing out of the civil rights movement. At a time when white America once again lost sight of its minorities, Young stood as a reminder of an ongoing struggle. His willingness to work within the system was a show of faith that most Black Americans could only share with great trepidation. They inevitably identified with Young's personal aspirations and could not avoid involving involving themselves in his endeavors. Black America might have feared his demise at the hands of the white establishment, but his unexpected resignation still caught most by surprise.

Although news of Young's resignation soon passed from public scrutiny, the lingering damage that it inflicted on race relations in the U.S. and abroad proved more permanent. The ouster of Young precipitated a confrontation between Blacks and Jews that exceeded the expected boundaries; but it was not the cause of these tensions, which had been simmering for years and which went far beyond the confines of international diplomacy. Blacks and Jews in the United States had been on a collision course for more than a decade. The conflict between them arose out of a long series of events which in total threatened the potential disintegration of a once powerful civil rights alliance. The only surprise was that Andrew Young served as an unwilling catalyst for the escalation of hostilities.

Throughout the entire episode Young conducted himself with the composure of a seasoned diplomat. He had already established a reputation as a skilled peacemaker during the civil rights era. His sometimes brash statements in no way meant that he was unwilling to seek a peaceful compromise solution to urgent problems. When Young saw the first sign of trouble brewing between Blacks and Jews, he publicly urged both sides to ease the tension. He always referred to the clash as "a confrontation between friends," and he spoke confidently of the fact that both groups had a long tradition of working together in spite of their occasional differences.[7] On the evening of his resignation, Young held nearly an hour-long telephone conference with the Black mayors of Los Angeles, Atlanta, Detroit, Newark, New Orleans and Washington, D.C. Mayor Tom Bradley of Los Angeles said Young asked city leaders to help "see there was no schism" between Blacks and Jews because of his resignation.[8]

But when it was announced publicly that Andrew Young was stepping down from his highly visible post as the United States' envoy to the United Nations, the word spread like wildfire through America's Black communities and the indignation was almost palpable. It seemed that Afro-America's highest ranking Black had been unceremoniously toppled for what appeared to fellow Blacks to be a peccadillo at worst.

Rightly or wrongly, Israel and its American Jewish advocates were held to be the culprits. No less than four thousand people in New Orleans who were attending a convention of Delta Sigma Theta dispatched angry letters of protest to President Jimmy Carter. Thelma Daley, the president of that public service sorority of Black women, conjured up the bugaboo of American Jews' loyalty to Israel and whether it took precedence over their loyalty to the United States. With uncharacteristic asperity Daley said of Jews, "We have been patient and forebearing in their masquerading as friends under the pretence of working for the common purpose of civil rights. The latest affront reveals clearly that their loyalties are not compatible with the struggles of Black Americans for equal opportunity under the law."[9]

Jesse Jackson interpreted Young's resignation as a "capitulation" to pressure emanating from Jewish leaders. A veteran of the civil rights era, Jackson explained, "When there wasn't much decency in society, many Jews were willing to share decency." The conflict began "when we started our quest for power. Jews were willing to share decency, but not power."[10] Young's withdrawal from the world body was also attributed to American Jewish influence by the *Afro-American*, which carried an editorial accusing Jews of "acting like spoiled children" because they could not unilaterally shape United States foreign policy on the Middle East. Jews were charged with paternalism in reminding Blacks of their past support for civil rights. To the *Afro-American* it looked as if Jews felt that it was obligatory for Blacks to back the Israeli position. Even more serious was the Jewish implication that Blacks lacked the intelligence to understand the tangled Middle East dispute. While lamenting the removal of Young, the *Afro-American* rebuked Israel for its "territorial expansionism" and its investments and involvement in South Africa. Furthermore, it expressed concern for the Palestinians as "darker-skinned peoples...in a white-controlled world."[11]

In a passionate piece published in the *Nation*, James Baldwin, the celebrated author, propounded the theory (which did not originate with him) that Israel had been brought into being not to save Jews but to safeguard Western interests. Jews have accepted the task of doing the Christians' dirty work, he wrote. But, Baldwin prophesied, without the involvement of the Palestinians, the victims of Middle Eastern imperialism, peace would remain elusive. As for Andrew Young, "out of tremendous love and courage, and with a silent, irreproachable, indescribable nobility, [he] has attempted to ward off a holocaust," and Baldwin proclaimed him a "hero, betrayed by cowards."[12]

Despite vehement denials by top Israeli officials, the Black Muslims and others trumpeted the "fact" that Tel Aviv had ousted Young.[13] Black columnist Dorothy Pounds also inveighed against Young's ouster. She expressed the belief that Israel's United Nations envoy violated "confidences Andrew Young shared with him about his meeting with a representative of the Palestine Liberation Organization" and "rushed to publicize this infraction of U.S. foreign Middle East policies to so embarrass the United States that it could not change its pro-Israeli stance." So deep was Pounds' rage over real or imagined Jewish responsibility for the firing of Andrew Young that she recited a litany of grievances against American Jewry and Israel. She fulminated against absentee Jewish landlords who bilked Black tenants, lacerated Jewish grocers who charged excessively high prices and chastised the Israelis for their racism in withholding "homeland rights" from the Black Hebrew Israelites.[14]

Among Blacks exercized over Young's untimely exit from his United Nations post, it was not uncommon to claim that an invidious double standard existed for Black public servants and their white counterparts. H. Carl McCall, a Black serving at the time in the New York State Senate, had no doubt that Young was "subjected to a double standard of administration reaction if not downright duplicity on the part of the State Department." Writing in the New York *Amsterdam News*, McCall observed that after Milton Wolf, America's ambassador to Austria, met with the PLO, he was just admonished to be more circumspect. To McCall, "the one clear difference between Ambassadors Young and Wolf is that Andy is Black."[15]

In an editorial entitled "Right On! Andy," the *Pittsburgh Courier*, normally congenial to Israel, pointed out that Young's bluntness had frequently stirred up hornet's nests, but only his secret meeting with the PLO official had elicited reprimands from President Carter and Secretary of State Cyrus Vance. In sharp contrast with Young's singular meeting with Terzi, Milton Wolf conferred three times in Vienna with a PLO spokesman. Yet Wolf was simply reminded of official U.S. policy, not rebuked, not forced to surrender his position.[16]

At a Black leadership meeting held at the NAACP national office in New York in late August, there was a demand to "know why the American Ambassador to Austria was given a mere reminder about U.S. policy prohibiting meetings with the PLO while Ambassador Young was harshly reprimanded." The civil rights stalwarts present called upon the Carter administration to "account for this gross double standard."[17]

Essentially the same point was made by *TransAfrica*, a non-profit membership organization incorporated in Washington, D.C., in 1977 which acts as a Black American lobby. It defines its purposes as attempting to "influence the formation of U.S. foreign policy vis-à-vis Africa and the Caribbean in a progressive fashion" and striving to "introduce the views of Afro-Americans into the decision-making process." In an open letter to the president of the United States, *TransAfrica* indicated its ire and dismay at the conduct of the Carter administration and at those Israeli actions which they charged led to Andrew Young's resignation. *TransAfrica* further alleged that backers of Israel had mounted misguided, albeit effective pressure to which the American government had acceded. In reviewing the circumstances surrounding Young's ouster, *TransAfrica* noted that his contact with Terzi was neither the first nor the only American exchange with a PLO representative and did not warrant the punitive action taken against Young. They remarked that "the Jewish community did not arouse a furor for the ouster of Ambassador Wolf, himself Jewish, who appears to have had discussions with PLO representatives that were even more substantive in nature than those Young was accused of conducting."[18]

Not every Black American has explicitly indicted Israel and American Jews in the matter of Andrew Young. In an October 11, 1979, fundraising letter for his SCLC, Joseph Lowery wrote that Young had been compelled to resign "while waging an agressive pursuit of peace." He was not clear about who compelled

"Andy" to resign. Asked for clarification several years later, Lowery said that President Carter and Secretary of State Vance were probably responsible. He speculated that Young may well have believed that his actions had placed the president in a difficult predicament, but he added that Jimmy Carter should have refused the resignation.[19] Florynce Kennedy, a Black feminist, blamed the white establishment as a whole. She believed that the outspoken Young was perceived as an iconoclast, an undiplomatic diplomat who had to be deposed at the first opportunity for his brash behavior. He had to be taught a lesson, and the Terzi incident provided a convenient pretext.[20]

Julius Lester went further. He took Black leaders to task for scapegoating Jews, for acting as if Jews had been responsible for the resignation. "I thought Andy was responsible for that," wrote Lester "and, with great dignity, he [Young] explained that he needed to be free to speak as he wished. But as Western history amply demonstrates, whenever something goes wrong it is easy to blame the Jews." Lester, an author, musician and teacher, railed against Blacks for not being appalled by Palestinian terrorism. Given the melancholy history of Black children murdered in 1963 in a Birmingham, Alabama, church, Lester argued that Blacks had not been sufficiently critical of Palestinian violence which claimed the lives of Jewish children at Ma'alot. Black leaders were guilty of "ethnocentric insensitivity." In addition, he cautioned Blacks about impugning Israel for dealing with South Africa when they themselves were indifferent to the persecution of Soviet Jewry and apathetic about the prospect that West Germany would set a limitation on the prosecution of Nazi war criminals. Lester's ideas were contained in a piece he published in the *Village Voice*.[21] Jewish agencies were so delighted with Lester's unequivocal defense of Jews and his spirited rebuttal to the Black assault that they reprinted his article and disseminated it widely. Forgotten by 1979 was the 1968–1969 controversy when Lester was pilloried as an anti-Semite because he allowed a crude anti-Jewish poem written by a fifteen-year-old girl to be read on a radio program he hosted in New York. After a second Black youngster who was a guest on the Lester program remarked that Hitler had not made enough lampshades of Jews, there were calls to curb anti-Semitic outbursts on the airwaves and a demand that the Federal Communication Commission suspend the license of the listener-supported station in question, WBAI. Who would have had the temerity to suggest then that Lester would surface a decade later championing the cause of American and Israeli Jews?[22]

Lester subsequently told of the intellectual odyssey which left him a committed Zionist. Interviewed by a journalist from a Long Island paper, the *Jewish World*, Lester described the metamorphosis in his thinking and ascribed his newfound appreciation of Israel to a study of the historical oppression of the Jews which culminated in the Holocaust. Although he received much notoriety, Lester was in the minority of Black Americans on the Young question.[23]

Most Jewish leaders in this country appeared shocked when first confronted by the heated accusations of offended Black Americans. By and large their initial reaction was simply to deny that they were in any way responsible for Young's ouster. Jack J. Spitzer, president of B'nai B'rith, was among the first Jewish officials to protest the fact that Young's resignation was being turned into a Black-Jewish issue. According to Spitzer, Young was solely responsible for his own fate since he acted against official United States policy by meeting with the PLO and then compromised himself even further by not telling his superiors the truth. With the exception of "some lone voices in the Jewish community," at no time did B'nai B'rith or any other major Jewish organization call for Young's firing. Therefore, to blame Jews for his ouster was "dishonest and demagogic." Spitzer sensed that much of the pent-up hostility which Blacks unleashed on Jews was a result of disagreements which mounted in recent years over such issues as affirmative action programs and quotas.[24]

Jewish leaders faced an uphill battle in trying to combat the wrath of Young defenders. Theodore Mann, then chairman of the Conference of Presidents of Major Jewish Organizations which considers itself the "United Voice of American Jewry," wrote to President Carter on August 16 and asserted that the American Jewish community "did not ask for Ambassador Young's resignation." When he added that Young's leaving was not an "issue in the relationship between the Jewish and Black communities," he was thinking wishfully.[25] Although Young met with representatives of the Jewish organizations which requested that he not step down, a fact which he subsequently verified, the Jewish image was already sullied in the eyes of many Black Americans.[26]

To reverse the damage, Henry Siegman, executive director of the American Jewish Congress, categorically rejected the "suggestion in some Black quarters that Ambassador Young was brought down by Jewish pressure." He branded that suggestion a "blatant falsification of the facts and an incitement to bigotry." Siegman said that "because he was Andy Young, because he was black and we realized the significance of that . . . we didn't call for his resignation."[27]

Many Jewish leaders spoke out sharply against the press for sensationalizing the story of Young's downfall. The fact that so much was made out of the possible complicity of Jews in bringing down Young was considered by many as anti-Semitic. Rabbi Wolfe Kelman, executive vice president of the Rabbinical Assembly, pointed out that pitting Blacks against Jews was "the oldest ploy of them all. The ruler dumps on the underclass and blames the Jews."[28] Kelman was only one of the many troubled leaders of the Jewish community to take a suspicious view of the fact that the long-time coalition of the Jews and Blacks in this country was being neatly undermined by the political establishment. The net effect of all this publicity was to drive a wedge in one of the nations's most powerful coalitions for social change.[29]

Whether there was, in fact, Jewish culpability is still not clear today. What can be ascertained is that only two top-ranking Jewish leaders asked for Andrew Young's resignation. Neither man pressed the matter after issuing initial statements.

One of the two was Bertram Gold, the executive vice president of the American Jewish Committee, under whose auspices Young had once visited Israel. Gold has confirmed that he commented at the time that if Ambassador Young had said and done what the press alleged and without White House sanction he ought to be dismissed. But, in retrospect, Gold does not believe that his statement caused Young's "discharge." Most Jewish organizations did not want Young to be forced out, Gold claims, and he strenuously denies that American Jews or Israelis covertly exerted pressure to bring about the resignation.[30]

A second Jewish spokesman who advocated Young's departure from the United Nations was Rabbi Joseph Sternstein, the president of the American Zionist Federation. Rabbi Sternstein heard the revelation about Ambassador Young's contact with the PLO representative while watching the news on television. Shortly thereafter he was called by the *New York Post*, which solicited his view. At that juncture Sternstein indicated his agreement with Gold that Young should be fired because he had violated the government's instructions. The following day, the *Post*, a sensationalist tabloid, summarized Sternstein's provocative opinion in banner headlines. Just before Young's resignation Rabbi Sternstein called for the delegate's ouster, saying, "The man has demonstrated he is totally unreliable."[31]

But Gold and Sternstein were atypical of Jewish leaders on the Young issue. Most held fast to a long-established faith in Young, who had been widely hailed in Jewish circles when he was awarded the prestigious post as United States ambassador to the United Nations. At that time Rabbi Wolfe Kelman congratulated Young and hoped that the appointment would signal a rebirth of the badly frayed Jewish-Black coalition. Rabbi Arthur Hertzberg, then president of the American Jewish Congress, voiced his "deep admiration" for Martin Luther King, Jr.'s, former comrade and remarked that "Andrew Young showed his strength, courage and commitment to racial justice on the battlefields of the civil rights movement." Rabbi Hertzberg was optimistic that Young would work on behalf of justice for Black Africa and for Israel too.[32]

There was no Jewish skepticism at first about former Congressman Young's credentials as one who was sympathetic to the Jewish people and the Zionist cause. Just the opposite was the case. As previously mentioned, Young had been one of the earliest members of Bayard Rustin's BASIC. In 1977 he was described in the Jewish press as "impeccable on all counts, including questions relating to Israel and Jews generally."[33] Young had been a sponsor of the O'Neill-Yates resolution which called for a reevaluation of America's role in the United Nations in the event Israel were to be suspended or expelled. He had supported military assistance to Israel during the Yom Kippur War, had denounced Arab terrorist assaults on northern Israel, had upbraided the United Nations' resolution classifying Zionism as racism and had consistently voted "aye" on bills to assist the Jewish state militarily and economically. In 1978, the year before his downfall, he had scolded the PLO for its unwillingness to accept Resolution 242 and the concept of negotiations.[34] That resolution which the Security Council adopted on November 22, 1967, and which all nations in the dispute accepted, although with widely varying interpretations, provided for the right of every country in

the region to exist in peace; for the withdrawal of Israeli forces from occupied
Arab lands; for the creation of permanent and secure frontiers; for the freedom
of navigation in the Straits of Tiran and the Suez Canal and for an equitable
solution to the dilemma of the Palestinian refugees.

Although few Zionist sympathizers in this country anticipated a head-on collision with Young over Middle Eastern policy in 1977 and 1978, the ambassador
modified his outlook during his service at the United Nations. The modification
was bound to alienate many supporters of Israel.

True, Young as United Nations ambassador had disappointed American Jews
with his revised outlook on the Middle East, but did Jewish displeasure bring
about the resignation? Not only Young himself, but President Carter, several
former aides to the president and Secretary of State Cyrus Vance have stressed
that there was no pressure brought to bear on the White House by the American
Jewish leadership to have Andrew Young removed. Nor did the Israeli government ask for Young's removal after its initial protest over the Terzi meeting.
Among those attesting to the foregoing were Hamilton Jordan, White House
chief of staff;[35] Charles Kirbo, a close friend, consultant and adviser to Jimmy
Carter;[36] Robert Lipshutz, the White House counsel who also served as liaison
with the Jewish community;[37] and Stuart Eizenstat, the chief domestic adviser
to the president.[38] Eizenstat, now an attorney in private practice in Washington,
D.C., remembers that there was no organized campaign, no active lobbying by
mainstream Jewish organizations to force Young out of office. They were, in
fact, quite nervous that they would be perceived as the villains in the matter,
and Eizenstat himself was alive to the likelihood that Young's leaving would
cause a chasm between Blacks and Jews.[39]

If the Jews didn't "get" Andy, what then explains his abrupt exile from the
United Nations? Zbigniew Brzezinski, Carter's national security adviser from
1977 to 1981, has recently written that "Young's violation of standing policy
was so clear that the President had no choice."[40] Secretary of State Vance has
disclosed that he actually urged Young to resign, although he insists that the
ambassador made the final decision. In other words Young resigned; he was not
fired.[41] Vance's explanation is as follows: because at the outset Young denied
that the meeting with the PLO had occurred, Vance told the press and the
American public something which was not entirely true.[42] Thus, what was at
stake was nothing less than the integrity of the State Department. Hamilton
Jordan agreed that "Andy's effectiveness in dealing with the State Department
was impaired. He knew it and took it upon himself to resign."[43] In his *Keeping
Faith* President Carter wrote that Young erred in not informing the Secretary of
State more fully about the controversial meeting, although United States policy
on the PLO had not been violated in his judgment.[44]

Atlanta attorney Charles Kirbo, a self-described "good friend of Andrew
Young," regards the PLO "flap" as the last in a series of incidents embarrassing
to the president and upsetting to Vance. In particular Young's "indiscreet"
remark that there were political prisoners in the United States peeved people

around the country and was viewed as potentially damaging to Carter's political future. Carter spoke to Young about his impolitic reemarks; and, according to Kirbo, Young knew that one more imprudent assertion would "finish" him. At the same time Young, due to his popularity with Black voters, was seen as a political asset by the administration. Furthermore, he could deal with African problems more effectively than anyone else. But, with the PLO "gaffe" Young realized that he had reached the "end of the trail." His usefulness had been irreparably undermined.[45]

Eizenstat has said in a recent interview that the president did not try to dissuade Young from resigning. Had Carter asked "Andy" to remain at his cabinet level post, he would have done so in Eizenstat's opinion. But State Department pressure was intense. Secretary Vance may well have threatened to resign himself if Young did not go. The State Department had had its feathers ruffled by a succession of events in which, it believed, Young's comments lacked sound judgment. If the meeting with the PLO representative had taken place a year or two earlier, it would not have put Young's job in jeopardy, according to Eizenstat.[46]

Confirmation of this theory of "cumulative grievances" against Young is contained in the Brzezinski memoirs. Vance confided to Brzezinski his "growing irritation about the various public pronouncements emanating from our irrepressibly outspoken and charmingly disarming U.N. Ambassador." Back in 1977 the Polish-born national security adviser observed that he had not seen Vance "so put off for quite a long time" and thought it obvious "that Andy is beginning to get under his skin." Thus it is justifiable to infer that the PLO incident was merely the "last straw." By August 1979 Andrew Young had emerged as a political and diplomatic liability.[47]

Many Jews felt as if President Carter did little to lessen the tension when he kept silent for two weeks as Blacks directed verbal assaults at both Israel and American Jewry. The first statement Carter made was on August 30 during a chapel ground-breaking ceremony at Emory University in Atlanta, Georgia. That morning a reference to the Black-Jewish conflict was added to his speech after his advisers concluded that it would be appropriate to the occasion. In the Emory speech Carter tried to smooth differences between Blacks and Jews to avert "deep and damaging divisions." "Black Americans and Jewish Americans have worked side by side for generations in the service of human rights, social justice, and general welfare," commented the president, who went on to say that both groups had "suffered too much pain, too much persecution, too much bigotry to compound that suffering in any way." When it came to the subject of Andy Young, Jimmy Carter spoke glowingly of his former chief ambassador, saying that Young had "helped millions of poor and oppressed people throughout the world to understand that we support their longings for justice and a better life." He extolled Young for speaking "from the heart, out of deep commitment, out of a religious conscience and with a preacher's eloquence."[48]

Later that same day Carter acknowledged the existence of Israeli intelligence in this country, although he did not confirm or deny the report that Israeli intelligence was responsible for revealing the Young-Terzi meeting. When asked by reporters if he was bothered by Israeli intelligence operations in the United States, Carter said there was "nothing abnormal about that" since "all countries have some form of intelligence operations in other countries." The president did say that there were "boundaries of legitimacy" which governed the world of international spying and that "the Israelis honor those boundaries, just as we do."[49] It was apparent from these comments that Carter did not think that the role of Israeli intelligence was an issue that ultimately mattered in his decision to accept Young's resignation. It was also clear that in an election year Carter wanted to stay clear of any conflict between Blacks and Jews. His effort at reconciliation not only came late but was also largely superficial in that most of what he had to say either celebrated the past or simplified the future by pretending that the recent bad feelings between Blacks and Jews were temporary and easily remedied.

Young's own statements, public and private, about a possible Jewish connection to his resignation have not cleared the air. "Who really forced your resignation?" asked an interviewer for *Penthouse*. Young's succinct response was "*The New York Post* headline—*Jews Demand Firing*. That made it a black-versus-Jew issue." Young went on to say that representatives of presidents of Jewish organizations asked him not to resign; President Carter asked him not to resign. But there was a danger of violence emanating from some Jews, e.g., "JDL hotheads from Brooklyn and New York" who might attack him at the U.N. A race riot would have hurt not only him but "everything I've been doing all along." He also cited a violent act by Hasidic Jews directed against a police station in Brooklyn.[50]

Yet Young, who was elected mayor of Atlanta in 1982, has stated privately on several occasions, sometimes to leaders of Jewish agencies, that Jews were not responsible for his U.N. resignation. To cite just one instance, he said so at a meeting held early in 1982 in Atlanta with both Jews and Blacks present and then reiterated that it was he who decided to tender his resignation. On that occasion he again mentioned sensationalist headlines in the *New York Post* as the source of Black anger and of the ensuing tension. Mayor Young remarked that at one point the New York tabloid had been owned by Jews; but subsequently, exactly when, he was not certain, it was taken over by non-Jews.[51] To be precise the *Post*, a voice of liberalism and a champion of racial justice when it was published by Dorothy Schiff, a Jew, was sold two and one half years before the Young controversy. In January 1977 ownership was transferred to the Australian newspaper magnate, Rupert Murdoch, a Gentile.

What may be most significant about this little-known 1982 Atlanta meeting was an assertion made there by Dr. Paul Smith, a local Black Presbyterian minister. He stated that many Afro-Americans continued to believe that Andrew Young stepped down only after Israel pressured the Carter White House. Blacks thought that they had been betrayed once again by Jews, said Reverend Smith.

With this distressing sentiment in mind and in the hope of improving deteriorating Black-Jewish relations, the Anti-Defamation League (ADL) in Atlanta urged Young to put to rest the "canard" that Israel or American Jewry forced the resignation. Young did not comply. He was subsequently implored again by the local ADL to set the record straight. In an open, honest, soul-searching session the mayor promised that he would deal with the matter in detail in his autobiography. But, from the ADL's vantage point, that was a long-term solution. For the short run he was beseeched again to dispel damaging misconceptions about Jewish involvement in the resignation by writing an "op-ed" piece for the *New York Times* or another influential medium. Young's failure to do so has left Jews "twisting in the wind," in the judgment of one Jewish leader.[52]

Nobody can state with absolute certainty why Young has not declared unequivocally in print that neither American Jews nor Israelis bore responsibility for his downfall. Conjecture that Young, who is something of a hero in the Arab world because of his unauthorized meeting with the PLO, might undermine his popularity and credibility there by speaking out cannot be substantiated. but it is no secret that Mayor Young hopes that some Arab petro-dollars can be lured to Atlanta, and in March 1983 he visited the United Arab Emirates to advertise the advantages of doing business in Georgia's rapidly growing capital city. In any case, it is still not too late for him to clarify the circumstances surrounding his regrettable departure from the United Nations. Were he to do so even now, his explanation, however tardy, might provide a much needed antidote to the poison that has infected Black-Jewish relations.

If Israel represents the principal foreign policy issue straining Black-Jewish relations, and it does, then "affirmative action" constitutes the major domestic concern generating friction between the two groups. That seems to be the assessment of both Black leaders and their Jewish counterparts. As long ago as 1973, Dr. Carlton B. Goodlett, the Black president of the National Newspaper Publishers Association, told a summit meeting of Jewish leaders and Black publishers that Afro-Americans were deeply disturbed over Jewish opposition to employment quotas for minority groups. Goodlett, a newspaper publisher in California, said that for many Black Americans the much resented Jewish posture was seen as a veiled manifestation of the "chosen people" mentality.[53]

Not infrequently, Blacks have said that affirmative action is as important to them and their survival as Israel is to most Jews. Affirmative action is an imperative, a must for achieving equality in fact as well as in law. Indeed, what is perceived as Jewish hostility to affirmative action has probably soured some Blacks on Israel, consciously or subconsciously. In the mind of Joseph Lowery, the "creation of Israel was itself an example of affirmative action" in the international sphere.[54] His words bespeak a significant juxtaposition of these two visceral issues in his thinking and in the thinking of Jesse Jackson, who has said the same thing publicly. Appearing on television in September 1979, Jackson explained why Israel itself was illustrative of affirmative action: "We support Israel as reparation for what Hitler did to the Jews in the Second World War." The five million dollars a day which he alleged was given by the United States to Israel was affirmative action. In this country when affirmative action is discussed as reparations for two and a half centuries of slavery and more than a century of racial discrimination, "we would not expect our former allies to be caught on the other side of the table."[55]

As a result of civil rights agitation, by the 1970's special plans had been implemented which gave Blacks and other designated minorities preferential treatment in university admissions, in union apprenticeship programs and in access to government aid for small businesses. To Blacks, Hispanics, Native Americans and Orientals these policies were no more than acts of historical reparations, long overdue attempts to overcome the consequences of centuries of discrimination and neglect. To white ethnic groups, including Jews, many of the policies were objectionable. They were not construed as delayed acts of justice but as discrimination in reverse. Such groups declared that they did not object to policies equalizing opportunity. Those previously discriminated against should henceforth be judged on the basis of merit rather than on race, ethnicity, religion or gender. They did not, in general, object to policies that required that special efforts be made to reach out to potential minority applicants. It was to the use of quotas and of race as the sole criterion for jobs or admission to universities that they objected most vehemently. They said that affirmative action and quotas were not synonymous. The former was acceptable, even desirable, the latter was not.

On the question of educational quotas, Jews in particular, with their strong tradition of learning, were in an historical straitjacket. That straitjacket predisposed them to equate quotas which are designed to exclude with "benign" quotas which are designed to include those previously excluded. In Czarist Russia Jews had been the targets of the *numerus clausus* (closed number), which severely limited their access to high school, university and professional education. Similar quotas were imposed on Jews in Poland between the world wars and even in the United States, especially at Ivy League schools. Consequently quotas, even those devised to remedy a wrong engendered by time-honored prejudice, were anathema. For most Jewish agencies they were unconstitutional and intrinsically unfair.

In a highly publicized case, Marco DeFunis, himself a Sephardic Jew, sued the president of the University of Washington Law School because his application for admission had been rejected, allegedly on the basis of race and in violation of the equal protection clause of the Fourteenth Amendment. Minority applicants had seats reserved for them and did not have to compete with those in the general pool of applicants. DeFunis, who had graduated from college magna cum laude and Phi Beta Kappa, argued that his qualifications were superior to those of some of the minority applicants who had been admitted.

Jews were divided on the case. The Union of American Hebrew Congregations and the National Council of Jewish Women supported the University of Washington and its plan; but the best-known Jewish agencies (the American Jewish Congress, the American Jewish Committee and the Anti-Defamation League of

B'nai B'rith) submitted *amici curiae* (friends of the court) briefs on behalf of DeFunis. The Congress contended that the Constitution prohibited treating "applicants differently, subjecting them to different standards and different bases of comparison, solely because of their race." However, in its view, factors such as cultural deprivation, poverty or inadequate scholastic preparation were all legitimate considerations for university admissions.[56]

Jewish agencies were by no means alone among ethnic organizations in lining up behind the petitioner. The Advocate Society consisting of Polish-American lawyers, the Joint Civic Committee of Italian Americans and UNICO National, a country-wide service group of Italian Americans, filed a brief jointly with the American Jewish Committee in support of DeFunis. Yet, the *New York Amsterdam News* in an analysis of the case, which it called crucial to Black survival, specifically took the major Jewish organizations to task for their "grave failure of leadership" in pursuing "organized court efforts to reverse the meager gains so hard won by Blacks over the last decade."[57] Writing in 1974 William Raspberry stated flatly that the "fight against 'affirmative action' programs designed to help blacks and other minorities into the American mainstream is being led by Jews." After noting that Jews are disproportionately represented in the ranks of faculty and college students, he speculated that "attempts at making the campuses more representative of the country are seen by Jews as attacks upon their special preserve."[58]

In 1971 when the litigation was initiated, the trial court judge ordered the University of Washington to admit DeFunis to its law school. The state appealed, sending the case on its tortuous way to the United States Supreme Court. But in the spring of 1974 that tribunal declared the matter "moot" because DeFunis was about to graduate.[59] The high court's decision not to decide left the quota question in a constitutional limbo.

In other celebrated litigation Allen P. Bakke, an unsuccessful applicant for admission to the medical school of the University of California at Davis, sued, contending that the school's affirmative action program was biased against white applicants like himself. Sixteen places in the entering class had been earmarked for minority candidates, and Bakke argued that his qualifications were superior to some of theirs. In other words, had there been a single pool for all applicants, he would have been admitted. In a somewhat ambiguous action, the Supreme Court in June 1978 upheld as constitutional college admission programs that gave an advantage to minorities which had previously been victims of discrimination. However, the Court held that the specific plan employed by the medical school at Davis was biased against whites and therefore impermissible. It ruled that Bakke was to be admitted. He has since graduated. Here, too, the American Jewish Congress, the American Jewish Committee and the Anti-Defamation League had all filed amicus briefs backing the petitioner, but they did so together with six other white ethnic societies, Greek-American, Polish-American, Italian-American and Ukranian-American.[60]

Given the diversity of white immigrants arrayed against "reverse discrimination,'' it is curious that most Black opprobium was directed at Jews. It may well have been that Jews ''cribbed, cabined and confined'' by their bitter historical encounter with quotas were actually in the vanguard of the opposition. Without doubt, some Jews were among the most vocal and outspoken on this thorny issue. In addition, it is not beyond the realm of possibility that Joseph Lowery is accurate when he says that Jewish academics were the most zealous in scrutinizing campus policies and practices and in ferreting out instances of ''reverse discrimination,''[61] Lastly, the blame focused on Jews may be rooted in the greater expectations that many Blacks have of Jews and the keener dismay that surfaces when those expectations are not fulfilled. What cannot be gainsayed is that the affirmative action/quota controversy is in the 1980's the primary domestic wellspring of the acrimony that pervades Jewish-Black relations.

The struggle to uphold affirmative action and racial quotas not only predisposed Blacks to blame Jews for Young's tribulations but also to see the Palestinian cause in a more favorable light. When Andrew Young first warned Israeli ambassador Yehuda Blum of a pro-Palestinian backlash among Black Americans, his foreboding seemed exaggerated and his theory farfetched. It appeared to be yet another example of Young's proclivity for overstatement. But it was not long after his resignation that signs emerged which suggested that Black Americans were growing more sensitive to the plight of the Palestinians. The small but noteworthy contingent of Black SCLC delegates, who shortly after Young's resignation accepted an invitation to visit the Middle East and sang ''We Shall Overcome'' holding hands with Yasir Arafat, was at least one early indication that Young's premonition should have been taken more seriously. With some exceptions Black leaders in this country stated that Young's downfall would have a major impact on their foreign policy outlook. In all likelihood this meant that Black Americans would abandon their customary enthusiastic support of Israel and start paying greater attention to the needs of the Palestinians.

One week after Young's resignation, a diverse group of Black leaders met at the New York headquarters of the NAACP to consider the impact of Young's departure. Before the meeting a number of its organizers questioned the wisdom of letting over two hundred participants from many organizations deal with an issue that was so deeply emotional. Almost immediately the session widened into a heated discussion of Black grievances. The anger which issued forth at the meeting was directed at both Israel and the American Jewish community for their alleged role in the Young affair. The statements drafted pointed out: the contribution of Andrew Young in advancing U.S. foreign policy in areas of the world that are crucial to American interests, the ''arrogance'' of those who questioned the right of Blacks to participate in shaping American policy, the ''callous, ruthless behavior'' of the State Department in dealing with Young, the ''racism'' of that agency in its hiring policies, the support given to preserving the racial status quo by some Jews and the alliance that allegedly existed between Israel and South Africa and Zimbabwe.[62]

What started as a freewheeling tirade against Young's supposed betrayers soon turned into a much more directed appraisal of Black issues. The group accomplished much that went beyond the issuing of resolutions, for there seemed to be a changed psyche among Black leaders. Many who participated viewed the event as a long-awaited opportunity to play a more formidable role in the shaping of American foreign policy. Young's downfall proved without the shadow of a doubt that Black Americans had to begin to assert themselves with greater force in foreign policy in order to look after their own interests. One participant predicted that Blacks would no longer be content to talk only about "ghetto politics." "The Andy Young affair is a benchmark," said Mayor Hatcher of Gary, Indiana. "Things will never be the same again. The Andy Young affair will cause the Black community to reassess and reconsider its commitment. . . and take another look at the whole question of Israel and Middle East policy."[63]

The assault on Young, which brought Black anger to a boil, was experienced as a rude and painful reminder that Jews no longer had to seek their identity among the "have-nots." Although none of the participants wished to be viewed as anti-Semitic, there was a very definite sense that many in the group were prepared to carry on their struggles without customary Jewish support. Noted sociologist Dr. Kenneth Clark referred to the Black unity meeting as "our Declaration of Independence,"[64] while Newark's mayor, Kenneth Gibson, described Young's departure as the beginning of "a new era for Black Americans."[65]

There was a near sense of euphoria as the meeting drew to a close. Before adjourning, conference members agreed that they would not discuss the issues in detail with reporters. Only a brief statement, which mainly included the resolutions, was read at a news conference at the New York Sheraton Hotel. Nothing more was supposed to be said about the angry remarks issued by those in attendance. However, in the tumult of the crowd leaving the hotel, a remark by Benjamin L. Hooks, executive director of the NAACP, was overheard: "There was no other way it could have gone, considering the depth of Black folks' feeling." Several other Black leaders at the meeting made impromptu remarks which were even more shocking than any of the resolutions. For example, one small group announced that they too would soon be meeting with Terzi. Among them was the Reverend Jesse L. Jackson, president of People United to Save Humanity (PUSH).[66] Following Young's example, a new generation of Black leaders were quite clearly in the process of devising a new foreign policy agenda.

Although obvious signs of strain existed earlier, the antagonism between Blacks and Jews in this country crystallized with Young's resignation. In many ways the precise details of Young's downfall never seemed to matter once the saga opened. After the first blows were struck, Blacks and Jews found themselves locked into an adversarial relationship. From that point on neither goodwill gestures nor new information about the cause of Young's calamity made a significant difference. Despite sincere efforts on both sides to alleviate this tension, there continued to be a bitter legacy of mistrust which made the prospect of reconciliation appear remote. Feelings of disappointment and anger have continued to linger.

There is reason to believe that even if the Young controversy had somehow been averted, some other source of friction might have touched off a dispute. There is ample reason why Blacks and Jews in this country no longer share the same political objectives, domestic or foreign, that they did during the civil rights era.[67] The Young controversy brought into sharp relief the frustrations of Blacks. Pace Law School professor Preston Green portrayed Young's departure as a great moment of truth between two groups which fared unequally in their pursuit of the "American Dream." He told *Amsterdam News* readers that the controversy was especially significant since it underscored "both the influence of the Israeli lobby and the relative powerlessness of Blacks in America." Green thought it something more than paradoxical that "three percent of the population has such immense influence and prestige while twelve percent of the population languishes in virtual obscurity."[68]

While Green's statement was exaggerated, it is true that the Black-Jewish alliance had historically been a partnership of unequals. Proverbially in the same boat, Jews and Blacks travelled on different decks with the latter confined to steerage. Nevertheless, both groups were faced with prejudice and discrimination and the alliance was based on mutual need. Although Jews wielded more economic power and political influence than Afro-Americans, they could confront their exclusion from the American mainstream by cooperating in the struggle for legal equality. Civil rights legislation and court decisions reaffirmed that equality, at least in law, which satisfied the aspirations of many Jews. However, most Blacks remained economically underprivileged. In the eyes of many Blacks, what followed in the 1970's and 1980's, as the civil rights crusade lost its momentum, was a movement by many Jews to disassociate themselves from powerless Blacks. The Andrew Young affair accelerated that movement as did events that flowed from his resignation.

NOTES

1. *New York Times*, 19, 20, and 21 October 1979.
2. Ibid., 15 and 19 August 1979.
3. Shortly after his resignation Young claimed that four days after he met with Terzi a virtually verbatim account of the conversation was circulating at the highest level of the State Department. Although Young declined to say whether he thought the meeting had been "bugged" by U.S. agents, he commented that he clearly understood how American intelligence forces operated since the FBI had closely monitored his activities throughout the 1960's when he was a leader of the SCLC.
4. *New York Times*, 16 August 1979.
5. Ibid., 20 August 1979.
6. Ibid., 16 August 1979.
7. *Jerusalem Post*, 19–25 August 1979, International edition.
8. *Afro-American*, 25 August 1979.
9. Quoted in Ethel Payne, "Young Affair Puts This All Against The Wall," *Afro-American*, 1 September 1979.

10. Robert Friedman, "The Spiritual Electricity of Jesse Jackson," *Esquire* (December 1979): 84.

11. *Afro-American*, 1 September 1979.

12. James Baldwin, "Open Letter to the Born Again," *Nation* (29 September 1979): 264.

13. *Bilalian News*, 31 August 1979.

14. *Journal American*, 27 October 1979.

15. H. Carl McCall, "The Political Lessons of August," *New York Amsterdam News*, 1 September 1979.

16. *Pittsburgh Courier*, 25 August 1979.

17. Statement, Black Leadership Meeting, August 22, 1979, NAACP National Office, New York City, New York.

18. "Message to the President on the Resignation of Ambassador Andrew Young and on United States Relations with the Middle East and Africa." (undated).

19. Joseph Lowery, Personal interview with the author, 15 March 1983.

20. Florynce Kennedy, Personal interview with the author, 22 February 1983.

21. Julius Lester, "The Uses of Suffering," *Village Voice* (10 September 1979; reprint, The United Jewish Appeal).

22. See the *New York Times*, 24 January 1969; 28 January 1969; and 7 February 1969. The poem was reprinted in the B'nai B'rith publication, the *Metropolitan Star*, 8 January 1969. The author of the poem said that she was "sick of hearing about the [Jewish] suffering in Germany" and she spoke of the hatred of "black Arabs" on the part of Jews.

23. *Kansas City Call*, reprint, 11 January 1980.

24. "The Aftermath of Young's Resignation," *The National Jewish Monthly*, October 1979.

25. "Report of the Conference of Major American Jewish Organizations For The Year Ending March 31, 1980" (New York, 1980), p. 7.

26. "Interview with Andrew Young," *Penthouse*, (February 1983): 142.

27. *New York Times*, 17 September 1979.

28. *Providence Journal*, 19 August 1979.

29. Malka Rabinowitz, "Two Shades of Anti-Semitism," *Jerusalem Post*, 9–15 September 1979, International Edition.

30. Bertram Gold, Personal interview with the author, 29 December 1982.

31. Rabbi Joseph Sternstein, Telephone interview with the author, 22 February 1983. In a draft statement issued at the time of the Young controversy, Rabbi Sternstein indicated his fears that "reports of clandestine contacts with the PLO, emanating from various parts of the world, only serve to buttress the suspicions of Israel that the real policy of the administration is to develop contacts with the PLO, while, for public consumption the State Department derides such reports."

32. *Kansas City Call*, 7 January–13 January 1977.

33. *The Jewish Week—American Examiner*, 2 January–8 January 1977.

34. *Atlanta Daily World*, 31 December 1978.

35. Hamilton Jordan, Telephone interview with the author, 17 March 1983.

36. Charles Kirbo, Personal interview with the author, 17 March 1983.

37. Robert Lipshutz, Personal interview with the author, 17 March 1983.

38. Stuart Eizenstat, Personal interview with the author, 18 May 1983.

39. Ibid.

40. Zbigniew Brzezinski, *Power and Principle—Memoirs of the National Security Adviser 1977–1981* (New York: Farrar, Straus, Giroux, 1983), p. 439.

41. Cyrus Vance, Telephone interview with the author, 22 March 1983.

42. Ibid.

43. Jordan interview, 17 March 1983.

44. Jimmy Carter, *Keeping Faith: Memoirs of a President* (New York: Bantam Books, 1982), p. 491.

45. Kirbo interview, 17 March 1983.

46. Eizenstat interview, 18 May 1983.

47. Brzezinski, *Power and Principle*, p. 37.

48. *New York Times*, 31 August 1979.

49. Ibid.

50. "Young," *Penthouse*.

51. Ibid.

52. Charles Wittenstein, Personal interview with the author, 17 March 1983.

53. *New York Amsterdam News*, 29 September 1973.

54. Joseph Lowery, Personal interview with the author, 15 March 1983. In May 1984 Benjamin Hooks told a convention of Reform Jews that "affirmative action is to the black community what Israel is to the Jewish community." See the *New York Times*, 21 May 1984.

55. Transcript of WABC-TV's Eyewitness News Conference, 23 September 1979.

56. Brief of the American Jewish Congress, Amicus Curiae, in Support of Petitioners, No. 73–235, Marco DeFunis et al., v. Charles Odegaard, Supreme Court of the United States (October term, 1973).

57. *New York Amsterdam News*, 9 March 1974.

58. William Raspberry, "Fighting Campus Discrimination," *Washington Post*, 15 March 1974.

59. *Boston Sunday Globe*, 28 April 1974.

60. Brief of American Jewish Committee, American Jewish Congress, Hellenic Bar Association of Illinois, Italian-American Foundation, Polish-American Affairs Council, Polish-American Educators Association, Ukranian Congress Committee of America (Chicago Division) and Unico National No. 76–811, The Regents of the University of California v. Allan Bakke, Supreme Court of the United States (October term, 1977).

61. Lowery interview, 15 March 1983.

62. Statements on Blacks and U.S. Foreign Policy and Black/Jewish Relations, Black Leadership Meeting, 22 August 1979, NAACP National Office, New York City. See also Ronald Walters, "The Young Resignation: What Does It Mean?" *New Directions*, 6, no. 4 (October 1979).

63. *New York Times*, 24 October 1979.

64. Ibid., 24 August 1979.

65. *New York Amsterdam News*, 25 August 1979.

66. Walters, "The Young Resignation," p. 10.

67. Joel Dreyfuss, "Such Good Friends: Blacks and Jews in Conflict," *Village Voice*, 27 August 1979, 11ff.

68. *New York Times*, reprint, 28 August 1979.

VII

Missions to the Middle East and Moshe Dayan

A direct outgrowth of the Andrew Young affair was heightened interest by some Blacks in the war-ravaged Middle East. Young had been scheduled to address the annual SCLC convention on non-violent approaches in American foreign policy when the unsettling news of his resignation reached the delegates assembled in Norfolk, Virginia.[1] The shocked convention proceeded to adopt a resolution extolling what it saw as Young's courageous peace initiative.[2] More specifically, Young's resignation was the catalyst for a much-publicized fact-finding mission to Lebanon undertaken by the SCLC.

Between the time of the convention and the mission, a meeting was arranged between Reverend Joseph E. Lowery, SCLC's president, and Zehdi Labib Terzi, the PLO observer. A separate meeting between Lowery and Yehuda Blum, the Israeli representative at the United Nations, was also arranged. Young's departure from his post at the world body was one of the principal topics to be discussed with both men, according to a spokesman for the civil rights organization. On August 20, after conferring with Terzi, Lowery told the press that the SCLC unconditionally supported the "human rights of all Palestinians, including the right of self-determination in regard to their own homeland." Later, he announced to newsmen that he had entreated the PLO to consider recognizing the "nationhood of Israel," a recognition contained in Security Council Resolution 242. Over the years the PLO had rejected that resolution, and the Lowery effort was to bring no change in their position.[3]

On August 21 the SCLC leaders spoke with Ambassador Blum, who was distressed about Lowery's declared backing for a Palestinian homeland. For Blum and most Israelis, unlesss otherwise stipulated, a homeland meant an independent Palestinian state located in occupied territory adjacent to Israel. Such a state, they fear, could come under Soviet influence and jeopardize Israeli security. Blum was quoted as saying that Lowery's comments signified a "misconception of the PLO's nature." He found the equation of Israel and the PLO absurd. "It's like equating criminals to a police force," he asserted.[4] Blum had wanted to meet Lowery first, perhaps in the hope of dissuading the Black leader from talking to Terzi. Consultation with PLO representatives is repugnant to the Israeli government because it lends legitimacy to and thereby strengthens a group it conceives of simply as a gang of terrorists.

Lowery has said that Terzi communicated with Yasir Arafat; and, as a consequence, the SCLC was invited to send a contingent to Beirut. Asked about how the mission was financed, Lowery has said that the participants paid their own way.[5] It is Lowery's contention that he wished to journey to Israel also, but the Israeli representatives in the United States found excuses for not inviting him. Finally, he was told explicitly that Prime Minister Begin would not see him.[6] As a result, the ten-person SCLC delegation, which included Lowery and Walter Fauntroy, chairman of the board of the SCLC and the Washington, D.C., non-voting representative in the United States House of Representatives, went only to Lebanon. There they met face to face with Yasir Arafat, the Cairo-trained engineer who had founded Al Fatah, by far the largest of the eight guerrilla entities that comprise the PLO, the umbrella organization, which he has led since 1970.

Lowery and Fauntroy, both ministers, described their trip as a mission of reconciliation. It aimed at initiating dialogue. Lowery and Fauntroy hoped to appeal to both parties to go to the peace table to resolve their differences non-violently. As a Christian, Lowery has written that he has a claim to the Holy Land because it was part and parcel of his faith.[7] With regard to their encounter with Arafat, who in Jewish eyes is the embodiment of evil and the epitome of intransigent opposition to Israel, Lowery and Fauntroy have been unrepentant. Fauntroy has said that he travelled to Lebanon not as a congressman but as a minister of the Gospel who sees all men, including Arafat, as brothers. Jesus taught mankind to "love the sinner," Lowery told one interviewer.[8] (Not that the SCLC regarded Arafat as a transgressor.) In fact, in his report to Congress about the junket, Fauntroy unambiguously denied that the chairman of the PLO was a wild-eyed terrorist or a bloodthirsty killer. "Mr. Arafat appears reasonable and open to dialogue within the framework of the interest of his own people," he concluded.[9]

Because the SCLC get-together with Arafat seemed to be characterized by warmth and genuine affection, it was all the more aggravating to many Jews, who classify the PLO chieftain not as a bona fide political leader of the Palestinians but as a "murderer of women and children" who, given the opportunity, would not hesitate to complete Hitler's "final solution." Therefore, when Lowery embraced Arafat, he became a would-be accomplice in genocide to many Jews who saw photographs of the embrace. Speaking to an historian in his modest SCLC headquarters in the Black section of Atlanta, Lowery pooh-poohed the exchange of kisses as just a matter of courtesy, the Middle Eastern equivalent of shaking hands.[10] It was completely devoid of political significance, said Lowery who further indicated his discomfit at cheek-kissing with men.

Some American Jews, not to mention Israelis, were also upset because at the conclusion of their session Arafat and the SCLC delegation linked arms and sang "We Shall Overcome," the stirring tune associated with the civil rights struggle, which Jews had disproportionately supported. Lowery has offered an explanation for the vocalizing. During his exchange of views with Arafat, Lowery suggested a non-violent march to Beaufort Castle near the Lebanese-Israeli border as a step towards peace. Arafat's immediate response was that the Israelis would massacre the marchers, but Lowery countered by saying that he would invite well-intentioned Israelis to cross the frontier and join the march. Although plans for the proposed march were quickly aborted, Lowery requested a sixty-day moratorium on violence from the PLO. Arafat supposedly agreed, with the stipulation that the Israelis refrain from acts of aggression during the prescribed period. At that juncture Lowery has said that he called on everyone present, Christian and Muslim alike, to pray. After the prayer one of Lowery's very emotional aides began to sing "We Shall Overcome," the song with which the SCLC had traditionally closed its gatherings. According to Lowery, the press gleefully reported the singing, and its meaning in that context was grossly perverted.[11] There are other, somewhat conflicting versions of the "We Shall Overcome" incident. In a syndicated column William Raspberry wrote that Walter Fauntroy had explained that "he was only responding to a specific request from a woman who had spent time in an Israeli prison." He denied to Raspberry that his singing constituted an endorsement of PLO tactics.[12]

Queried about this in his congressional office in May 1982, Fauntroy attempted to recall the atmosphere and the sequence of events of the parley with Arafat. He told an interviewer that members of the SCLC party spent two hours pleading with the PLO commander to disavow violence and to formally recognize Israel. Lowery, Fauntroy et al. urged him to go on the "moral offensive." Arafat reportedly agreed with the SCLC that bombing would not achieve their desired end. He agreed to try for a halt to the violence, although he conceded to his guests that others in his movement were less committed to a non-violent approach. As Fauntroy related the story, either Arafat himself or a Black Palestinian woman in his entourage—he couldn't remember which—called on the group to sing "We Shall Overcome." In retrospect Fauntroy believes that the request was probably made for propaganda purposes.[13] He is also convinced that the cheek kissing and the singing of the civil rights anthem were very damaging to Black-Jewish relations in the United States because they symbolized love for Arafat and agreement with the PLO.[14] For his part Lowery is of the opinion that the fundamental objection of those who reviled him was to the fact that he met directly with the leadership of the PLO and that he acknowledged its existence. It was not to what he said to Arafat or to the singing.[15]

Jewish reaction in the United States to the SCLC discussion with Arafat was swift and very negative, to no one's surprise. Phyllis Frank, president of the Jewish Community Council in Greater Washington which represents two hundred synagogue and other Jewish groups, railed against Fauntroy: "To recognize

Arafat, the most well-known terrorist, is morally reprehensible, politically fool-
ish, and can only result in abandoning the already difficult peace negotiations.''
She called the invitation allegedly extended to Arafat to visit this country ''an
outrageous affront to human decency.''[16]

Contributions to SCLC from Jews declined sharply in the ensuing months,
and Lowery and Fauntroy became personas non grata in most Jewish circles.
Lowery claims that a Jewish group refused to participate when he was scheduled
to speak at an NAACP banquet in New Jersey a few years after the mission.[17]
Since 1979 only on very rare occasions has Fauntroy been given the opportunity
to address synagogue audiences in the District of Columbia area.[18]

The junket to Lebanon even had implications for adoption of the District of
Columbia voting rights amendment to the United States Constitution. If adopted,
the amendment would give effective representation in the Senate and the House
of Representatives to the seven hundred thousand residents of the nation's capital,
mostly Afro-Americans, who are currently disfranchised. In January 1980 with
the amendment before the Maryland general assembly, Steven V. Sklar, who
represented a largely Jewish constituency in Baltimore, wrote to Walter Fauntroy
informing him that he would not support ratification as he had in the past. Why?
Because he was ''extremely distressed and disappointed'' over the SCLC's ''ill-
conceived journey to the Middle East to embrace Yassir Arafat.'' Sklar assumed
that if the amendment were ratified Fauntroy would be elected to the United
States Senate from the District of Columbia. He reasoned that ''those who
welcome an audience with Mr. Arafat either endorse or lend credibility to his
terrorist objectives and should not be relied upon to resolutely defend and advance
the security of the United States and its national interests in the legislative forums
of this country.''[19] In February 1980 Sklar reiterated his reason for opposing the
amendment using even stronger language: ''Fauntroy would be the first senator
from the PLO in this country. I would be damned if I would vote for the senator
from the PLO.''[20] A few other Maryland state solons concurred with Sklar's
misguided logic which, it seems, would have justified disfranchising the citizens
of South Dakota for electing the pro-Palestinian James Abourezk to the United
States Senate. Despite the exertions of Sklar, the amendment was ratified by the
Maryland assembly. It is noteworthy that at least nine national and local Jewish
organizations, including the American Jewish Committee, the American Jewish
Congress, the Anti-Defamation League and B'nai B'rith Women, came out in
favor of adoption. They understood that it is inherently unfair to deny nearly
three quarters of a million Americans the right to voting representation in Congress simply because Walter Fauntroy, who once conferred with Arafat, might
occupy a seat in the United States Senate.

Although Lowery and Fauntroy were stung by the passion of their critics,
they have not appreciably modified their views since 1979. Reverend Lowery,
who considers himself neither anti-Semitic nor anti-Zionist, continues to argue
that the Palestinians are entitled to a homeland but simultaneously avers that he

is "committed to a strong, secure Israel within the pre-1967 borders." For Lowery the 1975 resolution dubbing Zionism "racism" was objectionable, but some of Israel's policies in Judea and Samaria are equally objectionable. He has been critical of the Camp David accords because excluding the PLO from negotiations was "immoral, unrealistic and repeats the catastrophic errors of the 1947–48 U.N. action."[21] He favors some military aid to Israel but contends that the current level of assistance is excessive. Not surprisingly, he strongly criticized the Israeli invasion of Lebanon in June 1982.

Walter Fauntroy also rejects the anti-Israeli label which has been attached to him since 1979. Despite his disclaimer he is so perceived not just by proponents of the cause of Israel but by its opponents also. In 1982 James Abourezk, at the time serving as national chairman of the American Arab Anti-Discrimination Committee, held a reception honoring Fauntroy, then chairman of the Congressional Black Caucus. Abourezk's letter of invitation, dated July 6, acclaimed Fauntroy as the "one man I could point to in the House of Representatives who has been consistently fearless and 'out front' in his call for equal rights and a just peace for the Palestinian people and the people of Lebanon."[22] Fauntroy, who was one of the original members of Bayard Rustin's BASIC, does admit to disapproving of Prime Minister Begin's policies, which he says were antithetical to a just and lasting peace.[23]

More hostile toward Israel than either Lowery or Fauntroy has been Samuel F. Yette, a Black writer who was the sole journalist authorized by the SCLC to observe the mission from beginning to end. Although Yette's summary of the trip to Lebanon was entitled "Dr. King's Approach Pushed on Mideast Peace Mission" in the SCLC's national magazine, there was a great discrepancy between Dr. King's interpretations of the roots and nature of the Arab-Israeli conflict and those of Yette. Yette wrote that "While Palestine welcomed Jewish immigrants to settle there and to live peaceable [sic] with the existing Arab and Jewish population, world Zionists decided to take all of Palestine for themselves and to establish there a theocracy—a state based on one religion: Judaism." The foregoing presupposes with little justification that it was the Arabs who favored territorial compromise and the Zionists who were uncompromising because of their territorial greed. Yette also subscribed to the dubious idyllic notion that before the "Zionist seizure of Palestine, Lebanon had been a model of pluralism—a society in which many religions and races lived side by side in mutual respect and harmony."[24] In point of fact, sectarian conflict in Lebanon antedated not just Israel's birth but the founding of modern political Zionism in the 1890's. Thousands perished in bloody conflict between Druse and Maronite Christians in the mid-nineteenth century. In 1926 when the Lebanese Republic was created, representation in Parliament and the government in general was apportioned among the numerous religious communities comprising the human mosaic of Lebanon. For decades an uneasy equilibrium between Muslim and Christian was maintained. During the 1948 Arab-Israeli war, the influx of several hundred thousand Palestinian refugees, the vast majority Muslims, disturbed that equilibrium and eventually led to the tragic Lebanese civil war of the 1970's and the equally tragic Israeli invasion of June 1982.

The inaccuracy of Yette's version of Israeli history notwithstanding, it is most regrettable that the 1979 SCLC Middle East venture widened the chasm between Black Americans and Jewish Americans. Above all, the SCLC remains primarily a civil rights advocate whose main raison d'être is to improve the often desperate lives of Afro-Americans who are still victims of racial discrimination of the 1980's. In that praiseworthy cause they deserve the help of all, including Jews, who yearn for a just society.

A second Black expedition to the Middle East was undertaken in the fall of 1979 by the flamboyant Jesse Jackson, another protegé of the late Dr. Martin Luther King, Jr. Born into poverty in Greenville, North Carolina, in October 1941, Jackson, a Baptist clergyman, was appointed in 1967 to the post of national director of Operation Breadbasket, the economic wing of the SCLC. In the early 1970's after he had a falling out with the SCLC, Jackson founded People United To Save Humanity, better known by its acronym PUSH, with headquarters in Chicago. By dint of his evangelical eloquence and shrewd understanding of public relations, Jackson had made himself a figure of national importance by the late 1970's. Along with several others he has aspired to the mantle of Dr. King. Critics have focused on Jackson's vaulting ambition and vanity. Whatever his faults, even foes would concur with the following description of Jackson, which was offered after a brutally frank exchange of views with prominent Jews in Denver: "A man of electric presence, a totally compelling communicator, a dazzling combination of fire and ice.[25]

Before he embarked on his tour of several Arab countries as well as Israel, Jackson sought an appointment with Prime Minister Begin. Israel's ambassador in Washington, D.C., Ephraim Evron, and others had urged that the prime minister be hospitable.[26] Although it was reliably reported that Begin himself was initially inclined to receive Jackson, he was dissuaded from doing so by Foreign Minister Moshe Dayan. Dayan was allegedly irked by Jackson's anti-Israeli comments which were uttered publicly at the time of the Andrew Young imbroglio. An Israeli government spokesman said that Jackson had sharply assailed Israeli-South African ties, had called the prime minister a "terrorist" and had referred to Israel as a "theocracy" and a "state of oppressors."[27] A few of Jackson's remarks were construed as borderline anti-Semitism. Indeed, he had previously outraged some American Jewish communal leaders by stereotypical references to "Jewish slumlords."[28]

The Jerusalem government believed that Jackson's mind was already made up on the Arab-Israeli dispute and that he could not be swayed by anything he saw or heard in Israel. It became convinced that the ambitious Jackson was involved in a media event, not a fact-finding mission. There were other possible reasons for the snub. According to a *Washington Post* correspondent, Dayan contended that a meeting between Begin and the PUSH leader could undercut the delicate negotiations between Israel and Egypt.[29]

Probably the major reason for the official cold shoulder was that Dayan and others were opposed to third parties, especially private individuals, serving as mediators between Israel and the PLO. Jackson's perceived bias against Israel made him even more unacceptable as a mediator. As a matter of policy, Israel frowned on third parties speaking to both the PLO and Israel because such talks conferred upon the former the legitimate status of the second party. Israel has long maintained that the PLO is unrepresentative of the Palestinian people, that it engages in horrendous terrorism which targets innocent women and children and that, inasmuch as it does not even recognize the state of Israel, there is no basis for negotiations. Consequently, for Jackson or Lowery and Fauntroy to confer with Begin and then Arafat as if they were equals would create an unacceptable diplomatic symmetry. President Jimmy Carter interceded with the Israeli government on Jackson's behalf. He hoped to convince the prime minister to meet personally with the Black leader, but to no avail.[30]

American Jews were divided on the wisdom of Begin's shunning of Jackson. That division was dramatized when the Jerusalem representative of the Anti-Defamation League, Zev Furst, indicated his disagreement with the Israeli government's decision, which he believed would damage Israel's image in the United States. However, within a couple of days, the league's national director, Nathan Perlmutter, announced that Furst spoke only for himself. "The position of the Anti-Defamation League is that we don't disagree with Prime Minister Begin's refusal to meet Rev. Jackson," he told the press.[31] Behind the scenes there were many Jews who feared that Israel's cool treatment of Jackson would likely drive another wedge between the Black and Jewish communities in this country.

Despite the Begin government's snub, Jackson, unlike the SCLC delegation, opted to go to Israel anyway. Teddy Kollek, Jerusalem's extroverted mayor, sent Jackson a cable agreeing to meet with him, although he took exception to the reverend's "offensive" comments about Israel and Begin, who was no political ally of Kollek's. The mayor said he would welcome Jackson to Jerusalem where he would have the chance to see for himself the "infrastructure of peace and tolerance."[32] In addition, at the proverbial eleventh hour, "logistical assistance" was provided by personnel of the foreign ministry.

During the course of his visit, Jackson revealed himself to be inadequately informed about the history and geography of the region. For example, he seemed to be under the mistaken impression that the Jordan River separated Lebanon and Israel instead of Jordan and Israel. More than once he spoke of halting the violence on both banks of the Jordan River, when in fact the Israeli-Jordanian frontier was tranquil.[33] It was along the troubled Lebanese border that violence periodically erupted. Jackson's wife erroneously believed that the West Bank was inside the old city of Jerusalem. Jackson himself was unaware of the fact that the PLO was an umbrella group of which Arafat's Al Fatah was by far the largest constituent member. Moreover, in simplistic fashion he compared Israeli policies on the West Bank and Gaza with antebellum chattel slavery in the United States. Although the sometimes draconian Israeli occupation would not warm the cockles of a civil libertarian's heart, it is a far cry from the "peculiar institution" which stripped Black bondsmen of the most basic human rights until the Civil War.

To some observers it appeared that Jackson was not particularly eager to educate himself about the Arab-Israeli dispute. Israelis were disturbed that he could not find time to meet with Jews from Arab lands[34] or with Lebanese Christians, who would undoubtedly have given Jackson and his retinue new and different perspectives. The PUSH leader did not even appear to be interested in hearing from the West Bank Arabs who gave him a tumultuous welcome.[35] It was more a matter of seeing, of being seen and of being photographed than of exchanging ideas. "Articulate preacher, bad listener," was the title of a *Jerusalem Post* editorial, which was meant to characterize Jackson, the would-be peacemaker.[36]

Most of Jackson's comments raised Israeli hackles. When he toured a West Bank refugee camp, he said that the open sewers and the poor educational facilities conjured up memories of his childhood in Chicago. "I identify with the underdog because I am one of the underdogs," he declared.[37] He castigated the American government for donating less money to Palestinian refugees than they gave to Israel.[38] Jackson also opined that the Israelis had to relinquish Jerusalem's Old City as an essential step toward peace.[39]

While in Jerusalem Jackson was taken to Yad Vashem, the Holocaust memorial, on a tour which is virtually mandatory for dignitaries visiting Israel. For some, Jackson's responses to the memorial were insufficiently sympathetic. In his defense, Jackson has written that the tour guide stated that the Holocaust was unique in world history. Jackson conceded that it was tragic but not necessarily unique. "For while 6 million Jews had died in the Holocaust, more non-Jews than Jews were killed. American genocidal treatment of the Indian and the deaths of 60 million African blacks during slavery were also tragic, but not necessarily unique events.[40] Because Jackson was reported to have quipped on the flight to the Middle East that he was "sick and tired of hearing constantly about the Holocaust" and that Jews didn't have a monopoly on suffering but merely wanted to put Americans in a "position of having to take a guilt trip,"[41] his defense fell on deaf ears.

If Jackson had been trying to say that more media attention is paid to the martyrdom of Jews in the 1940's than to Black suffering, he would have been correct. For centuries death was the constant companion of Africans wrenched from their homeland and transported against their will across the Atlantic in the nefarious slave trade. Their agony is familiar to few today. Lynchings in the United States, a national pastime for decades, is rarely mentioned, not even in classrooms. And grisly episodes, such as the genocide perpetrated against the Congolese by King Leopold of the Belgians in the late nineteenth and early twentieth centuries, are remembered only by historians. If Jackson did in fact speak in good faith and without malice, he should have chosen different language to make his point—a valid one—because Jews are understandably hypersensitive about the Holocaust, *the* apocalyptic event in Jewish history. Hitler's "final solution" not only claimed the lives of six million of their brethren, but it aimed at the physical annihilation of all Jews.

A permanent Holocaust memorial and museum has been established in our nation's capital for very good educational and ethical reasons. However, some Black Americans are grumbling because there is no slavery memorial and museum to remind Americans that for almost a century after the Declaration of Independence pronounced all men free, equal and entitled to life, liberty and the pursuit of happiness the people and government of this nation sanctioned slavery.

Behind Jackson's intemperate aircraft outburst is the dissatisfaction of American Blacks with their position of impotence relative to that of American Jews. It was reminiscent of a column entitled "Why worry so much about Russian Jews?" which had appeared in the Black press six years earlier. The columnist, Ollie Stewart, said he was "sick and tired of reading about the constant headlines on Russian Jews." It was apparent that Stewart was miffed because the United States, which had tolerated no external interference with the segregation, discrimination and violence directed against Black Americans, was now meddling in internal Soviet affairs on behalf of Jews. Washington, D.C., was not truly interested in aiding the oppressed, otherwise it would have championed the cause of Blacks in Zimbabwe or abetted the enslaved Africans in "South Africa where millions are treated worse than dogs," wrote Stewart.[42] Stewart was certainly right in suggesting that righteous indignation along the Potomac is selective and politically motivated. One often hears about the "refusenik" Anatoly Shcharansky, a Jewish prisoner of conscience prevented from leaving the Soviet Union, whose plight concerns the United States government. Indeed, Jewish pressure in this country convinced the government in 1975 to link preferential trade benefits for the Soviet Union to the Kremlin's willingness to implement a more relaxed emigration policy for Jews.[43] In contrast, that same United States government cares not at all about Nelson Mandela, the leader of South Africa's subjugated Black masses who has languished for more than twenty years in Robben Island prison. Surely Mandela is no less a prisoner of conscience than Shcharansky. but the latter is imprisoned by Communists and the former, by a fervent anti-Communist regime. And Afro-Americans lack the power to influence the government on behalf of their brothers and sisters in southern Africa. Therefore Stewart's annoyance was justified, but his conclusion that the "Jew issue is phoney" was unwarranted.

Graphically illustrating the disparate American reactions to the woes of Soviet Jews and the troubles of South African Bantu was a cartoon published in the *New York Amsterdam News*. It showed a mustachioed, pith-helmeted white imperialist, labelled South Africa, holding a revolver in one hand while choking a Black figure with his other hand. In front of "South Africa" was a mound of skulls. Adjacent to that sketch was another of a man representing the Soviet Union, who was pushing a trunk. Its contents were Jewish emigrants, and its destination was Israel. Uncle Sam admonished the Soviet Union to be "careful of that trunk" while remaining completely oblivious of homicidal South Africa.[44]

Black Americans should be angry about this state of affairs but not with the Jews who have employed political clout to convince the government to take cognizance of Jewish suffering, past and present. This is a case where Jesse Jackson and Ollie Stewart should emulate Jewish tactics rather than revile their achievements.

After his sojourn in Israel and a brief tour in Jordan, where he called for an Israeli withdrawal from all lands occupied since the Six Day War, Jackson and his entourage travelled to Beirut. The PUSH president was given a hero's welcome by Palestinians in the Lebanese capital. He was warmly hugged by Yasir Arafat, who intoned the "We Shall Overcome" slogan of the civil rights struggle to emphasize his kinship with the American Blacks. Jackson said that "fighting for Palestinian justice is a way of fighting for the security of Israel" and expressed his hope that his mission would establish a "beachhead" for dialogue between the PLO and the United States government.[45] Jackson concluded his visit in Beirut by asserting that the PLO had proclaimed a ceasefire in southern Lebanon when in fact it had simply restated its willingness to abide by a five-week-old truce sponsored by the United Nations. Although the reverend had previously stated that one of his objectives was to have the PLO renounce guerrilla warfare against the Israelis, no statement along those lines was forthcoming from Arafat.

Shortly after Jackson's return to the United States, it became clear that his efforts were not appreciated any more by some PLO elements than they were by Israelis, American Jews or certain Afro-Americans. A member of the PLO's executive committee accused Jackson of dividing "the Arab and Palestinian ranks by demanding a freeze in the Palestinian armed struggle, recognition of Israel and participation in the Camp David accords.[46]

To say that certain segments in the American Jewish community were offended by Jesse Jackson's foray into the Middle Eastern morass is to be guilty of understatement. Violence-prone Jewish Defense League stalwarts, wielding baseball bats, reacted most strongly of all. Half a dozen of them raucously stormed into PUSH's Los Angeles headquarters for the purpose of delivering a live pig symbolic of their disapproval of Jackson's diplomatic initiative. Owing to Black restraint, bloodshed was averted, but there were some Afro-Americans who were deeply affronted by the JDL's strong arm tactics. At least a few wanted an apology from the general Jewish community.[47] Almost a year later, a truce of sorts was worked out by the local PUSH and JDL groups.[48]

Stung by the many unfavorable comments disseminated by the media, Jackson retorted that his journey to the Middle East had been misrepresented by the American press. Jewish journalists who lacked the capacity to be objective about Arab affairs and who could not transcend their emotional links to Israel were the villains in Jackson's eyes. He suggested that he had been criticized by the Chicago media because "there are no Arabs and no Palestinians writing for a major newspaper or television station downtown."[49]

Jackson denied having called Prime Minister Begin a "racist" for rebuffing him. In "The real story of my Mideast mission," Jackson wrote that Begin's attitude in refusing to meet Fauntroy, Lowery and himself "reflected racial insensitivity."[50]

As to the purported remark about being "sick and tired of constantly hearing about the Holocaust," which Newsweek quoted,[51] Jackson implied that he had made no such remark. He faulted Newsweek for not checking the matter with him prior to publication: "Such questionable journalism says much about the Newsweek reporter's degree of professionalism."[52]

Unanimity in the Black community on the peace expedition was non-existent. Blacks were sharply divided on the justification for the trip. According to a survey conducted toward the end of 1979, four of five Blacks polled thought it appropriate that Black leaders be involved in American foreign policy and two-thirds believed that the Jackson and SCLC missions to the Middle East furthered the peace process.[53] Of course, there was no shortage of Black critics willing to take Jackson to task.[54]

Both the Jackson and SCLC delegations and specifically their encounters with Arafat elicited a sharp demurrer from the Urban League's Vernon Jordan. In remarks delivered in Kansas City, Missouri, to the National Conference of Catholic Charities, Jordan warned against "ill considered flirtations with terrorist groups devoted to the extermination of Israel." He added that non-violence was a guiding moral principle of the civil rights movement. "It has nothing in common with groups whose claim to legitimacy is compromised by cold-blooded murder of innocent civilians and school children,"[55] he asserted, obviously with the PLO in mind.

For Jordan and other objectors the Jackson Mideast junket was a "sideshow" that distracted the civil rights struggle from "vital survival issues" and jeopardized relationships between Blacks and Jews. He lamented the fact that in the preceding weeks "we've seen more concern exhibited about Palestinian refugee camps than about America's ghettos. We've seen more concern about the PLO's goals than about Black America's aspirations for equality. And we've seen more concern about Yasir Arafat's future than about the future of millions of Black kids growing up in poverty."[56]

If Jordan was convinced that Jackson was being manipulated by the PLO, the Afro-American hinted strongly that Jordan himself was being managed by the Israelis. A cartoon portrayed the two Black activists as puppets in combat, Jackson under PLO influence and Jordan under Israeli control. Arrayed below the puppets were Black figures—the poor, the unemployed, the oppressed.[57]

Thus, by the autumn of 1979 there was not only a rift between Blacks and Jews over the Arab-Israeli conflict, but a serious split had developed over the issue among Blacks. The Afro-Americans, mostly youngsters, who protested

Jordan's position by picketing Urban League offices in New York were the visible symbol of that split.[58]

Speculation about the major reason for Jackson's involvement in the Middle East quagmire has been rife. Critics have charged that the incentive was pecuniary, i.e., Arab money. Indeed, a staff correspondent for the *Christian Science Monitor* wrote in September 1979 that Jackson had met with local Arab businessmen at PUSH headquarters and threatened that unless there was an infusion of money into the Black community from the Arab world by October 1 no Black leader would champion the cause of the Palestinians. "We will all learn to recite the alphabet without three letters, P–L–O," he warned.[59] Jackson subsequently said that he was quoted out of context for "slanderous purposes" in the *Monitor*, but in October he ostensibly confirmed that Arab interests had pledged ten thousand dollars to PUSH at a breakfast meeting.[60]

This financial arrangement angered Dr. J. H. Jackson, who was president of the country's largest Black denomination, the National Baptist Convention. Both Dr. Jackson and the *Atlanta Daily World* objected to the ultimatum that Black support for the cause of the Palestinians would be given only in exchange for Arab money. "It is a reflection on our country and our race to indicate that money can be given to influence foreign policy," editorialized the *World*. It further argued that the formulation of foreign policy was the responsibility of the president of the United States under our Constitution, and the PUSH leader ought not to have interfered.[61]

On this question of "interference," the *World* was in the minority in Black America. In fact, few things about the missions to the Middle East seem to have galled Blacks as much as the viewpoint sometimes implied, sometimes stated explicitly, that Afro-Americans had no legitimate concerns in that part of the world or that the complexities of the Arab-Israeli confrontation were beyond their ken. This was seen as racist and arrogant, as an expression of the time-honored desire to keep Blacks in their place. When a white owned Oregon daily flailed the SCLC for playing the role of self-appointed international peacemaker, the editor of a Black newspaper, the *Portland Observer*, angrily replied: "What arrogance leads the white press to praise the occasional United Nation [*sic*] visits and peace proclamation of the Popes, while ridiculing the peace efforts of Black ministers? Is it because they still believe the place for Black people is within their 'regional boundaries'—or in the back of the bus?"[62] The editor proceeded to add that because Blacks had long endured racial indignities they were especially well qualified to "understand and interpret the inhuman conditions under which three million Palestinian people live." It would be a mistake to attribute the foregoing to the *Observer*'s pro-Palestinian bias. Vernon Jordan, an ardent partisan of the Israeli cause, was also annoyed that there were people who would circumscribe the involvement of Black citizens in shaping foreign policy.[63]

Blacks have several good reasons to want to influence the direction of American foreign policy and several good reasons to be anxious about developments in the volatile Middle East. If the powder keg which is the Arab-Israeli dispute were to explode and if American troops were to participate in the fighting, a scenario which is by no means farfetched, then the Black American community would be involved willy-nilly. "A disproportionate number of blacks died in the Vietnam War," Reverend Lowery reminded an interviewer in 1979. "If war comes in the Mideast, that's apt to be repeated."[64] Jesse Jackson made precisely the same point to CBS correspondent Dan Rather on "Sixty Minutes": "If there's a hot war in the Middle East, blacks will die first. We're 35 percent of the ground forces."[65] Both Jackson and Lowery know that the paucity of employment opportunities in civilian life causes Blacks to seek places in the military where, as a racial group, they are overrepresented, particularly in frontline forces.

Black criticism of the Vietnam War was rooted in many of the same apprehensions enumerated by Jackson, Lowery, Fauntroy et al. CORE, for example, at first hesitated to become entangled in international affairs, fearing that to do so would obfuscate crucial domestic issues and retard the freedom struggle. But it became clear that the war in Southeast Asia had implications that were racial in nature. In a position paper on the war, CORE pointed to "inequities in the draft" which resulted in a disproportionate number of Blacks being drafted. Among Blacks the casualty rate was higher, and proportionately more Afro-Americans were dying in the jungles and rice paddies. In addition, tax revenues that should have been used to cure the social ills afflicting the decaying inner cities were funnelled to finance a war eight thousand miles from home. For these reasons a CORE convention in Baltimore adopted a resolution condemning the war and urging the United States government to withdraw.[66]

As American citizens and as taxpayers, Blacks have a vested economic interest in the Arab-Israeli conflict. For years Israel has been the recipient of congressional largess. Israel is the single largest beneficiary of the yearly foreign aid appropriation.[67] Billions of dollars in economic and military aid have been channelled to the Jewish state in the form of grants and loans. To some Black spokesmen every dollar allocated to assist foreign countries is a dollar less which is available for ameliorating conditions in America's ghettos. As Reverend Lowery commented in an interview published in *U.S. News & World Report* on October 15, 1979, "military and foreign aid expenditures have serious implications for domestic programs designed to fight unemployment, provide housing, health care etc." According to Walter Fauntroy's calculations, from fiscal year 1946 to fiscal year 1979, economic and military assistance to ten countries in the Middle East had cost the American taxpayer more than twenty-five billion dollars; and Israel, he claimed, had received three-fifths of the total outlay. Therefore, Blacks already ravaged by joblessness and inflation were "extremely sensitive to the linkage between international problems, the foreign policy decisions of our government in this region, and the consequent impact such decisions have upon our domestic life chances."[68]

Spiralling energy costs, which had a calamitous impact on the poor, also linked the Middle East conundrum and the dilemma of American Blacks. But this was a secondary, even a tertiary consideration, at least for Congressman

Fauntroy, who argued that a cutoff of oil supplies would have a "devastating effect on America but a fatal effect on black America." However, he was convinced that rising oil prices were mainly the fault of gouging oil companies.[69] In a Middle East position paper Jackson contended that peace in the Middle East was essential because Arab-dominated OPEC supplied 43 percent of the free world's oil requirements and a serious interruption in the flow of that oil would touch off a major depression.[70] Perhaps so, but *if* Jackson believed that a gesture of friendship to the PLO by Black American organizations would melt the hearts of OPEC's Arab members, that belief was surely chimerical. Economic self-interest and market forces, not gratitude or goodwill, determine the price of oil which that international cartel charges.

All factors considered, it was a tactical error for the Begin government to ignore the Jackson and SCLC delegations. The prime minister or a high-ranking cabinet member, perhaps Moshe Dayan, could have met with the visitors and used the occasion to argue Israel's case and to disabuse their guests of some of their misconceptions about the Middle East. For example, Walter Fauntroy said that it was a matter of racial justice that impelled him to seek dialogue with "millions of displaced and homeless Palestinians...of darker color than the Jews who displaced them."[71] Many Blacks, including educated and knowledgeable ones, believe the Palestinians to be much darker than Jews. Chances are that most members of the SCLC delegation have never seen a Jew from Yemen, Morocco or India, nor have they laid eyes on a Falasha. Because the vast majority of American Jews are Ashkenazim, i.e., European Jews, most Americans overlook this simple truth: a majority of the Israeli populace is Oriental in origin with roots in North Africa and southwest Asia and many of them are as dark-skinned as the "typical" Palestinian Arab. This fact should have been empirically demonstrated to the SCLC contingent on the streets of Tel Aviv and Jerusalem.

Other myths and misconceptions about Israel harbored by the SCLC people could have been dispelled. Several years after Reverend Lowery's journey to the Middle East, he ingenuously asked a Jewish interviewer if it was true that no Black could become a citizen of Israel. This question undoubtedly sprang from his misunderstanding of the Black Hebrew Israelite affair.[72]

Whether Jesse Jackson himself was educable on the Arab-Israeli conflict is a matter of speculation. What is fact is that after being snubbed by Begin his criticism of Zionism became shriller. "Judaism is a beautiful religious flower just as are Islam and Christianity," he wrote in 1980, "but Zionism is a poisonous weed that's choking the flower of Judaism." Zionism, he continued, in a statement that brought to mind the infamous 1975 United Nations resolution, "is a political philosophy based on race."[73] We will never know if a more hospitable reception from Begin might have averted such a diatribe.

It is not being suggested here that Jackson and Lowery should have been given ticker tape parades down Jerusalem's Ben Yehuda Street. But certainly political prudence dictated a course of action other than the cold shoulder. Instead, the prime minister was guilty of a public relations blunder. It was neither his first nor his last in dealing with American public opinion. Several Hebrew language newspapers, ranging from the anti-Herut left to the usually pro-government right, saw Begin's policy as impolitic. The *Jerusalem Post* insightfully editorialized as follows: "Even if it were true that Lowery and Jackson should be written off as implacable foes of Israel which is questionable, the decision of how to handle their overtures for meetings should have been measured as well in terms of its public consequences, chiefly in the United States. And here certainly there is room to doubt the wisdom of the government's position."[74] Andrew Young, whose influence with the Israeli government was non-existent at that point, concurred with the *Jerusalem Post*. As the recipient of the Black Caucus' International Award in September 1979, Young said if Prime Minister Begin failed to receive Jesse Jackson, he would make a very serious "public relations error." When he pointed out that the Israeli government had previously greeted South Africa's premier, Mr. Vorster, the contrast was so stark and telling that the former ambassador received a standing ovation.[75] Both Reverend Lowery and Reverend Jackson have invidiously compared Begin's snub with the willingness of Prime Minister Rabin to host Vorster. Actually Lowery was under the mistaken impression that it was Begin who invited the South African.[76]

Since 1979 Begin has met with some odd visitors to Israel, one being the Reverend Baily E. Smith, president of the Southern Baptist Convention. That meeting occurred as a result of the fact that in 1980 the fundamentalist minister announced with almost papal certainty that "God Almighty does not hear the prayer of a Jew." In this case crude anti-Semitism did not alienate the prime minister. Rather it paved the way for an invitation to Jerusalem and a warm reception. In response to Smith's parochial assertion regarding selective acoustics in heaven, the Anti-Defamation League sponsored a trip in the hope of enlightening the benighted reverend about Jews and the Jewish state. Dismayed by what is construed as the unfriendliness of liberal Protestantism toward Zionism, as exemplified by the National Council of Churches, Israel and its supporters have cultivated evangelical Protestantism. The latter, represented for example by the so-called Moral Majority (it may not actually be moral or a majority), has often expressed pro-Zionist sentiments. Their backing for Israel is not based on a love for Jews. Instead, it is anchored in a literal interpretation of biblical prophecy and the eschatological notion that the ingathering of the Jews in Israel will be followed by Armageddon, the second coming of Christ and the mass conversion of Jews to Christianity.[77] Nevertheless Begin has eulogized Moral Majority leader Jerry Falwell and has given him a medal. It is also worthy of note that Prime Minister Begin found time in January 1983 to chat with actress Elizabeth Taylor when she undertook a solo peace venture that also entailed a meeting with Lebanon's president Amin Gemayel.[78]

What Israel and its American Jewish supporters should have seen as the overriding considerations in September 1979 were how millions of Afro-Americans reacted to the twin rebuffs to Jackson and the SCLC, what the Congressional

Black Caucus thought about it and what future opinion molders in the Black community felt upon learning that Prime Minister Begin saw fit to ignore Black American representatives. After all, the SCLC is still highly esteemed by Blacks, who associate it with the venerable Dr. King. And Jesse Jackson, whatever his imperfections, is widely if not universally admired in Black America. Results of a 1980 *Black Enterprise* magazine poll among middle-class Afro-Americans revealed that more than 30 percent of the sample viewed Jackson as the Black who best voiced the aspirations of Black Americans. In separate surveys carried out to ascertain who was the most admired Black, Jesse Jackson came in first in the Data Black National Opinion poll and the *Ebony* magazine poll. He trailed front-runner Andrew Young in the *Essence* magazine poll.[79]

Blacks in the United States are periodically reminded of the low priority that is given Africa and Afro-America by *their* government. An incident in 1970 involving President Kenneth Kaunda of Zambia is illustrative. Mr. Kaunda was in the United States to speak to the General Assembly and reportedly was eager to confer with President Nixon. No mutually convenient appointment could be arranged. President Nixon was only able to see the Zambian at the hour when the latter was scheduled to address the United Nations. The American chief executive was then devoting much of his time to campaigning for Republican candidates in the upcoming elections. Black Americans were perturbed and insulted by what was indubitably an act of discourtesy to one of the African continent's most respected statesmen. They had good reason to feel upset. Is it conceivable that Mr. Nixon would have behaved with comparable tactlessness and insensitivity had the foreign dignitary been the chief of state or head of government of Israel, Ireland or Italy, three nations with strong ethnic bonds to segments of the American populace?

By extension, the rudeness displayed towards Kaunda was viewed as insensitivity towards Black Americans, many of whom continuously lament the fact that they get no respect. When African statesmen and Black Americans are ignored, it is a reminder that people of African descent in this country can be treated with contempt, that they need not be taken seriously. Begin's failure to see Jesse Jackson and the SCLC delegation was undoubtedly seen by Black Americans as an insult to all of them. It is not the effect of the snub on the fortunes of PUSH or SCLC that should concern Israel but the long-term impact on Black America.

Black political clout on the municipal, state and national levels can be expected to grow in the future. There are currently twenty-one Black congressmen compared to just thirteen in 1972, and they no longer function on the fringes of Capitol Hill power bases. As of 1983 four standing committees were chaired by members of the Black Caucus. There is every reason to believe that the Black Caucus will increase in number and influence as the Afro-American population is augmented in absolute terms and in percentage of the general U.S. population. Black political consciousness will surely be raised in the coming years, and more and more Blacks will be going to the polls on election day. The Black vote will make the difference between victory and defeat in many crucial electoral contests, so that those candidates ambitious to hold high office and those lobbies eager to influence legislation will be forced to cater to the Black voter so largely ignored in the past. Simultaneous with the enhancement of Black political muscle, one may see a diminution of Jewish political power as the American Jewish population declines in proportion of the overall population. No crystal ball is needed to know that Jews may have to be more dependent on Black political support for various Jewish concerns, including Israel. Blunders such as mishandling the Jackson and SCLC trips can only worsen the situation.

More bizarre than either the Jackson or SCLC missions to the Middle East was a third Black expedition to that perennially troubled region. In September 1979 in the company of almost a score of Blacks—academics, clergymen, politicians and others—the Reverend Hosea Williams, a Georgia state representative and former aide to Martin Luther King, Jr., undertook a twelve-day excursion to Libya. The press reported that while in the oil-rich North African country, Reverend Williams, one of the leaders of the famous Selma-to-Montgomery civil rights march and a man whom Dr. King called my "able and courageous associate,"[80] bestowed the "decoration of Martin Luther King" on Colonel Muammar el Qaddafi, the Libyan strongman. According to Jana, the official Libyan news agency, Qaddafi in turn pledged the support of his Libyan revolution for the Black Americans' "honorable struggle for the abolition of racial discrimination practiced against them and for achieving freedom and equality between them and other men."[81]

Needless to say, Qaddafi has not played a constructive role as peacemaker; not in the Middle East, not in Africa nor anywhere else. In fact, he has bankrolled terrorists on several continents, given haven to hijackers and provided the likes of Idi Amin with succor. In a part of the world where reasonableness is the scarcest of commodities, Qaddafi is easily the most intransigent of rulers. Characteristically intemperate was his depiction of Israelis of European background as "criminals, foreigners, mercenaries and fighters who came and set up a criminal society that poses a grave threat to peace."[82] Simply stated, his objective for years has been the obliteration of the Jewish state.

Consequently, the Afro-American junket and what allegedly transpired in Libya had far-reaching implications for Black-Jewish relations. When Jews and many others heard that a man widely regarded as the premier impresario of international terrorism and a man rabid in his opposition to the idea of a Jewish homeland had been given a prize honoring the memory of Martin Luther King, Jr., they were appalled. One Jew, confused by news reports, told a meeting of the Delegate Assembly of Atlanta's Jewish Federation that he had received a solicitation from the Martin Luther King, Jr. Center for Non-Violent Change, but he would refuse to donate a cent because of the medal awarded to Qaddafi. Others present at the meeting indicated that they felt the same way. Although the Israeli consul general explained to the assemblage that neither the King Center nor Mrs. Coretta King nor the King family had anything to do with the medal, some Jews who were unaware of the fact that Hosea Williams was not affiliated with the King Center, were alienated.[83] Mrs. King belatedly dissociated herself from the medal reportedly given to Qaddafi which she said ought not be confused with the authentic Martin Luther King, Jr., non-violent peace award. The latter had been given in the past for outstanding humanitarian work to Jimmy Carter, Andrew Young and Cesar Chavez.[84] Despite Mrs. King's disclaimer, Jewish anger was not assuaged.

Even before he left Libya, Williams, an ordained Baptist minister, a research chemist and a man with a reputation for erratic behavior, was disparaged because of what the press wrote about his friendly encounter with Qaddafi.[85] One Jewish letter writer, a self-described volunteer civil rights lawyer in the 1960's, was deeply disturbed that Williams had given the mysterious King medal to the Libyan leader who "supports. . . the murderers of Jews in Israel in the same way Hitler destroyed them in Europe." He accused the reverend of betraying Martin Luther King, Jr.'s, memory and declared that Hosea "will have to live with a conscience now smeared with oil and the blood spilled by the murderers you seek to honor."[86] Another Jewish letter writer who had seen an article about the Libyan venture said he was "shocked and outraged" and also asserted that Dr. King's ideals had been perverted.[87]

Williams' peregrinations probably received more publicity in Atlanta, where he is based, than anywhere else. A columnist in the *Atlanta Constitution* wrote that for Qaddafi a peace medal was much less appropriate an award than a loaded machine gun or the head of a Jew or Irishman on a silver platter. He said that the expeditions of Williams and Lowery both "had the scent of itchy palms."[88] An editorial in the *Atlanta Journal* hinted that Williams was a headline grabber and thought Qaddafi unworthy of honor, recognition or association with the ideals of Dr. King.[89] An Atlanta radio station, WGST, also took Williams to task reminding him that Martin Luther King, Jr., stood for non-violence whereas Qaddafi promoted terrorism.[90]

There were several Blacks who objected to the putative presentation of the Martin Luther King, Jr., peace medal, which no one had actually seen. Syndicated columnist William Raspberry was one. He was "outraged" and stated flatly that Reverend Williams had "profaned America's foremost black hero," the leading apostle of non-violence and peace. What prompted Williams' "obscene gesture?" Raspberry asked rhetorically. "The crucial fact, from Williams' point of view, is that Libya has accumulated a lot of money from its petroleum resources, and that money apparently has Williams smacking his lips."[91]

Williams has not denied that he hoped to exploit Libya's wealth for the benefit of Black Americans. Specifically, he sought jobs for Blacks in Libya in the oil industry, in agriculture and in education. He also tried to arrange a faculty and student exchange between Libyan and Black American universities. But, and it is a big "but," Williams has insisted that newspaper accounts of the mission to Libya were grossly distorted. Interviewed at his chemical plant in Atlanta, he stated emphatically that he was just one member of the delegation, not its leader or organizer. Available evidence suggests that Williams is accurate on this score. The organizer of the pilgrimage was Talmadge Anderson of the Black Studies program at Washington State University. However, the flamboyant Williams was the best-known and most-outspoken member of the delegation and may well have tried to project himself as the spokesman of the group.[92]

In addition, Williams contended that no Martin Luther King, Jr., decoration was ever bestowed on Colonel Qaddafi. What he did give to the Libyan chieftain was a brass medallion, roughly two and a half inches in diameter, bearing a likeness of Dr. King, a black hand and a white hand clasping one another and the inscription "I Have A Dream." Almost four years after the trip, Williams revealed to a researcher that he had once purchased twenty thousand such medallions at a cost of thirty cents each. Ordinarily they were sold for fundraising purposes by his Metropolitan Atlanta SCLC, an entity wholly independent of Lowery's SCLC which expelled Williams. Before informally presenting this gift to Qaddafi, Williams said he gave the same medallions to an accommodating bellhop, an efficient driver and a Libyan student he had met at a university in Tripoli.[93] Another participant in the mission has confirmed that there was no formal presentation ceremony during the contingent's one meeting with Qaddafi.[94] The medallion then was either a personal gift from Williams or something given on behalf of his Metropolitan Atlanta SCLC.[95] It was not given on behalf of the Black American delegation much less in the name of all Afro-Americans.

Reverend Williams blames the Anti-Defamation League of B'nai B'rith for circulating misinformation about the expedition and the decoration,[96] but the source of most of the articles in the American newspapers was the Libyan press agency. It probably sought to exploit the Black Americans' visit, which Libya financed for propaganda purposes. It fabricated or at least embellished the tale of the King medal in the hope of partially rehabilitating Qaddafi's badly tattered image as an international terrorist and troublemaker. Williams, perhaps because he was so eager to ingratiate himself with the opulent Libyans, refrained from correcting media accounts. To hold B'nai B'rith responsible for the mythology that the trip engendered is patently unfair. After all, B'nai B'rith has neither a news agency, nor a branch nor much of a following in Libya.

In all probability the full unvarnished story of the Martin Luther King, Jr., decoration will never be unravelled, but we can be reasonably sure that Reverend Williams' press releases issued during and after the junket damaged his already frayed credibility with the Jewish community. For example, in a statement issued in Tripoli, Williams called racism "the other face of Zionism" and said that he sought an international coalition to "eliminate Racism and Zionism" which would "hasten the reality of the Dream of our great, beloved fallen leader—Dr. Martin Luther King, Jr."[97] Upon his return, in another press release, Williams voiced his goal of freeing all "African people from the imperialistic powers of both Racism and its inextricably-bound twin Zionism." The reverend also indicated his belief that the PLO was not anti-Semitic but anti-Zionist. "They unquestionably differentiate between Jews and Zionism, just like we do between

white people and racism."[98] He explained the PLO's aspirations as follows:
"...all they want is democratic self-rule for the citizens of Palestine; not just
the Arabs, but for all Palestinians, Palestine Jews as well as Palestine Christians."[99]

Evidently Williams was repeating the PLO's position that it no longer wishes
to drive the Jews into the sea, the avowed aim of Ahmed Shukeiry, the organization's first chairman. Rather its aim is the creation in Palestine of a democratic, pluralistic, secular state in which Jews, Christians and Muslims will live
in peace and harmony. However, Israeli supporters would point out to Williams
that in the Arab world all countries, save Lebanon, have established Islam as
their official faith. Moreover, they would remind him that the new PLO position
is clearly contradicted by the Palestinian National Covenant, amended in 1968,
article six of which states that only Jews who were living permanently in Palestine
until the beginning of the "Zionist invasion" will be considered Palestinians.
Others would be aliens and since several Palestinian pronouncements say that
1917, the year of the Balfour Declaration, marks the beginning of the Zionist
invasion, few Jews would be eligible to live in their pluralistic state.

One famous *sabra* or native-born Israeli who would have qualified for Palestinian citizenship even under the highly restrictive terms of the Palestinian
National Covenant was the late Moshe Dayan. Dayan was born in Kibbutz
Degania in 1915, the year after his parents had migrated from Russia. Sixty-
five years later Dayan, in the twilight of his checkered and controversial career
as a soldier and statesman, inadvertently immersed himself in the proverbial
hornet's nest. The hornets were Afro-Americans. He managed to do so with a
single off-the-cuff remark uttered in Tel Aviv. It happened in November 1980
during an interview for Israeli television, and it further debased Israel's standing
among Black Americans.

A closer look at the unfortunate Dayan incident is very much in order. On
that occasion in November 1980 the former minister of defense expressed support
for a military draft in the United States. In the absence of conscription the United
States Army was composed of volunteers. Therefore, Dayan observed that up
to the rank of sergeant "most of the soldiers are Blacks who have a lower
education and intelligence." The army ought to be attracting "better blood and
brains," he added.[100]

Needless to say, Dayan's bigoted assertion infuriated countless Black Americans and was widely reported in the Black press. The *Bilalian News*, formerly
Muhammad Speaks, the organ of the Black Muslims, was irritated and found
Dayan's comments "typical of the thinking within the Israeli hierarchy who
view Bilalians [Blacks] in the same light they view Palestinians who were pushed
out of Palestine by Zionists."[101] Of course, the Black Muslims have supported
the Palestinian Arab cause for decades and their reaction was no surprise. But
in the Dayan contretemps the Muslims had plenty of company. "Dayan Maligns
Intelligence of Black Troops" screamed a headline on the front page of the
Sentinel, which serves Los Angeles' Black community.[102]

Reverend Jesse Jackson sent a telegram calling Dayan's opinions "unkind, insensitive and an insult." He also requested a public apology. Jackson found Dayan's views even more upsetting in light of Israel's improving relations with South Africa and the "harassment of Blacks in Israel," an allusion to the predicament of the Black Hebrew Israelites.[103]

Carl Rowan, the syndicated Black columnist and former United States ambassador to Finland, wrote that Jackson had underreacted. For Rowan, Dayan's opinions were "stupid, racist, ill-informed and inimical to Israel's security interests." In a column entitled, "Moshe Dayan Insults Black GI's," Rowan reminded his readers that Black Americans will question anew why the United States government gives billions of dollars in aid to Israel, much more than it gives to all of Black Africa. Rowan also pointed out that a higher percentage of Black enlistees in the United States Army has earned high school diplomas than white enlistees. Those same Black enlistees might have to jeopardize their lives in Middle East fighting for Israel. It was especially galling to Rowan that this "racist. . . crap comes from a foreigner whose country's very existence may ultimately be dependent on the very soldiers he is slandering."[104] Clifford Alexander, then secretary of the army and himself a Black, confessed his annoyance with the aspersion Dayan had cast and vigorously defended his branch of the service.[105]

Blacks were not the only ones to take exception to Dayan's portrayal of the Black GI. Mike Royko, a white journalist, devoted an entire column entitled "It's Moshe-ly racist" to the incident. He echoed Jesse Jackson's assessment: "Dayan's remarks—whatever his motives might have been—were insensitive, unkind and an insult. And I'd add arrogant and racist to that." They were a slap at Blacks, said Royko, who could not conceive of any well-known American voicing comparably crude sentiments about Israelis without being subjected to an avalanche of criticism, including charges of anti-Semitism. He also wondered aloud about the response of the Black GI to Dayan "considering that it is his black behind that might be shot off some day in defense of Israel." As to Dayan's recommendations that the draft be re-instituted in the United States, Royko was of the opinion that opposition to conscription would be spearheaded by upper-middle-class families which would encompass most Jews.[106]

Initially, Dayan refused to disavow his views. He was quoted as saying the following: "What I said, I said. Can't I say what I think? Whoever thinks differently is welcome to speak out."[107] Subsequently, however, he did apologize, not once but twice. Speaking to the Rotary Club at the Tel Aviv Hilton on December 8, 1980, he blamed his "poor English" and said that press reports had distored his meaning. He did not intend to judge Blacks or say anything that could be construed as discriminatory but rather wished to support the idea of compulsory military service.[108]

In late January 1981 at the Knesset, he met a pro-Israeli Black American delegation headed by Bayard Rustin. Dayan apologized and repudiated his remarks which had originated, he said, in a regrettable misunderstanding. "Especially with you gentlemen, I do not want to have a misunderstanding." Rustin

declared that Dayan's comments had apparently stemmed from inaccurate information about the social composition of the United States Army.[109] As is usually
the case with such matters, Dayan's apologies were hardly mentioned in the
American press, neither the general press nor the Black press.[110]

Why Dayan made his racially provocative comments in the first place remains
a mystery. After all, he could have simply indicated that in his professional
military judgment, America needed a draft. Without ever mentioning race he
could have made his point. Had he done so, no brouhaha would have ensued.
Rightly or wrongly, millions of Americans agree with the notion that a purely
volunteer army results in an impaired fighting force.

Discretion was never one of the strong points of Dayan, who frequently stirred
controversy with his iconoclastic ideas and his gratuitous remarks. It is ironic
in light of his disparagement of Black soldiers that in 1974 Dayan antagonized
some whites in South Africa when he upbraided the republic's apartheid legislation which prohibits interracial marriage. He did so after concluding a two-
week sojourn in South Africa, where the Jewish community was his host.

Just prior to his departure from Jan Smuts Airport in Johannesburg, Dayan
told reporters, "I can understand some of South Africa's problems...military,
economic and so on. And I sympathize with them. But I find it impossible to
understand how, in 1974, a government can believe it has the right to dictate
that certain couples, because they are of different races, are not permitted to be
friends or to marry." Dayan commented specifically on the case of a colored
man who committed suicide because the republic's marriage laws prevented him
from marrying his Afrikaner sweetheart.[111] One livid South African wrote that
the Pretoria government did not derogate Dayan for his blunders as defense
minister during the Yom Kippur War because it does not meddle in the domestic
affairs of another country. "It is therefore shocking," he continued, "that Mr.
Dayan has left a bitter taste when he left South Africa and criticized our marriage
law."[112]

Why Dayan commented at all on miscegenation in South Africa remains as
much an enigma as his reason for discussing the racial composition of the United
States military. Baffled by Dayan's motives, the author of one letter to the editor
of a widely read Black weekly, the Baltimore *Afro-American*, speculated that
Dayan might have been trying to curry favor with the "new right" by insulting
Black Americans.[113] This was not very probable. In all likelihood Dayan, with
his habit of speaking bluntly, was just insensitive to the sensitivities of Blacks
in this country. Despite his high intelligence, he did not appreciate the fact that
because of their long history of persecution and humiliation Black Americans
are easily hurt by real or imagined slights. Jews in particular should understand
this as they are among the most thin-skinned of peoples.

To their credit, several Jewish agencies in the United States were quick to
criticize the Dayan statement. The American Jewish Committee, a pioneer human
relations organization, called it "as unseemly and as untrue as it is reprehensible
and irresponsible." They deplored "this slander of our fellow Americans who

are voluntarily serving our country."[114] "Thoughtless," "meanspirited," "outrageous" and "indefensible" were the adjectives employed by the American Jewish Congress in their emphatic rejection of the Dayan comment.[115] B'nai B'rith's Anti-Defamation League has said that as soon as the statement was brought to their attention they made representations both to the Israeli government and to Dayan himself through some mutual friends. Moreover, the midwestern regional office of the ADL wrote to the editor of the *Chicago Sun-Times* about this "startling statement" which had the "ring of bigotry."[116]

It is disturbing indeed that other Jewish agencies such as the Zionist Oranization of America, which is so intimately involved in Israeli affairs, saw fit not to issue any statement at all.[117] Initially, at least, Ehud Gol, an Israeli consul in Chicago, denied that Dayan had made the racist remark attributed to him. "This is a complete distortion of the truth. We have been notified from Jerusalem that he never said those things regarding Blacks in the American army." Gol also told the local Black press that news harmful to Israel was being manipulated to distract attention from the Iraqi-Iranian war.[118] Meanwhile, the Israeli Embassy in Washington, D.C. remained silent since Moshe Dayan spoke as a private citizen and was not then a representative of the Israeli government.[119]

It is true of course that Moshe Dayan did not speak officially for the Israeli government when he evaluated the United States Army. He spoke for himself. Dayan had resigned from the cabinet in October 1979 because he and Prime Minister Menachem Begin had irreconcilable differences over Israeli policy in the occupied Gaza Strip and West Bank. Still, when he offered his thoughtless evaluation in November 1980, he was a member of the Knesset. And not just any member of the Knesset but a former chief of staff and erstwhile defense minister and foreign minister, a famous war hero and diplomat. Indeed, although he held no cabinet post on the day he made his defamatory remark, in the United States he may actually have been the best-known and most recognizable Israeli. His eyepatch was as much a symbol of Israel as the Star of David.

Consequently, Dayan's indisputable racist slur should not have been ignored by the Israeli Embassy in our nation's capital, for it could have far-reaching implications both for American support for Israel and for the chronically delicate Black-Jewish relations in the United States. The embassy should have issued a terse, straightforward explanation of Dayan's status in Israeli political life, accompanied by an official governmental disavowal; and these should have been sent to Black newspapers, Black radio stations, Black politicians, civil rights leaders and other notables. As events unfolded millions of Americans of African descent, including their congressional representatives, and by implication millions of Blacks in Africa and the Caribbean, may have been offended and needlessly so.[120]

A disturbing postscript to the Dayan episode was made public in June 1982 at a scholarly conference on Blacks in the American armed forces, held in Racine, Wisconsin. A high-ranking Pentagon official disclosed to the gathering that some of the United States' allies in Europe, in the main West Germans, were increasingly concerned about "cultural differences" and the problem of absorbing greater numbers of Afro-Americans into white populations. Reservations had also been expressed about relying on an American military force, one-third of which was Black, to protect western Europe. The rejoinder of Edwin Doran of the Joint Center for Political Studies, a Black research organization in Washington, D.C., focused on the unremitting prejudice among Germans: "They have a sensitivity to race that's not too different from that of Moshe Dayan or many people in this country. They think anything black is low-quality, undependable and undisciplined."[121] Given the martyrdom of European Jews at the hands of the Nazis, how tragic it is that a recent German expression of racism should call to mind the mindless comment of one of Israel's most esteemed personages.

NOTES

1. Unpublished report of the Honorable Walter E. Fauntroy, Chairman, Board of Directors, SCLC, on Fact-Finding Mission to Lebanon, 17–21 September 1979. Released 11 October 1979, p. 3.

2. "Statement by Dr. Lowery...Following S.C.L.C.'s Middle East Peace Initiative," *S.C.L.C.* (November/December 1979): 34.

3. *New York Times*, 21 August 1979.

4. Ibid., 22 August 1979.

5. Rev. Joseph Lowery, Personal interview with the author, 15 March 1983. Four years after the trip, Nabeel Abraham, executive director of the Association of Arab-American University Graduates, said that he had paid the travel costs for Lowery's trip. *New York Times*, 17 October 1983.

6. Lowery interview, 15 March 1983. In response to a query on this matter, in April 1983 the Israeli Embassy in Washington, D.C. stated, "There are no records here at the Embassy of correspondence relating to a 1979 event. Documents are not kept for such a long period. Also, there is no one on our staff now who was at the Embassy in 1979." Letter from Harry Z. Hurwitz, minister of information, to the author, 13 April 1983. When the Israeli ambassador to the U.N. was contacted, he remembered "meeting with the Reverend Lowery in August 1979 in the wake of the resignation of Ambassador Andrew Young and discussing with him developments related to that episode. The setting up of meetings between officials of the Israel government and persons or organizations unrelated to the United Nations and its activities is not dealt with by this Mission." Letter from Judith Varnai-Dranger, first secretary, permanent mission of Israel to the United Nations, to the author, 20 July 1983.

7. Rev. Joseph Lowery, "All Children of Abraham," *Afro-Americans Stand Up for Middle East Peace*, ed. James Zogby and Jack O'Dell (Washington, D.C.: Palestine Human Rights Campaign, 1980), p. 16. Jack O'Dell is director of international affairs of Jesse Jackson's Operation PUSH.

8. Fauntroy report, p. 3; Lowery interview, 15 March 1983.

9. Fauntroy report, p. 17.

10. Lowery interview, 15 March 1983.

11. Ibid.

12. *Washington Post*, 27 September 1979.

13. Walter Fauntroy, Personal interview with the author, 19 May 1983.

14. Ibid.

15. Ibid.

16. *Washington Star*, 25 September 1979.

17. Lowery interview, 15 March 1983.

18. Fauntroy interview, 19 May 1983.

19. Letter from Steven V. Sklar to Congressman Walter Fauntroy, 23 January 1980.

20. David Silverberg, "The D.C.-P.L.O. Connection," *Baltimore Jewish Times*, 1 February 1980, pp. 44–48.

21. Lowery interview, 15 March 1983; and Lowery, "All Children," p. 17.

22. Letter of invitation from James Abourezk, 6 July 1982.

23. Fauntroy interview, 19 May 1983.

24. Samuel Yette, "Dr. King's Approach Pushed on Middle East Mission," *S.C.L.C.* (November/December 1979): 26. This piece originally appeared in the *Afro-American*.

25. American Jewish Committee Memo on "Jesse Jackson Meeting In Denver," 17 September 1979.

26. *Jerusalem Post*, 30 September–6 October 1979, International edition.

27. *Washington Post*, 25 September 1979; and *New York Times*, 21 September 1979.

28. Ibid., 27 August 1979. See also Colman McCarthy, "Jesse Jackson, Surfing Along on the Latest Wave," *Washington Post*, 7 October 1979. At a White House reception Hyman Bookbinder, the American Jewish Committee's Washington representative, admonished Jackson not to use emotionally loaded words such as "Jewish slumlords." Hyman Bookbinder, Personal interview with the author, 17 May 1983. Back in 1969 during a *Playboy* interview, Jackson indicated that he saw the confrontation between Jews and Blacks in the North in terms of "economic colonialism." The Jew had been revealed as a shopowner and a landlord, but he characterized the mood of Afro-Americans as one of "anti-colonialism" not anti-Semitism.

29. *Washington Post*, 25 September 1979.

30. *New York Times*, 4 October 1979. The Israeli government denied that President Carter had requested that it receive Jackson. Ibid., 9 October 1979.

31. Ibid., 24 September 1979.

32. Ibid., 21 September 1979; and the *Jerusalem Post*, 23 September–29 September 1979, International edition.

33. *New York Times*, 9 October 1979.

34. *Washington Post*, 26 September 1979.

35. *New York Times*, 28 September 1979.

36. *Jerusalem Post*, 26 August 1979.

37. Ibid., 30 September–6 October 1979, International edition.

38. *New York Times*, 27 September 1979.

39. Ibid., 28 September 1979.

40. Jesse Jackson, "The real story of my Mideast mission," *Los Angeles Herald Examiner*, 20 October 1979.

41. Eliahu Salpeter, "Courting The PLO—Jesse Jackson's Pilgrimage," *The New Leader* (22 October 1979): 4.

42. *Afro-American*, 13 October 1973.

43. This linkage was made by the Jackson-Vanik amendment to the 1974 Trade Reform Act. See Paula Stern, *Water's Edge—Domestic Politics and the Making of American Foreign Policy* (Westport, Conn.: Greenwood Press, 1974).

44. *New York Amsterdam News*, 6 October 1973.

45. *New York Times*, 28 September 1979; and *Providence Sunday Journal*, 30 September 1979.

46. *New York Times*, 7 October 1979.

47. *Los Angeles Sentinel*, 4 October 1979.

48. Ibid., 28 August 1980.

49. *Chicago Tribune*, 7 October 1979.

50. Jesse Jackson, "The real story," 20 October 1979.

51. *Newsweek*, 8 October 1979.

52. *Los Angeles Herald Examiner*, 20 October 1979. Blazer confirmed that Jackson had indeed made the Holocaust remark en route to Israel.

53. The results of this Data Black Poll were summarized in the *Atlanta Daily World*, 24 January 1980.

54. Not atypical was the sentiment expressed by Charles Kenyatta who asked rhetorically, "What is Jesse Jackson doing rabble-rousing abroad when 35 million Blacks in this country cry out for human rights and nationhood?" *New York Amsterdam News*, 20 October 1979.

55. *Kansas City Globe*, 18 October 1979.

56. *Afro-American*, 20 October 1979 and 27 October 1979; *New York Times*, 15 October 1979.

57. *Afro-American*, 23 October–27 October 1979.

58. Ibid., 27 October 1979.

59. Christopher Swan, "Jesse Jackson—A Man with PUSH," *Christian Science Monitor*, 25 September 1979.

60. JTA Daily Bulletin, 17 October 1979; Roger Simon, "Jesse Raises $10,000 in Arab Cash," *Chicago Sun-Times*, 16 October 1979; and *New York Times*, 17 October 1979. At the breakfast meeting Jackson is reported to have said that he accepted the PLO as a government in exile and not simply as a terrorist gang.

61. *Atlanta Daily World*, 28 October 1979. Founded in 1918, the *World* claims to be the oldest continuously Black-owned, Black-controlled daily Black newspaper in the United States. In sharp contrast with the *World* was the position taken by the director and co-chairman of the American Jewish Congress' Commission on Law and Social Action. When fourteen congressmen called for the prosecution of Reverend Jackson under the Logan Act, which defines unauthorized communication with a foreign power to influence that power with regard to a controversy involving the United States as a crime, they called for the scrapping of the law. They did so despite their belief that Jackson's involvement in the Middle East was "inimical and damaging to this country's welfare and national interests." See letter from Nathan Z. Dershowitz and Abraham S. Goldstein to editor, *New York Times*, 11 October 1979.

62. *Portland Observer*, 27 September 1979.

63. *New York Amsterdam News*, 20 October 1979.

64. "Black's Role in Mideast Talks—Right or Wrong?" *U.S. News & World Report*, 15 October 1979.

65. Transcript of "60 Minutes," 16 September 1979, p. 16.

66. Martin Luther King, Jr. Library and Archives, CORE Papers, Box 42, Series 111 (undated).

67. Comptroller General of the United States, report on U.S. Assistance to the State of Israel, GAO/ID-83-51, 24 June 1983, p. i. One justification offered for the substantial aid to Israel is that it is a highly reliable ally and acts as a surrogate for U.S. interests

in the Middle East. Hyman Bookbinder of the American Jewish Committee has argued that the "funds appropriated for Israel as 'aid' should in fact be thought of as part of U.S. defense outlays. In adding to Israel's self-defense, the U.S. is contributing to furtherance of its own national interests in that crucial area." See Hyman Bookbinder "The Jewish Lobby—Myths and Reality," speech delivered at Commonwealth Club, San Francisco, 25 March 1983. Egypt is the second greatest beneficiary of U.S. aid.

68. Fauntroy report, p. 12.

69. Ibid.; *New York Times*, 22 August 1979; and letter to the editor, *New York Times*, 31 August 1979.

70. Jesse Jackson, "A Quest for Peace in the Middle East—and the Vital Interests of Black People." A position paper, 20 August 1979.

71. Letter from Walter Fauntroy, *New York Times*, 31 August 1979.

72. Lowery interview, 15 March 1983.

73. "Interview—Jesse Jackson," *Arab Perspectives* (September 1980): 28.

74. *Jerusalem Post*, 23 September—29 September 1979, International edition.

75. *Los Angeles Sentinel*, 27 September 1979.

76. "Blacks' Role," 15 October 1979.

77. Balfour Brickner, "America's Religion: What's Right, What's Left," *Present Tense*, 8, no. 3 (Spring 1981): 41.

78. *Jerusalem Post*, 2 January–8 January 1983; and 9 January–15 January 1983, International edition.

79. See *"Ebony* Interview with the Rev. Jesse Jackson." *Ebony* (June 1981): 155.

80. David L. Lewis, *King—A Critical Biography* (Baltimore: Penguin Books, 1970), p. 275.

81. *Atlanta Constitution*, 17 September 1979; *Providence Journal*, 17 September 1979; *New York Times*, 17 September 1979; and *Atlanta Journal*; 18 September 1979.

82. Zdenek Cervenka, "The World of Muammar Qaddafy," *Africa Report* (March–April 1982): 14.

83. Anti-Defamation League Memo, Stuart Lewengrub to Irwin Suall, 7 November 1979.

84. Ibid.; and Maxine Cheshire, "VIP—Qaddafi Peace Medal Surprises Mrs. King," *Washington Post*, 25 October 1979.

85. For insight into Williams' life and career, see David S. Morrison, "The Pro and Con of Hosea Williams," *Atlanta Weekly*, 24 May 1981, 10ff.

86. Letter from David J. Halperin to Hosea Williams, 18 September 1979.

87. Letter from Albert Varner to Hosea Williams, 17 September 1979.

88. Bill Shipp, "Why Did Joe and Hosea Go to Mideast?" *Atlanta Constitution*, 21 September 1979.

89. *Atlanta Journal*, 20 September 1979.

90. WGST, Editorial 124, 20 September 1979.

91. *Washington Post*, 27 September 1979.

92. Hosea Williams, Personal interview with the author, 17 March 1983. Two other members of the delegation have verified that Williams did not lead the mission. William Nelson, Telephone interview with the author, 23 March 1983; and Robert Cummings, Telephone interview with the author, 10 May 1983.

93. Williams interview, 17 March 1983.

94. Nelson interview, 23 March 1983. Nelson, who heads the Black studies program

at Ohio State University, kept a diary on the trip to Libya. Robert Cummings, who teaches African history at Howard University, could not recall any award ceremony either.

95. A Williams aide said in fact that the medallion was given on behalf of his local SCLC chapter. See Angelo Lewis, "Hosea Williams Gives Medal to Libyan Moammar Khadafi," *Atlanta Constitution*, 17 September 1979.

96. Williams interview, 17 March 1983.

97. Metro Atlanta SCLC press release #1, 19 September 1979.

98. Metro Atlanta SCLC press release #2, 19 September 1979.

99. Ibid.

100. Carl Rowan, "Moshe Dayan Insults Black GI's," *New York Amsterdam News*, 20 December 1980.

101. *Bilalian News*, 12 December 1980.

102. *Los Angeles Sentinel*, 4 December 1980.

103. *Pittsburgh Courier*, 27 December 1980, National edition.

104. Rowan, "Moshe Dayan."

105. *Los Angeles Sentinel*, 4 December 1980.

106. Mike Royko, "It's Moshe-ly racist," *Chicago Sun-Times*, 26 November 1980.

107. *Jerusalem Post*, 28 November 1980.

108. Samuel W. Lewis, U.S. ambassador to Israel, letter to the author, 3 November 1981. See also Foreign Broadcast Information Service Daily Report on Middle East and Africa, 27 January 1981. This report was a translation of a Jerusalem Domestic Service item in Hebrew of 26 January 1981.

109. Foreign Broadcast Information Service . . . , 27 January 1981.

110. One notable exception among the Black press was the *Atlanta Daily World*, which reported the Dayan apology on 16 December 1980.

111. *Rand Daily Mail*, 9 September 1974.

112. *Jerusalem Post*, 23 August 1974 and 14 November 1974. For another critical letter, see *The Star* [Johannesburg], 24 September 1974.

113. *Afro-American*, 29 November 1980.

114. Press release, 6 December 1980. This statement issued by the president of the American Jewish Committee was published in the Black press. See also the *Afro-American*, 27 December 1980. In a letter to the editor of the *Chicago Defender* the president of the Chicago chapter of the American Jewish Committee also regretted "this . . . calumny against patriotic Americans who have chosen to serve their country." *Chicago Defender*, 10 December 1980.

115. Press release, 11 December 1980.

116. Theodore Freedman, letter to the author, 14 September 1981; and *Chicago Sun-Times*, 8 December 1980.

117. Ivan J. Novick, president of the Zionist Organization of America, letter to the author, 22 October 1981.

118. *Chicago Defender*, 29 November 1980. In January 1983 Gol, then a consul for information in New York, was unwilling to retract his November 1980 statement and declared that "There was nothing in Moshe Dayan's comments in the way of racial or bigoted statements." He insisted that "Absolutely no anti-Black sentiments were intended, quite the contrary." Ehud Gol, letter to the author, 14 January 1983.

119. Avraham Benjamin, First Secretary (Information), Embassy of Israel, letter to the author, 17 November 1981.

120. Dayan's racial indiscretion did not make him persona non grata among all Blacks

familiar with his comment. Shortly after his death, the *Chicago Defender* eulogized him in an editorial, "Dayan peace apostle" and described him as an "irresistible crusader for peace and understanding." *Chicago Defender*, 22 October 1981.

121. *New York Times*, 6 June 1982.

Epilogue

Two events in 1983 epitomized the escalated significance of the Arab-Israeli conflict in Black-Jewish relations. One was connected with the twentieth anniversary demonstration commemorating the historic August 1963 march on Washington, D.C., which is best remembered for Martin Luther King, Jr's., eloquent "I Have a Dream" address. While heartily applauding the concept of commemorating the original march and renewing Dr. King's vision of justice and dignity for all, several Jewish organizations were loath to endorse the 1983 rally. They were reluctant to do so not so much because it was scheduled for the Jewish sabbath but because one of the co-chairpersons, Joseph Lowery, and a few of the conveners (including Congressman John Conyers, Walter Fauntroy, Jesse Jackson and particularly former Senator Abourezk) were considered unsympathetic to Israel.

In Jewish circles there was concern that anti-Zionist sentiments might be voiced from the podium. Feeding that concern was the crucial fact that the wide-ranging "Call to the Nation" that accompanied the letter inviting participation in the memorial march dealt with various issues that were seemingly unrelated to civil rights. Especially worrisome in that manifesto was the ambiguous allusion to the Middle East which implied that a reduction in military assistance to Israel was desirable: "We oppose the militarization of internal conflicts, often abetted and even encouraged by massive U.S. arms exports, in areas of the world such as the Middle East and Central America, while their basic human problems are neglected."[1]

In the end at least a few Jewish organizations took part, and one of the prayers at the rally was offered by the head of the Union of American Hebrew Congregations, Rabbi Alexander Schindler. Other groups that declined to participate sponsored alternative activities that paid tribue to Dr. King and reaffirmed support for racial equality.[2]

The second event was a maelstrom at the Stony Brook campus of the State

University of New York. At the center of the storm was a Black from South Africa, Ernest Dube, who is a member of the Africana Studies Program at Stony Brook and is also affiliated with the African National Congress. A visiting professor from Israel charged Dube with teaching that Zionism was a form of racism comparable to Nazism in his course on the "Politics of Race." The allegation triggered a prolonged and highly emotional debate about academic freedom, the validity of Black studies, the true nature of Zionism and whether anti-Zionism was synonymous with anti-Semitism. Before long those involved in the academic brouhaha included politicos, such as New York Governor Mario Cuomo, as well as sundry Black and Jewish organizations. Least helpful of all was a spokesman for the Jewish Defense Organization, described as a "more militant offshoot of the Jewish Defense League," who threatened to "get Dube" and called for his dismissal from the faculty.[3]

Certainly by the 1980's the image of Zionism and the aura that surrounded the fledgling State of Israel a few decades earlier had been sullied among Afro-Americans. Several factors were responsible. Adverse publicity associated with the woes of the Black Hebrew Israelites, some of which were surely of their own making, had hurt Israel's standing, but it is by no means the major issue that has poisoned relations between the Jewish state and Black America. By itself, it would not have done irreparable damage. There has been some appreciation of the fact that few nations would cheerfully accept two thousand newcomers who claim to be the rightful owners of their adopted homeland while accusing the host government and citizenry of being usurpers.

To be sure, one still hears the occasional grumbling about the plight of the Black Hebrew Israelites. Sometimes it is muted. For example, Wyatt Tee Walker, a Black minister who has been sharply critical of Israel in recent years, saw Israeli policy concerning the Chicago-based sect as "a program of only mild harassment and surveillance."[4]

However, in May 1984 the issue of the Black Hebrews boiled over when Dov Shilansky, the deputy minister in the office of Prime Minister Yitzhak Shamir, told a reporter for the *Jerusalem Post* that in a very short time the sect would no longer be in Israel. This was an official declaration, Shilansky said, and he went on to describe the Black Hebrews as "worse that the P.L.O.," a group that wanted to take over.[5]

Fearful of a mass deportation, the Black Hebrews and their allies in the United States lost no time in reacting. A press conference was called in Chicago by their spokesman, Asiel Ben Israel. Standing in front of a large sign that read "Black Americans Are Not Welcome In Israel—End Racism In Israel," he voiced his fears of a "wholesale slaughter" of men, women and children.[6] An attack on the community was imminent, he said, but vowed that they would remain in Israel.[7] Black religious leaders flanking Ben Israel called for an end to discrimination against Black Americans. There were also demands for Shilansky's removal.

In the wake of the Shilansky statement, Robert Farrell, a Black member of the Los Angeles City Council, was just one of several Afro-Americans who made inquiries in Israel about the presumed deterioration of Black Hebrew fortunes. The American Embassy in Tel Aviv received numerous calls expressing concern.

In June, Prime Minister Shamir indicated that the Black Hebrews were not, in fact, a high priority item on his agenda. Interviewed in Jerusalem, Yehoshua Kahane, the deputy director general of the Ministry of Interior, confirmed that although the Black Hebrews are in the country illegally, although they will not be given legal status as a group, "no decision has been made to deport them," Shilansky to the contrary notwithstanding.[8] Kahane stated unequivocally that had the sect been white they would have been expelled long before as had sundry messianic groups bent on proselytizing in Israel. Concern about alienating Blacks in the United States and Africa had prevented ejection of the Hebrew Israelites.

Even before this latest flap, Congressman Gus Savage, a Democrat from Illinois, was upset by what he told a PUSH conference was Israel's denial of the rights of the Black Hebrew Israelites. Savage, who began a congressional career in January 1981 as the first Black to represent his Chicago costituency, described the leader of the sect as "charismatic" and "brilliant." He asserted that the Blacks living in the Negev had been "denied the right to send their children to school, denied citizenship and deprived of a living." Voting rights were also allegedly withheld from those whom Congressman Savage called "our black brothers and sisters in Israel."[9]

Since his arrival on Capitol Hill, Savage, a longtime gadfly on the Chicago political scene, has been conspicuously cool toward Israel. In a divided Black Caucus, he typifies those who argue for a more evenhanded approach to the Arab-Israeli conflict which would entail recognition of the legitimate rights of the Palestinian people, including the right to a homeland. For Savage, whom Israeli lobbyists view as a member of the small, "mean-spirited" anti-Israeli coterie in the Black Caucus, Israel receives an excessive amount of foreign aid while needful Black African states are ignored. "More money for arms is going to one little nation than to all the half billion of our hungry black brothers and sisters in 47 sub-Saharan African nations put together," he wrote in 1983.[10]

This contention, which is frequently expressed by Black spokesmen, is a crucial one. Scarce resources seem to them to be allocated unfairly. Black Africa is shortchanged, and Black American needs go unmet while military and financial aid is lavished upon the Jewish state. The counterargument often adduced by backers of Israel that the assistance to Israel is justified because not only is it the United States' most reliable ally in the Middle East, but it also sacrifices its blood and treasure in the global struggle against Communist expansion, is unconvincing to many Blacks.

If opposition to Communism is the overriding criterion for determining whom the United States regards with favor, and it frequently is just that, then the pigmentocracy which is the Republic of South Africa deserves our unflagging support. However, that white supremacist regime, obsessed with maintaining political monopoly and economic privilege for four million Caucasians, subjugates its non-white populace.

Because Israel has established not just correct, but cordial relations with the apartheid government, the Jewish state has been the object of blistering attacks by Afro-Americans who regard the millions of oppressed Blacks in the republic as racial kin. It is true that many of the critics ignore the fact that prior to the 1970's Israel often took a more assertively anti-apartheid stance at the United Nations than most Western democracies. It is true that the Israeli rapprochement with South Africa was prompted by the animosity of sub-Saharan African states that ruptured relations with Jerusalem. It is true that much of the denunciation of Israel is based on a hypocritical double standard which chides Israel for trading with Pretoria when most of the rest of the world including African and Arab countries does the same thing. It is also true that the South African head of state and/or the prime minister have met not just with the Israeli prime minister, Yitzhak Rabin, in 1976, but with many other world leaders including several prominent African leaders.[11] P. W. Botha, South Africa's prime minister, undertook a grand tour to eight West European democracies in the spring of 1984. His itinerary included the Vatican where he met with Pope John Paul II. Even if allegations of extraordinary Israeli military succor to South Africa and persistent rumors of nuclear collusion are baseless (a big ''if''), it is equally true that diplomatic relations are often defined by tone as well as by substance, and those between Pretoria and Jerusalem are unusually warm at this juncture in history.

In addition, because Jews have long been persecuted and since World War II have talked ceaselessly about the western world's dereliction of moral duty during the Holocaust, it is often expected that Jews will do more than pay lip service to ethical concerns. Black novelists, such as Richard Wright and James Baldwin, have voiced their disappointment that not all Jews have been ''ennobled by oppression,'' to use Baldwin's phrase.[12] Julian Bond has made essentially the same point about how more is expected from Jews, given their tragic past, than from other whites.[13] That expectation is not fulfilled in the matter of Israel's links with South Africa.

More than any other single incident, Andrew Young's resignation from his post as U.S. ambassador to the U.N. projected the question of Blacks and Israel into the limelight. When pollster Lou Harris asked a sample of Americans if Andrew Young had been victimized by Jewish American and Israeli pressure on the White House, 40 percent of the Blacks asked answered in the affirmative. An additional 20 percent of the Black sample was not sure.[14] This notion of American Jewish and Israeli culpability was largely attributable to the sensationalist treatment given the incident by some of the media, for it was not supported by the facts. Most Blacks thought Young innocent of any wrongdoing. A poll conducted by ABC News–Lou Harris in August 1979 disclosed that whereas only a third of all whites believed Young was right to sit down and talk to the PLO representative at the U.N., among Blacks 62 percent approved of his behavior.[15] It was not surprising that a third poll carried out a week later revealed that the PLO enjoyed much more popularity among Black Americans than among their white counterparts, despite the fact that 52 percent of Blacks in the survey sympathized more with Israel than the PLO.[16]

It is noteworthy that Donald McHenry, President Carter's choice to succeed Young, was less satisfactory than Young from the Zionist perspective. If anything, he lacked the warmth towards Jewish organizations that Young had always displayed.[17] McHenry's "Blackness" may well have determined his selection. The administration wanted to placate the Black community because so many had taken offense at what they perceived as the unwarranted firing of Andrew Young. Another factor was that the president wanted to minimize friction between Blacks and Jews—two of his most reliable political constituencies. A third consideration was that McHenry, who was Young's deputy, would provide continuity for Carter's human rights program and his policy on South Africa.[18]

As for Young, he certainly has not allowed the resignation to silence him as a spokesman on world affairs. He has continued to speak out on the Middle East, sub-Saharan Africa and other global trouble spots. On an African tour in the fall of 1979, he took issue with Jesse Jackson's comments which had equated apartheid with Zionism. At a press conference in Tanzania, the former ambassador said it was unfair to use Israel as a scapegoat because of her ties with South Africa when the United States, Japan, West Germany and Britain all behaved in a similar fashion. He also asked Black African countries to renew their severed diplomatic relations with the Jewish state and to act as moderators in the ongoing Arab-Israeli dispute.[19]

Late in September Young conferred in New York City with Israeli foreign minister Moshe Dayan. Articles in the Black press said that the meeting had been held expressly for the purpose of dispelling rumors of Israeli responsibility for Young's abrupt departure from the United Nations. A few days earlier when the former ambassador had spoken at funeral services for an old Jewish ally in the civil rights movement, Stanley D. Levison, he had identified Dayan as the individual who had made public the meeting with the PLO's Terzi. Dayan denied this when he and Young met in New York.[20] After they talked Young was quoted as saying that "the events of the past month were something I blamed nobody for, certainly not him or his country."[21]

American Jews who learned of those statements must have been pleased, but they received little coverage. Needless to say, the *New York Post* did not believe that they merited screaming headlines on the front page.

Despite the foregoing, relations between Young and some segments of the Jewish community have been sporadically tempestuous. For example, the Lebanese conflagration in 1982 put many Jews and the newly elected mayor of Atlanta at swordspoint again. Israel had invaded its northern neighbor in June, and the Lebanese capital was under siege. Young evoked the wrath of some Jews in Atlanta and elsewhere by signing an open letter, published in the *New York Times*, asking "Must Beirut Be Destroyed?" The *Times* message compared the saturation bombing of Beirut with the destruction of Warsaw, Dresden and Hiroshima during World War II.[22] Disappointment and anger was the reaction of the Atlanta Jewish Federation to Young's position on the sanguinary Lebanese crisis. He was charged with having a selective double standard on moral issues for criticizing the Israelis while ignoring the PLO's "murder and mayhem" and the slaughter carried out by Syrian forces.[23] An estimated fifteen hundred Atlanta Jews at a mass rally applauded speakers who reproached Young for not having denounced PLO terrorism in Israel.[24]

Talking to reporters, Young explained that he signed the open letter because it signified a "genuine humanitarian concern." He elaborated as follows: "Certainly there's nothing like the killing of some six million Jews. But the silence now is just as deafening as it was then." And he condemned that silence.[25]

In August, still under verbal assault, Young wrote to a Jewish constitutent that throughout his career he had "spoken out consistently in behalf of Israel's security and survival as a humanitarian, democratic, biblical state." In two terms in the House of Representatives he said his voting record had been 100 percent supportive of Israel. But he did not feel obligated to back all of Israel's policies and indicated that he disapproved of the "present militaristic approach of Prime Minister Begin [which] is markedly different from the approach of David Ben-Gurion and other historic leaders." Young noted approvingly that the peace movement in Israel itself was challenging the "militarism which threatens Israel as much as it threatens the Lebanese and Palestinians."[26]

Tensions continued to simmer in Atlanta. The following year the Nigerian government's arbitrary ouster of one and a half to two million resident aliens provided critics of Young with another opportunity to make barbed comments. Where were the newspaper advertisements rebuking Nigeria, asked Stuart Lewengrub of the Anti-Defamation League in Atlanta. Where were Mayor Young and the Reverend Ralph Abernathy who had faulted Israel the previous year? Arguing that the double standard was alive and well, Lewengrub declared, "If Israel expels two Palestinians for terrorist activities, the eyes and judgement of the world are focused on it. When Nigeria expels two million workers and their families, c'est la vie."[27]

Young's reply was that the Israeli invasion of Lebanon and the Nigerian expulsions were not comparable phenomena. Dislocation, while regrettable, was not the same as destruction. Young conceded that the mass deportations were crude and tragic, but they did not involve the killing of civilians by the Nigerian military. In contrast, the siege of Beirut "included more than a month of bombardment, strafing by warplanes and the kind of irresponsible military actions which even the Israeli people and the Israeli press have vigorously condemned."[28]

Mistrust of the Reverend Jesse Jackson on the part of many Jews was not dissipated between his Middle East junket, taken in 1979 shortly after the Young affair erupted, and his announcement in the fall of 1983 that he was a candidate for the Democratic nomination for the presidency of the United States. In fact, Meir Kahane, the JDL's contentious leader, attempted to disrupt the Washington,

D.C. session at which Jackson formally announced his candidacy, and the rabbi was unceremoniously evicted by local police.[29] In addition, the JDL which had taken violent umbrage over Jackson's meeting with Arafat four years earlier, labelled the founder of PUSH an "enemy of the Jewish people" and publicized the formation of a new organization to combat the Jackson candidacy, viz., "Jews Against Jackson."[30] Approximately a week later the anti-Jackson group published an advertisement in the *New York Times*. Under a photograph of Arafat and Jackson embracing were several flattering statements Jackson had made about the PLO chairman and other "Jacksonisms" critical of Israel and American Jews. "Jews Against Jackson" declared its belief that the reverend was "No Good For Jews, For Israel Or For America." All were endangered by Jackson, and his opponents expressed their intention to exert pressure on influential politicians to publicly denounce and withhold funds from Jackson.[31]

Within twenty-four hours heads of national Jewish agencies assailed the advertisement, terming it "unwise," "unproductive," "counterproductive" and an "attempt to pick a fight." It was abundantly clear that the Anti-Defamation League, the American Jewish Congress and the American Jewish Committee (all establishment organizations which the JDL had disdained for years) feared that the provocative ad would generate more bitterness and drive still deeper the wedge between the Jewish and Black communities in the United States.[32]

Hyman Bookbinder, the American Jewish Committee's veteran Washington representative, wrote that Jackson's right to run for president could not be challenged even though his record on Jewish and Israeli issues was a troubling one. In order to become a credible candidate in Jewish eyes, the reverend would have to disavow some of his previous assertions.[33] With his need to achieve credibility and respectability among Jews in mind, Jackson held an unpublicized off-the-record meeting with American Jewish Committee representatives in November 1983. Apparently it bore little fruit.

Presidential-hopeful Jackson did manage to enhance his stature among others early in January 1984. Taking advantage of his rapport with the Arab states, he won the release of a Black American flier, Lieutenant Robert O. Goodman, Jr., who had been captured by the Syrians when the United States involved itself in the sectarian fighting in Lebanon. Although the regime of President Hafez Al Assad was probably motivated by a desire to improve its disfigured human rights profile rather than by a wish to promote Jackson's candidacy, the reverend scored a significant coup with his unofficial mission to Damascus. Shortly after his return home, Jackson, Walter Fauntroy and the Syrian ambassador to the United States, Rafic Jouejati, made a joint appearance at a Black church in Washington, D.C. There the Syrian diplomat received a standing ovation from the Black assemblage appreciative of the fact that the Black pilot had been released and the Black candidate treated with respect. However, Jackson did irk some Arabs with statements attributed to him to the effect that the "Arab war against Israel must be stopped." It was also reported that he had voiced a hope that the Jewish state would become the Middle Eastern center of commerce and democracy.[34]

But neither Jackson's coup in Damascus nor his sympathetic statement about Israel seemed to endear him to most Jews. Nathan Perlmutter, ADL's national director, was angry because prior to departure Wyatt Tee Walker, who accompanied Jackson to Syria, asserted on television that if Lieutenant Goodman had been "white or Jewish" more would have been done on his behalf by the U.S. government. Perlmutter saw this as an intrusion of racism into the Goodman case. Walker was almost certainly wrong. But in all likelihood his assertion was another expression of frustration engendered by relative Black political impotence rather than racism or anti-Semitism. Perlmutter wondered aloud if Reverend Walker would have travelled to the Syrian capital if Lieutenant Goodman had not been a Black.[35] The answer is obvious. The Jackson campaign would have been strengthened even more if Jackson, Walker et al. had been able to win the release of a white prisoner of war.

Confirming Jewish apprehension about Jackson's "pro-Arab bias" was the revelation that a few years earlier PUSH-related organizations had received two previously undisclosed donations totalling $200,000 from the Arab League, an umbrella grouping of twenty-one Arab states. Jackson's claim that he knew nothing of the donations sounded disingenuous—and not just to Jews. Although they were perfectly legal, the contributions nonetheless deepened Jewish anxieties about Jackson.[36] Edgar Bronfman, president of the World Jewish Congress, wrote that "strident bellowing about gifts to legitimate organizations confuse and distort rather than ameliorate. Only Jewish rhetoric can make this mole hill into a mountain."[37] Bronfman added that both he and his company, Joseph E. Seagram and Sons, had contributed to the same PUSH affiliates. However, it should be emphasized that the reaction of Bronfman, who is something of a maverick in Jewish circles, was atypical.

In February 1984 a *Washington Post* story about the rift between Jews and Jackson divulged that the reverend had made a derogatory reference to Jews as "Hymies" and to New York City with its sizeable Jewish population as "Hymietown."[38] The revelation was made by a Black staff writer for the *Post*, Milton Coleman. It turned out that the slurs were voiced on January 25 during an off-the-record conversation with Black reporters at the Washington National Airport. Jackson was deploring the fact that his controversial views on the Middle East were given so much prominence and said something to the effect that "All Hymie wants to talk about is Israel; every time you go to Hymietown, that's all they want to talk about."[39]

Initially, Jackson claimed that he could not recall having used the offensive language[40] but subsequently admitted he had done so. Speaking at a Manchester, New Hampshire, synagogue just before the primary in that state, Jackson confessed and apologized. He had indeed used the word "Hymie," but he had not done so "maliciously." "However innocent and unintended, it was insensitive and wrong," he conceded. Jackson's candor won him praise from both Jewish and Black spokesmen.[41] At the same time the incident unquestionably hurt his candidacy. It and much that followed further exacerbated Black-Jewish tensions.[42]

As primary followed primary in the spring of 1984, the "Hymie" remark continued to dog Jackson. Mired in a kind of impalpable quicksand due to his verbal slip, Jackson struggled to extricate himself, but his defensive explanations only seemed to make things worse. In a freewheeling interview with *Newsweek* editors, Jackson denied that "Hymie" was a derogatory term compararable to "kike." "It's non-insulting colloquial language," he asserted. Asked when he first used "Hymie" and in what context, the beleaguered reverend replied that he had initially heard it upon arrival in Chicago twenty years earlier. "There's a place down off Maxwell Street called 'Jewtown.' Understand? 'Jewtown is where Hymie gets you if you can't negotiate them suits down,' you understand? That's not meant as anti-Semitic.... If you can't buy any suits downtown, you go down to Jewtown on Maxwell Street, and you start negotiating with Hyman and Sons.... And if Hyman and Sons show up they're called Hymie. There's no insult even to them."[43] It is a virtual certainty that the average American Jew would find Jackson's choice of language, especially the use of the word "Jewtown," insulting, offensive, insensitive and perhaps anti-Semitic.

Throughout the campaign for the coveted Democratic nomination, Jackson was harassed and heckled, mainly by members of "Jews Against Jackson," the JDL offshoot. His life was also threatened. Louis Farrakhan, the leader of one Black Muslim faction and a Jackson supporter, expressed concern for the reverend's safety. Fearful that his "champion" might fall victim to an assassin's bullet, Farrakhan warned Jews that if they harmed Jackson "in the name of Allah, that will be the last one you will harm. Leave him alone."[44]

Jackson defended Farrakhan's remark about retaliation, which was construed by many Jews as a direct threat. For Jackson it reflected the anger Afro-Americans felt about the assassination of other Black luminaries such as Martin Luther King, Jr., and Malcolm X. Blacks would no longer be victims. Jackson observed that "Jews went to the chambers silently. They should have gone fighting if they had to go at all."[45] That comment was also deemed inappropriate by some Jews. Edward Koch, New York's contentious mayor who was already rather unpopular among Gotham's Blacks, said that Jackson's historical allusion was "in poor taste" and inaccurate. Moreover, he would not endorse Jackson if he were to be the Democratic standard-bearer.[46]

Jackson later explained and qualified his comment by citing the Warsaw ghetto uprising in 1943. His point was that, given their respective histories of persecution, Jews and Blacks both resolved "never again" to be victimized.[47] Jackson's original reference to the lack of Jewish resistance to Nazi oppression is debatable. The scope and nature of Jewish resistance has been the subject of much heated debate among historians, especially Jewish historians, since the end of World War II. Decades later it is still a very sensitive issue in the Jewish community. Just as many Blacks are nettled by statements that the ordinary Black slave on the typical antebellum plantation was a "Sambo," i.e., docile and childlike, many Jews take offence at suggestions that Jews went to their deaths like sheep to the slaughter during the Holocaust.

In the climate of mistrust that prevailed between Jackson and a sizeable portion of American Jewry, the reverend made several indiscreet comments. At one point Jackson was peeved by questions posed to him by Lesley Stahl, a CBS television reporter, about his reputed affinity for the PLO. Asked if he objected to Stahl's queries because she was Jewish, Jackson, surprised to learn of Stahl's ethnic background, retorted, "She doesn't look like she's Jewish. She doesn't sound like she's Jewish."[48]

For a time during the campaign there were uncorroborated rumors that Jackson had told Walter Mondale, then the frontrunner for the Democratic nomination, that he would be willing to stay out of the race if the former vice president would favor recognition of the PLO and its demand for a Palestinian homeland. Jackson denied that he had proposed such a deal. A spokeswoman for Mondale said that allegations that Jackson and Mondale had discussed the PLO were "totally false, a total fabrication."[49]

At the same time that candidate Jackson was grappling with accusations that he was anti-Semitic, anti-Zionist and pro-Arab, he in turn charged that three years earlier, his daughter Santita had opted to attend Howard University rather than Harvard University. Her decision was determined by the fact that she had been hectored by a Jewish interviewer at Harvard, an alumnus. In Jackson's version, which was not contradicted by Harvard, the interviewer specifically asked Santita to disavow her father's position on the Arab-Israeli dispute which he interpreted as anti-Jewish.[50]

People of goodwill could only lament the sorry state of Black-Jewish relations in early 1984. In contrast, some of the media appeared to relish the recriminations and even helped to make matters worse. For example, a syndicated cartoon which first appeared in the *Chicago Tribune* would have warmed the cockles of Hitler's heart. It could have come from the pages of Julius Streicher's *Der Stürmer*. Two bearded, long-nosed stereotypically caricatured Jews condescendingly admonished Jackson: "Well, Just see that it dosen't happen again...Okay, Boy?" Readers could justifiably assume that the cartoonist's intention was malicious.[51]

That the Jews-versus-Jackson matter was an unmitigated disaster for Jewish-Black friendship is crystal clear in retrospect. Indeed it was crystal clear as the controversy unfolded. Boston's Black newspaper, the *Bay State Banner*, published an editorial whose title "Anti-Afro-Americans!" capsulized its perception of the hounding of Jackson. To the *Banner*, Jackson's use of the term "Hymie" was not defamatory. Jews had overreacted and their attacks on Jackson were "gratuitous." Formation of a "Jews Against Jackson" organization, it noted, was unnecessary as Jackson posed no threat to the Jewish community. Unfortunately the splinter anti-Jackson group was seen by the *Banner* as typical of American Jewry. What Jackson's critics failed to understand was that "Jackson is the political Moses...the one who has been annointed [*sic*] to lead blacks out of the political wilderness to a greater realization of their potential political power."[52] In other words, Jackson's candidacy was symbolic and ought to have been recognized as such.

The irrepressible and seemingly ubiquitous Louis Farrakhan made that difficult for many Jews. In the weeks before the Democratic party convened in San Francisco, Jackson's campaign, remarkable in so many ways, was still bedevilled by provocative remarks uttered by Farrakhan. In a radio address, the Black Muslim declared the establishment of Israel to have been an "outlaw act" that involved expelling the original inhabitants. Backing Israel's existence meant participating in a "criminal conspiracy." Israel itself could enjoy no peace "because there can be no peace structured on injustice, thievery, lying and deceit...." In his philippic against the Jewish state, Farrakhan also described Judaism as "your gutter religion." This crude, blatantly anti-Jewish language understandably caused a furor. Though reluctant to publicly rebuke other Black leaders, Jackson was belatedly compelled to repudiate Farrakhan's comments as "reprehensible and morally indefensible."[53] For many Jews, Jackson's repudiation was too little as well as too late. They wanted him to disavow Farrakhan's political support and to denounce the Muslim leader personally. Almost on the eve of the Democratic conclave, Jackson alleged that Mondale had not given him serious consideration as a vice-presidential nominee because Jewish leaders were struggling to make him a pariah and to separate him from the masses.[54] If anything, the gulf between Jackson and the Jewish community, opened in 1979, was widening.

At the core of the *initial* acrimony between Jackson and many Jews was a fundamental difference in outlook on the Middle East. Many Blacks, including Jackson who had previously gone further in his criticism of Zionism than other Afro-Americans of national repute, resent the fact that when they advocate consultation between the United States and the PLO or between Israel and the PLO, they are accused of being anti-Israel or, worse still, anti-Semitic. In just about all other international disputes, India versus Pakistan, Greece versus Turkey, Iraq versus Iran, the United States versus the Soviet Union, to mention a few, dialogue is considered the first step towards resolution. Even in the Levant, the Arab states' belligerent policy of non-recognition of Israel is deplored by the United States and Israel alike. The lone exception, Egypt's Anwar Sadat, was hailed as a realist and a man of peace when he journeyed to Jerusalem and eventually signed the Camp David Accords. But because of the PLO's long-standing commitment to terrorism and its continued unwillingness to recognize the Jewish state, the Israelis argue that there is nothing to discuss with them.

For Blacks such as Andrew Young, Jesse Jackson, Joseph Lowery, Walter Fauntroy and countless others, this should not foreclose an exchange of views, a search for areas of potential agreement or possible compromise. To them the avowed policy of the United States and of Israel is ostrich-like. It inflames Arab opinion and bodes ill for peace in the tinderbox which is the Middle East. The failure to foster negotiations between the Israelis and the Palestinians increases the likelihood of a war in which America may well become militarily involved and is therefore inimical to the country in general and Black citizens in particular.

This perception of the Arab-Israeli conflict and America's responsibility in it has curtailed Jewish backing for civil rights groups. By the 1980's Jewish support is often made contingent upon the position in the conflict taken by the organization in question. Insufficiently enthusiastic support for Zionism has often been construed as hostility to Jews. Klanwatch, a project of the Southern Poverty Law Center based in Montgomery, Alabama, has received so many inquiries about suspected anti-Semitism that it has developed a form letter in which it reassures prospective contributors that its anti-Klan work as frequently focuses on counteracting anti-Semitism as on racism. It has also noted that one of the center's co-founders and several members of its staff are Jewish.[55] To questions dealing specifically with the position of Julian Bond on the Middle East, the Georgia senator routinely replies, ''I am a strong believer in Israel's right to exist. I am a lifelong opponent of terrorism; whether directed at tourists, Olympic athletes, or anyone. I yield to no one in my commitment to equal rights and human dignity.''[56]

After the Young controversy and the Jackson and SCLC initiatives in the Middle East, both Arab governments and Arab-American organizations sensed that the time was ripe to woo Black American support. Illustrative of their efforts was the distribution by the American-Arab Anti-Discrimination Committee, based in Washington, D.C. of a sixty-seven page book entitled *Afro-Americans Stand Up For Middle East Peace*. It was edited by James Zogby, chairman of the Palestine Human Rights Campaign which had sought since its founding in 1977 to build a coalition of religious and ''peace'' groups plus Black organizations to back the PLO. Jack O'Dell, director of international affairs for Operation PUSH, was co-editor. The contents of the book included: Congressman Fauntroy's report to Congress, an editorial from the Black quarterly *Freedomways* which supported the rights of the Palestinian people and the legitimacy of the PLO, remarks by Jesse Jackson and Joseph Lowery, resolutions on Palestinian rights by sundry Black religious groups and statements drawing parallels between the situations in South Africa and Israel.[57]

In 1983 *Freedomways* devoted two entire numbers to the Middle East question. Virtually all of the articles were pro-Arab. The *Journal of Palestine Studies* and the American-Arab Anti-Discrimination Committee were among the advertisers.[58]

It is by no means coincidental that the *Journal of Palestine Studies*, a quarterly on Palestinian affairs and the Arab-Israeli conflict, which was published in Beirut, devoted its Winter 1981 issue to Black Americans. ''Afro-Americans and Arabs: An Alliance in the Making?'' was the title of one of the articles in that issue.[59]

In the wake of the Young wrangle, an Arab-Black American Dialogue Committee was created. Its avowed objective was to cement ties between Blacks in this country and Arabs. Dr. M. T. Mehdi, a well-known Arab lobbyist in the United States, and James R. Lawson, a veteran Black nationalist, became cochairmen. Lawson used the pages of the *Chicago Defender* to say that both

Mehdi and he had believed for years that the "Jewish Zionist lobby" had exerted undue influence on American foreign policy and that United States military aid to Israel was excessive. Lawson urged Libya and the Arab states to invest in redeveloping Harlem and other Black American communities.[60]

Actually even before Young's downfall Afro-Americans had endeavored unsuccessfully to attract Arab petro-dollars to minority-owned businesses. On January 20, 1979, Los Angeles hosted what was billed as the First Annual Saudi Arabian-Black American Business Conference, the stated goal of which was to enable Black American entrepreneurs to forge commercial ties with the oil-rich Arab world. Roy Innis of CORE told the assemblage that the Black community was a sound investment for the Arabs and asked them to pressure white firms doing business in the Middle East to hire Black Americans.[61]

Other conferences, some with an obvious anti-Zionist thrust, involving Black Americans and Arabs have been held. One on the theme of "War and Peace in the Holy Land—What Does Biblical Justice Require of Us?" met in May 1983 in Atlanta. Arab lobbyists have also been active on the campuses of several predominantly Black colleges and universities.

Occasionally the Arab effort to win Black American sympathy has been lacking in subtlety. In 1979 at the annual dinner of the Atlanta branch of the NAACP, traditionally a social rather than a political affair, a representative of the Arab League indicated his willingness to make a thousand-dollar contribution on condition that he be allowed to make a speech. Julian Bond, president of the branch, refused and the contribution was not forthcoming.[62]

Nevertheless, it is undeniably true that in the past decade and a half the Arabs have made inroads in the Black community and not just among Black nationalists and radicals, those who invoke the mystique of Third World solidarity. Events in 1979, previously described in detail, accelerated a process already underway in the 1960's. Some would argue that after 1977 the pugnacious personality and programs of Prime Minister Begin contributed in some measure to the alienation of Black Americans from the Zionist cause. In any case ties between Black Americans and Jewish Americans have become increasingly strained as Blacks have increasingly been viewed as pro-Arab.

In a comprehensive 1983 national survey of the attitudes of American Jews toward Israel and Israelis, of fifteen groups in the United States Blacks emerged as the most unfriendly to Israel. Both a cross section of Jews and, to an even greater extent, a sample of Jewish communal leaders rated Blacks much lower on a "friendly index" than the State Department or corporations which were deemed somewhat hostile.[63]

Despite the chill that has permeated Black-Jewish relations in general, there have been some encouraging signs of fraternity and understanding. Jewish electoral support for Black candidates has been noticeably strong. Three out of four Jewish voters cast their votes for Tom Bradley, the Black mayor of Los Angeles, in his abortive bid for the governorship of California in November 1982. In the envenomed atmosphere surrounding the highly publicized Chicago mayoralty election in April 1983, an exit poll revealed that while Harold Washington, the victorious Black candidate, managed to garner only 18 percent of the overall white vote, he attracted 43 percent of the Jewish vote. What makes these statistics even more remarkable is that Washington's Republican opponent, Bernard Epton, was himself Jewish.[64]

A similar pattern emerged in the hard-fought municipal race in Philadelphia where a Black candidate, Wilson Goode, was eventually elected. He was disproportionately supported by Jews, not once but twice. Whereas 75 percent of all Caucasian voters pulled the lever for former mayor Frank Rizzo in the Democratic primary, half of the Jewish voters favored Goode.[65] In the general election held in November 1983, Goode received a higher percentage of votes in Jewish neighborhoods than in other white ethnic neighborhoods.[66] Of course, in these local contests the Middle East played no role. And it is in the international sphere that Jewish wariness of Blacks is keenest.

In order to refurbish Israel's image and to counter Arab propagandizing on college campuses, the youth division of the American Israeli Public Affairs Committee (AIPAC) has stepped up its activities vis-à-vis young Blacks. In the fall of 1983 it and the youth division of the NAACP held a conference at which Jewish and Black spokesmen discussed their respective concerns. Past misunderstandings were lamented, and more than one speaker called for closer cooperation between Blacks and Jews. Julius Lester declared, "We have been brutalized too much to start brutalizing each other."[67]

Jews and Blacks alike would do well to ponder Lester's words. For centuries each group has suffered inordinately. Despite differences over the prickly conundrums of the Middle East and quotas in America, they share a fundamental vision of a just society devoid of racial or religious hatred. Moreover, both are still confronted by a common enemy: the bigot in whom anti-Semitism and racism are integral elements. Blacks and Jews who forget this do so at their peril.

NOTES

1. Letter from Walter Fauntroy to the National Jewish Community Relations Advisory Council, 26 April 1983.

2. *Time*, 5 September 1983. See also Hasia Diner, "Can a Broken Alliance Be Repaired?" *The Jewish Monthly* (August–September 1983): 30ff.

3. Walter Ruby, "Fort Stony Brook," *Village Voice*, 20 December 1983: 21.

4. Wyatt Tee Walker, "Liberation Theology and the Middle East Conflict," *Freedomways*, 23, no. 3 (1983): 150.

5. *Jerusalem Post*, 6 May–13 May 1984 International edition.

6. *Washington Afro-American*, 26 May 1984.

7. Transcript of press conference, 17 May 1984.

8. Yehosha Kahane, Personal interview with the author, 17 June 1984.

9. Gus Savage, "America in the Wrong," *Freedomways* 23, no. 3 (1983): 174.

10. Ibid., p. 172.

11. Tom Bradley, the Black mayor of Los Angeles, has even presented the key of his city to the South African counsul, Sean M. Cleary. See the *South African Digest*, 7 January 1983.

12. Richard Wright, "The Man Who Went To Chicago," *Eight Men* (Cleveland and New York: World Publishing Co., 1940), p. 239; James Baldwin, "Negroes are Anti-Semitic Because They're Anti-White," *New York Times Magazine* (9 April 1967): 140.

13. Julian Bond, Personal interview with the author, 17 March 1983.

14. ABC News—Harris Survey, vol. I, no. 108, released 3 September 1979.

15. ABC News—Harris Survey, vol. I, no. 104, released 24 August 1979.

16. ABC News—Harris Survey, vol. I, no. 105, released 27 August 1979. A 1976 Yankelovich poll showed that the Israelis had a significantly higher standing among Afro-Americans. Seventy-one percent characterized the Israelis as "people we can get along with." Only 48 percent so characterized the PLO. Blacks also saw the Israelis as much more democratic and freedom-loving then the PLO.

17. Bertram Gold, Personal interview with the author, 29 December 1982.

18. Robert Lipshutz, Personal interview with the author, 17 March 1983.

19. *The Atlanta Inquirer*, 13 October 1979; and *Kansas City Call*, 5 October 1979. Both newspapers cited a report in the *Chicago Defender* as the source of their information.

20. *New York Times*, 27 September 1979.

21. *Kansas City Call*, 5 October 1979.

22. *New York Times*, 25 July 1982.

23. Letter from the Atlanta Jewish Federation to Andrew Young, 26 July 1982.

24. *Atlanta Journal*, 27 July 1982. See also Tom Houck, "Interview with Mayor Young," *Atlanta Magazine* (December 1982): 82ff.

25. *Atlanta Journal*, 26 July 1982.

26. Letter from Andrew Young to Douglas W. Kessler, 12 August 1982.

27. Letter to the editor of the *Atlanta Constitution*, 11 March 1983.

28. Letter to the editor of the *Atlanta Constitution*, 17 March 1983.

29. *Near East Report*, vol. XXVII, no. 46 (18 November 1983).

30. *New York Times*, 3 November 1983.

31. Ibid., 11 November 1983.

32. Ibid., 12 November 1983.

33. Hyman Bookbinder, "More Questions on Jesse Jackson," *Washington Jewish Week* (17 November 1983).

34. Wolf Blitzer, "Assad-Jackson coup," *Jerusalem Post*, 8 January–14 January 1984, International edition; and *New York Times*, 4 and 6 January 1984.

35. Nathan Perlmutter, "Fabricating Racism," *ADL Bulletin* (February 1984): 2.

36. *New York Times*, 29 and 31 January 1984. In both an editorial and a cartoon the *New York Amsterdam News*, 4 February 1984, lambasted the *New York Times* for calling Jackson a "carpetbagger" because of his mission to Syria. It also railed against the *Times* for its front-page story announcing that the Arab League had made a sizeable donation to Jackson's PUSH Foundation. The cartoon strongly suggested that the *Times* attack on Jackson as an Arab sympathizer was carried out on behalf of the cause of Israel.

37. *New York Times*, 8 February 1984.

38. *Washington Post*, 3 February 1984.

39. *New York Times*, 8 March 1984. See Milton Coleman's account of the "Hymie" controversy in the *Washington Post*, 8 April 1984.

40. *New York Times*, 20 February 1984.

41. Ibid., 28 February 1984; *Providence Evening Bulletin*, 27 February 1984; and *New York Amsterdam News*, 3 March 1984. Mayor Kenneth Gibson of Newark, New Jersey, a Jackson supporter, deplored "Jackson's insulting references to the Jewish people" and found it "very, very frustrating to have to read and hear of his insensitivities, ignorance or possibly worse." Letter from Kenneth A. Gibson to Nathan Perlmutter, 8 March 1984. See also the *New York Amsterdam News*, 17 March 1984.

42. See Jack Newfield, "Blacks and Jews: The Tragedy of Jackson, the Logic of Coalition," *Village Voice* (20 March 1984): 1ff.

43. *Newsweek* (9 April 1984).

44. *New York Times*, 27 February 1984. Farrakhan, who is a rival of Wallace Muhammad's, told a gathering of Black journalists that according to reports of the secret service, there had already been no fewer than one hundred threats to kill Jackson. He added that ten people were already incarcerated because of their efforts to hurt Jackson. See the *New York Amsterdam News*, 17 March 1984. Gibson also dissociated himself from "the implied threats by Muslim Minister Farrakhan [which] do not represent the thinking of myself or other Blacks who know the difference between righteousness and rhetoric." Gibson to Perlmutter, 8 March 1984.

45. *New York Times*, 28 February 1984.

46. Ibid., 29 February 1984.

47. Ibid., 5 March 1984.

48. *Boston Globe*, 28 February 1984.

49. *New York Times*, 23 February 1984.

50. Ibid., 27 February 1984.

51. *Providence Evening Bulletin*, 2 March 1984.

52. *Bay State Banner*, 8 March 1984.

53. *New York Times*, 29 and 30 June 1984. Black leaders such as Benjamin Hooks swiftly and unequivocally criticized Farrakhan's outburst. The *Amsterdam News* in its June 30, 1984, issue disavowed Farrakhan's comments in the "strongest possible terms" and condemned them as "intemperate, obscene, ill advised and incendiary." Having repudiated Farrakhan, the paper rhetorically asked who would repudiate Mayor Edward Koch, New York's flamboyant chief executive who was frequently at swordspoint with the Black community.

54. *New York Times*, 11 July 1984.

55. Letter from Marie Johnson, Klanwatch staff assistant, to the author, 18 March 1983.

56. Bond interview, 17 March 1983.

57. James Zogby and Jack O'Dell, *Afro-Americans Stand Up for Middle East Peace* (Washington, D.C.: Palestine Human Rights Campaign, 1980).

58. *Freedomways*, vol. 23, nos. 2 and 3 (1983).

59. Robert G. Newby, "Afro-Americans and Arabs: An Alliance in the Making?" *Journal of Palestine Studies*, X, no. 2 (Winter 1981): 50–58.

60. *Chicago Defender*, 25 July 1981. Clovis Maksoud, a well-known Arab lobbyist, brought Blacks and Arabs together in January 1981 for a memorial tribute to Martin Luther King, Jr. Maksoud twice addressed PUSH conventions, in 1981 and 1982. See *Pro-Arab Propaganda In America: Vehicles and Voices* (New York: The Anti-Defamation League of B'nai B'rith, 1983), p. 82.

61. *Los Angeles Sentinel*, 21 December 1978 and 25 January 1979.

62. Bond interview, 17 March 1983.

63. Steven M. Cohen, *Attitudes of American Jews Toward Israel And Israelis—The 1983 National Survey Of American Jews And Jewish Communal Leaders* (New York: Institute On American Jewish-Israeli Relations—The American Jewish Committee, 1983), pp. 14–16. A 1981 Yankelovich poll on *Antisemitism in the United States*, commissioned by the American Jewish Committee, concluded that 40 percent of Blacks were high or moderate in anti-Semitism compared to 20 percent of whites. Other polls have yielded similar results. See Geraldine Rosenfield, "The Polls: Attitudes Toward American Jews," *Public Opinion Quarterly*, vol. 46 (1982): 433.

64. See William Raspberry, "On Blacks, Jews and Quotas," *Providence Journal*, 15 June 1983; and Rachel Abrahamson, "Blacks, Jews and the Chicago Election," *Genesis*, 2 (July–August 1983): 3.

65. Raspberry, "On Blacks."

66. *New York Times*, 10 November 1983.

67. *Near East Report*, vol. XXVII, no. 47 (25 November 1983). Other projects to deepen Black American understanding of Israel are underway. Representative Mickey Leland (D., Tex.), one of the Black Caucus' members most supportive of Israel, has co-sponsored a Kibbutz Internship Program which sends high school students from inner-city communities to Israel for summers. *The Facts* (Seattle), 25 August 1982.

Selected Bibliography

BOOKS

Abrahams, Israel. *The Birth of a Community*. Cape Town: Hebrew Congregation, 1955.

Amir, Shimeon. *Israel's Development Cooperation with Africa, Asia, and Latin America*. New York: Praeger Publishers, 1974.

Aptheker, Herbert, ed. *Writings in Periodicals Edited by W.E.B. Du Bois—Selections from The Brownie's Book*. Millwood, N.Y.: Kraus-Thomson Organization Ltd., 1980.

Baraka, Imamu Amiri [Le Roi Jones], ed. *African Congress—A Documentary of the First Modern Pan-African Congress*. New York: William Morrow and Co., 1972.

Begin, Menachem. *The Revolt*. New York: Dell Publishing Co., 1978.

Beshir, Mohamed Omer. *Israel and Africa*. Khartoum: Khartoum University Press, 1974.

Blyden, Edward W. *From West Africa to Palestine*. Freetown, Manchester and London, 1873.

———. *The Jewish Question*. Liverpool: Lionel Hart and Co., 1898.

Breitman, George, ed. *Malcolm X Speaks*. New York: Grove Press, 1965.

Brotz, Howard. *The Black Jews of Harlem—Negro Nationalism and the Dilemmas of Negro Leadership*. New York: Schocken Books 1970.

Brzezinski, Zbigniew. *Power and Principle. Memoirs of the National Security Adviser 1977–1981*. New York: Farrar, Straus, Giroux, 1983.

Carmichael, Stokely. *Stokely Speaks—Black Power Back to Pan-Africanism*. New York: Vintage Books, 1971.

Carson, Clayborne. *In Struggle: SNCC and the Black Awakening of the 1960's*. Cambridge, Mass.: Harvard University Press, 1981.

Carter, Jimmy. *Keeping Faith: Memoirs of a President*. New York: Bantam Books, 1982.

Clark, Elmer J. *The Small Sects in America*. Nashville: Cokesbury Press, 1937.

Cleage, Albert B., Jr. *The Black Messiah*. New York: Sheed and Ward, 1968.

Cohen, Steven M. *Attitudes of American Jews Toward Israel and Israelis—The 1983 National Survey of American Jews and Jewish Communal Leaders*. New York:

Institute on American Jewish-Israeli Relations—The American Jewish Committee, 1983.

Cruse, Harold. *The Crisis of the Negro Intellectual*. New York: Morrow, 1967.

Decter, Moshe. *"To Serve, To Teach, To Leave"*: *The Story of Israel's Development Assistance Programs in Black Africa*. New York: American Jewish Congress, 1977.

Diner, Hasia R. *In the Almost Promised Land—American Jews and Blacks 1915–1935*. Westport, Conn.: Greenwood Press, 1972.

Fauset, Arthur Huff. *Black Gods of the Metropolis—Negro Religious Cults of the Urban North*. Philadelphia: University of Pennsylvania Press, 1944.

Feuerwerger, Marvin C. *Congress and Israel: Foreign Aid Decision-Making in the House of Representatives 1969–76*. Westport, Conn.: Greenwood Press, 1979.

Foner, Philip, ed. *Paul Robeson Speaks—Writings, Speeches, Interviews 1918–1974*. New York: Bruner/Mazel Publishers, 1978.

Forman, James. *The Making of Black Revolutionaries*. New York: The Macmillan Company, 1972.

Franklin, John Hope. *From Slavery to Freedom*. New York: Vintage Books, 1969.

Garvey, Amy Jacques, ed. *Philosophy and Opinions of Marcus Garvey or Africa for the Africans*. London: Frank Cass and Co., 1967.

Harlan, Louis, ed. *Booker T. Washington Papers*. Vols. 10 and 11. Champagne-Urbana: University of Illinois Press, 1972.

Hertzberg, Arthur, ed. *The Zionist Idea*. Garden City, N.Y.: Doubleday and Co., Inc. and Herzl Press, 1959.

Herzl, Theodor. *Old-New Land*. Translated by Lotta Levensohn. New York: Bloch Publishing Co., 1941.

Hess, Moses. *Rome and Jerusalem—A Study in Jewish Nationalism*. Translated by Meyer Waxman. New York: Bloch Publishing Co., 1945.

Hill, Norman. *The Black Panther Menace—America's Neo-Nazis*. New York: Popular Library, 1971.

Hurewitz, J. C. *The Struggle for Palestine*. New York: Schocken Books, 1976.

Israel's Program of International Cooperation. Jerusalem: Ministry for Foreign Affairs, 1967.

Jacobs, Steve, and Windsor, Rudolph. *The Hebrew Heritage of Our West African Ancestors*. Wilmington, Del.: Rose-Lee Inc., 1971.

Kalb, Marvin and Kalb, Bernard. *Kissinger*. Boston: Little, Brown and Co., 1974.

Laqueur, Walter. *A History of Zionism*. New York: Holt, Rinehart and Winston, 1972.

Lewis, David L. *King—A Critical Biography*. Baltimore: Penguin Books, 1970.

Lincoln, C. Eric. *The Black Muslims in America*. Boston: Beacon Press, 1963.

Lounds, Morris, Jr. *Israel's Black Hebrews: Black Americans in Search of Identity*. Washington, D.C.: University Press of America, Inc., 1981.

Lynch, Hollis R. *Edward Wilmot Blyden, Pan-Negro Patriot 1832–1912*. London: Oxford University Press, 1967.

Malcolm X. *The Autobiography of Malcolm X*. New York: Grove Press, 1966.

Marsh, Zoë and Kingsnorth, G. W. *An Introduction to the History of East Africa*. Cambridge, Eng.: Cambridge University Press, 1965.

Meir, Golda. *My Life*. New York: Dell Publishing Co., 1975.

Miller, Jake C. *The Black Presence in American Foreign Affairs*. Washington, D.C.: University Press of America, 1978.

Munger, Edwin S. *Jews and the National Party*. New York: American Universities Field Staff, 1956.

Myrdal, Gunnar. *An American Dilemma*. 2 vols. New York: McGraw-Hill Book Company, 1964.

Oil Tankers to South Africa. Amsterdam: The Shipping Research Bureau, 1981.

Osia, Kunirum. *Israel, South Africa and Black Africa: A Study of the Primacy of the Politics of Expediency*. Washington, D.C.: University Press of America, Inc., 1981.

Ottley, Roi, *"New World A-Coming"—Inside Black America*. Boston: Houghton Mifflin Co., 1943.

Patai, Raphael. *The Vanished Worlds of Jewry*. New York: The Macmillan Company, 1980.

Peretz, Don. *The Middle East Today*. New York: Holt, Rinehart and Winston, 1978.

Pinsker, Leo. *Auto-Emancipation*. Masada Youth Zionist Organization, 1935.

Ploski, Harry A. and Kaiser, Ernest, eds. *The Negro Almanac*. New York: The Bellweather Co., 1971.

Pro-Arab Propaganda in America: Vehicles and Voices. New York: The Anti-Defamation League of B'nai B'rith, 1983.

Rapoport, Louis. *The Lost Jews—Last of the Ethiopian Falashas*. New York: Stein and Day, Publishers, 1980.

Redkey, Edwin S., ed. *Black Exodus—Black Nationalist and Back-To-Africa Movements, 1890–1910*. New Haven and London: Yale University Press, 1969.

————. *Respect Black: The Writings and Speeches of Henry McNeal Turner*. New York: Arno Press, 1971.

Reynolds, Barbara A. *Jesse Jackson—the Man, the Myth, the Movement*. Chicago: Nelson-Hall, 1975.

Robeson, Paul. *Here I Stand*. Boston: Beacon Press, 1958.

Robins, Eric. *This Man Malan*. Cape Town: South Africa Scientific Publishing Co., 1953.

Rogers, J. A. *100 Amazing Facts About the Negro with Complete Proof*. New York: Futuro Press, 1957.

Sellers, Cleveland and Terrell, Robert. *The River of No Return—The Autobiography of a Black Militant and the Life and Death of SNCC*. New York: William Morrow, 1973.

Selzer, Michael. *Israel as a Factor in Jewish-Gentile Relations in America: Observations in the Aftermath of the June 1967 War*. New York: American Council for Judaism, 1968.

Shimoni, Gideon. *Jews and Zionism: The South African Experience 1910–1967*. Cape Town: Oxford University Press, 1980.

Silverman, Morris, ed. *High Holiday Prayer Book*. Hartford, Conn.: Prayer Book Press, 1951.

Stern, Paula. *Water's Edge—Domestic Politics and the Making of American Foreign Policy*. Westport, Conn.: Greenwood Press, 1974.

Stevens, Richard P. and Elmessiri, Abdelwahab M. *Israel and South Africa—The Progression of a Relationship*. New Brunswick, N.J.: North American, Inc. 1977.

Teplinsky, Leonid. *Tel Aviv Fails in Africa*. Moscow: Novosti Press Agency Publishing House, 1975.

Thirty Years of Lynching in the United States 1889–1918. New York: National Association for the Advancement of Colored People, 1919.

Tomeh, George J. *Israel and South Africa—The Unholy Alliance*. New York: New World Press, 1973.

U.S. Assistance to the State of Israel. Report by the Comptroller General of the United States, GAO/ID-83-51, 24 June 1983.

Vance, Cyrus. *Hard Choices—Four Critical Years in America's Foreign Policy*. New York: Simon and Schuster, 1983.

Walker, Alice. *In Search of Our Mother's Gardens: Womanist Prose*. New York: Harcourt Brace Jovanovich, 1983.

Washington, Booker T. *The Future of the American Negro*. New York: Negro Universities Press, 1969.

Webb, James Morris. *The Black Man—The Father of Civilization*. Seattle: Acme Press, 1910.

———. *The Black Man Will Be the Coming Universal King Proven by Biblical History*. Chicago: n.p., 1919.

Wedlock, Lunabelle. *The Reaction of Negro Publications and Organizations to German Anti-Semitism*. Washington, D.C.: Howard University Press, 1942.

Weisbord, Robert G. *African Zion: The Attempt to Establish a Jewish Colony in the East Africa Protectorate 1903–1905*. Philadelphia: Jewish Publication Society, 1968.

———. *Ebony Kinship: Africa, Africans, and the Afro-American*. Westport, Conn.: Greenwood Press, 1973.

Weisbord, Robert G., and Stein, Arthur. *Bittersweet Encounter: The Afro-American and the American Jew*. Westport, Conn.: Greenwood Press, 1970.

White, Walter. *A Man Called White—The Autobiography of Walter White*. New York: The Viking Press, 1948.

Whitfield, Thomas. *From Night to Sunlight*. Nashville, Tenn.: Breadman Press, 1980.

Williams, John A. *The King God Didn't Save—Reflections on the Life and Death of Dr. Martin Luther King, Jr.* New York: Coward-McCann, 1970.

Williams, Joseph J. *Hebrewisms of West Africa: From Nile to Niger with the Jews*. New York: The Dial Press, 1930.

Windsor, Rudolph R. *From Babylon to Timbuctoo—A History of the Ancient Black Races Including the Black Hebrews*. New York: Exposition Press, 1973.

World Armaments and Disarmament—Stockholm International Peace Research Institute Yearbook. London: Stockholm International Peace Research Institute, 1975, 1978, 1980, 1981.

Wright, Richard. *Eight Men*. Cleveland and New York: World Publishing Co., 1940.

Zogby, James and O'Dell, Jack. *Afro-Americans Stand Up for Middle East Peace*. Washington, D.C.: Palestine Human Rights Campaign, 1980.

Zucker, Norman. *The Coming Crisis in Israel—Private Faith and Public Policy*. Cambridge, Mass.: The M.I.T. Press, 1973.

ARTICLES

Abrahamson, Rachel. "Blacks, Jews and the Chicago Election," *Genesis*, 2 (July–August 1983): 3.

"Africa, the Middle East and South Africa," *Africa Report* (September/October 1975): 18.

"The Aftermath of Young's Resignation," *The National Jewish Monthly*, (October 1979).

Axelrad, Rabbi Albert S.; Goldburg, Rabbi Robert E.; Newton, Huey; Schappes, Morris U.; Wald, George, eds. *The Black Panthers, Jews and Israel*, A Jewish Currents Reprint, no. 9, New York, 1971.

Ayal, Eli. "Dynamite in Dimona," *Ma'ariv*, 6 April 1973.

Bakst, Jerome. "Negro Radicalism Turns Antisemitic—SNCC's Volte Face," *Wiener Library Bulletin* (1967–1968): 20–22.

Baldwin, James. "Negroes Are Anti-Semitic Because They're Anti-White," *New York Times Magazine*, 9 April 1967: 27ff.

———. "Open Letter to the Born Again," *Nation*, 29 September 1979: 263-264.

"B.A.S.I.C. Statement," *Congress Monthly*, October 1975.

Bernstein, Edgar. "Israel, the O.A.U. and South Africa," *Jewish Affairs*, 26, no. 7 (July 1971): 8–11.

"Blacks' Role in Mideast Talks—Right or Wrong?" *U.S. News & World Report*, 15 October 1979.

Blitzer, Wolf. "Assad-Jackson Coup," *Jerusalem Post*, 8 January–14 January 1984, International edition.

Bookbinder, Hyman. "More Questions on Jesse Jackson," *Washington Jewish Week*, 17 November 1983.

Breytenbach, Willie J. "Israel/South Africa—Isolation and Cooperation," *Africa Report* (November–December 1980): 39–43.

Brickner, Balfour. "America's Religion: What's Right, What's Left," *Present Tense*, 8, no. 3 (Spring 1981): 40–43.

Cale, Ruth. "Israel Grapples with a 'Black Hebrew' Problem," *Baltimore Sun*, 6 November 1971.

Cervenka, Zdenek. "The World of Muammar Qaddafy," *Africa Report* (March–April 1982): 11–14.

Chazan, Naomi. "Israel in Africa," *The Jerusalem Quarterly*, no. 18 (Winter 1981): 29–44.

———. "Israel's Shortsighted Policy in South Africa," *Jerusalem Post*, 13 April 1976.

Cheshire, Maxine. "VIP—Qaddafi Peace Medal Surprises Mrs. King," *Washington Post*, 25 October 1979.

"Conversation with Martin Luther King," *Conservative Judaism*, XXII, no. 3 (Spring 1968): 1–19.

Co-operation Between South Africa and Israel. Information bulletin no. 384. Pretoria: Department of Agricultural Technical Services, 1977.

Crockett, George W., Jr. "An Open Letter on the Middle East," *Freedomways*, 23, no. 3 (1983): 176–178.

Curtis, Michael. *Israel and South Africa—Middle East Review Special Report*, no. 1 (October 1983).

Decraene, Philippe. "Is the Romance with Israel Over?" *Africa Report* (May–June 1973): 20–23.

Delany, Hubert. "Hubert T. Delany Reports on Israel," *Crisis*, 63, no. 9 (November 1956): 517ff.

Diner, Hasia. "Can a Broken Alliance Be Repaired?" *The Jewish Monthly* (August–September 1983): 30ff.

Drake, St. Clair. "The Black Diaspora in Pan-African Perspective," *The Black Scholar* (September 1975): 2–13.

Dreyfuss, Joel, "Such Good Friends: Blacks and Jews in Conflict," *Village Voice*, 27 August 1979: 11ff.

Du Bois, Shirley Graham. "Egypt Is Africa," *The Black Scholar* (September 1970): 28–34.

———. "The Liberation of Africa: Power, Peace and Justice," *The Black Scholar* (February 1971): 32–37.

Du Bois, W.E.B. "A Case for the Jews," *Chicago Star*, 8 May 1948.

———. "Jews and Arabs," *Phylon*, V, no. 1 (1944): 86.

———. "Suez," *Black Titan—W.E.B. Du Bois*. Ed. John Henrik Clarke, Esther Jackson, Ernest Kaiser, J. H. O'Dell. Boston: Beacon Press, 1970: 296–298.

———. "Winds of Time." *Chicago Defender*, 15 May 1948.

"*Ebony* Interview with the Rev. Jesse Jackson," *Ebony* (June 1981): 155ff.

Edwards, Dick. "The Kibbutz—A Model for Black Collectives," *National Council of Jewish Women* (October–December 1970): 8–10.

Eytan, Walter. "Will Africa Resume Relations with Israel?" *Hadassah Magazine*, 61, no. 8 (April 1980): 4–6.

Flory, Ishmael. "What I Think," *Pittsburgh Courier*, 1 May 1976.

Friedman, Robert. "The Spiritual Electricity of Jesse Jackson," *Esquire* (December 1979): 80ff.

Frye, Thelma Ruby. "Golda vs. Apartheid," *Present Tense*, 6, no. 3 (Spring 1979): 5–7.

Garvey, Marcus. "The Case of the Negro for International Racial Adjustment, Before the English People." London: Poets' and Printers Press, n.d.

Gilliam, Angela. "An Afro-American Perspective on the Middle East," *Freedomways*, 23, no. 2 (1983): 81–89.

Goodman, Walter. "When Black Power Runs the New Left," *New York Times Magazine*, 24 September 1967: 28ff.

Griggs, Tony. "Angry Black Jews Return Here," *Chicago Daily Defender*, 27 September 1972.

Grose, Peter. "The Partition of Palestine 35 Years Ago," *New York Times Magazine*, 28 November 1982: 88ff.

Hakim, Najib J. and Stevens, Richard P. "Zaire and Israel: An American Connection," *Journal of Palestine Studies*, XII, no. 3 (Spring 1983): 41–53.

Houck, Tom. "Interview with Mayor Young," *Atlanta Magazine* (December 1982): 82ff.

"Interview—Jesse Jackson," *Arab Perspectives* (September 1980): 23–28.

"Interview with Andrew Young," *Penthouse Magazine* (February 1983): 122ff.

Jabara, Abdeen. "The American Left and the June Conflict," *The Arab World*, 14, nos. 10–11, Special Issue, n.d.: 73–80.

Jabara, Abdeen and Saleh, Noel J. "Blacks and Iraquis Collide in Detroit," *Freedomways*, 23, no. 3 (1983): 179–185.

Jackson, Jesse. "The real story of my Mideast mission," *Los Angeles Herald-Examiner*, 20 October 1979.

Jacobovici, Simcha. "Israel and Ethiopian Jews," *The Globe and Mail* (Toronto), 12 March 1983.

Jacobs, Paul. "Watts vs. Israel," *Commonweal* (1 March 1968): 649–654.

"Jesse Jackson—Candid Conversation," *Playboy* (November 1969): 85ff.

"Jewish Leader Pledges Work in the Spirit of Dr. Martin L. King," *Wichita Times*, 15 January 1976.

Jones, Le Roi. "Black Art," *Black Fire, An Anthology of Afro-American Writing*. Edited by Le Roi Jones and Larry Neal. New York: Morrow & Co., 1966: 302–303.

Katzew, Henry. "How the Nationalists View the Jews." *Jewish Chronicle*, 15 October 1965.

———. "Israel's Reaction to the Contribution," *Jewish Affairs*, 26, no. 7 (July 1971): 12–14.

Kent, Clark. "Dashikis in the Promised Land," *Israel Horizons* (May–June 1972): 8–12.

Kenyatta, Charles. "Consistent Ties between Blacks and Jews," *New York Amsterdam News*, 20 October 1979.

King, Martin Luther, Jr. "Of Rights and Wrongs Against Jews," *S.C.L.C. Newsletter*, 2 (July–August 1964): 11.

Knee, Stuart E. "The Impact of Zionism on Black and Arab Americans," *Patterns of Prejudice*, 10, no. 2 (March–April 1976): 21–28.

Korn, Shulamit. "Dimona—A Black Misunderstanding," *Jerusalem Post*, 15 October 1971.

Kurtis, Bill. "Strangers in the Holy Land," *New York Times Magazine*, 22 March 1981: 64ff.

Lane, Bill. "people—places 'n' situwayshuns," *Los Angeles Sentinel*, 6 April 1978.

Lankin, Doris. "Law Report—Leonia Clark and others v. Minister of the Interior," *Jerusalem Post*, 9 January 1983.

Lenhoff, Howard. "You are our brothers; you are our blood and flesh," *Present Tense*, 9, no. 4 (Summer 1982): 39–41.

Lens, Sid. "The New Politics Convention: Confusion and Promise," *New Politics*, VI, 1 (1967): 4–12.

Lester, Julius. "The Uses of Suffering," *Village Voice*, 10 September 1979.

Lev, Yehuda. "Strange Odyssey: Jesse Jackson, from Skokie to the West Bank," *Israel Today*, 25 October 1979, 2–5.

Levin, Nora. "Israeli Models for Black Co-ops," *The Progressive* (June 1972): 23–26.

———. "The Southern Cooperatives—Working to Save Rural America," *Tuesday Magazine* (June 1971): 2–6.

Lewis, Angelo. "Hosea Williams Gives Medal to Libyan Moammar Khadafi," *Atlanta Constitution*, 17 September 1979.

Lewis, Larry. "Black American Soldier in the Israeli Army," *Sepia* (October 1975): 18–24.

Lipset, Seymour Martin. "The Socialism of Fools—The Left, the Jews and Israel," *Encounter* (December 1969): 24–35.

Lowery, Rev. Joseph. "All Children of Abraham," *Afro-Americans Stand Up for Middle East Peace*. Edited by James Zogby and Jack O'Dell. Washington, D.C.: Palestine Human Rights Campaign, 1980: 16–20.

Manheimer, Aron. "The Black Israelites of Dimona," Part II, *Davka*, II, no. 3 (May–June 1972): 48–53.

"Mayor Hatcher Speaks," *The Sunday Post-Tribune*, 2 February 1969.

McCall, H. Carl, "The Political Lessons of August," *New York Amsterdam News*, 1 September 1979.

McCarthy, Colman, "Jesse Jackson, Surfing Along on the Latest Wave," *Washington Post*, 7 October 1979.

McDougall, Harold A. "Namibia and Palestine: Focal Points of Afro-American Soli-
    darity," *Freedomways*, 22, no. 4 (1982): 213–222.
Meeley, Fred. "The Chicken or the Egg of the Middle East," *AfroAmerican News for
    You*, July 1967.
"Middle East Powder Keg," *New York Amsterdam News*, 20 October 1973.
Miller, Jake C. "Black Viewpoints on the Mid-East Conflict," *Journal of Palestine
    Studies*, X, no. 2 (Winter 1981): 37–49.
Milstein, Tom. "A Perspective on the Panthers," *Commentary*, 50, no. 3 (September
    1970): 35–43.
Moleah, Alfred T. "Violations of Palestinian Human Rights: South African Parallels,"
    Journal of Palestine Studies, X, no. 2 (Winter 1981): 14–36.
Morrison, David S. "The Pro and Con of Hosea Williams," *Atlanta Weekly*, 24 May
    1981: 10ff.
Newby, Robert G. "Afro-Americans and Arabs: An Alliance in the Making," *Journal
    of Palestine Studies*, X, no. 2 (Winter 1981): 50–58.
Newfield, Jack. "Blacks and Jews: The Tragedy of Jackson, the Logic of Coalition,"
    Village Voice, 20 March 1984: 1ff.
O'Dell, J. H. "Editorial—The Silence Is Broken," *Freedomways*, 23, no. 2 (1983): 66–
    69.
Payne, Ethel. "Young Affair Puts This All Against the Wall," *Afro-American*, 3 Sep-
    tember 1979.
Perlmutter, Nathan. "Fabricating Racism," *ADL Bulletin* (February 1984).
"Playboy Interview: Malcolm X," *Playboy* (May 1963): 53ff.
"Playboy Interview: Muhammad Ali," *Playboy*, (December 1975): 65ff.
Price, Larry. "Black Jews in the Promised Land," *Chicago Today Magazine*, 8 November
    1970: 8ff.
Puddington, Arch. "Jesse Jackson, the Blacks and American Foreign Policy," *Com-
    mentary*, 77, no. 4 (April 1984): 19–27.
Rabinowitz, Malka. "Two Shades of Anti-Semitism," *Jerusalem Post*, 9–15 September
    1979, International edition.
Raspberry, William. "The Cost of Jackson's Slur," *Washington Post*, 2 March 1984.
———. "Fighting Campus Discrimination," *Washington Post*, 15 March 1974.
———. "Israel and South Africa: Toward U.S. Tensions," *Washington Post*, 21 April
    1976.
———. "More to the Story," *Washington Post*, 19 November 1980.
———. "On Blacks, Jews and Quotas," *Providence Journal*, 15 June 1983.
———. "Unholy Time in Holy Land," *Jerusalem Post*, 7 November 1980.
Reed, Beverly. "Black, Beautiful and Free," *Ebony* (June 1971): 45ff.
Reynolds, Barbara. "The Reverend Push," *The New Republic*, 27 October 1979: 14–
    16.
Rogers, Barbara. "South Africa Gets Nuclear Weapons Thanks to the West," *Dirty Work
    2—The C.I.A. in Africa*. Edited by Ellen Ray, William Schaap, Karl Van Meter,
    Louis Wolf. Seacaucus, N.J.: Lyle Stuart Inc., 1980: 276–280.
Rosenfeld, Stephen S. "Will Africa and Israel Patch It Up," *Present Tense*, V, no. 2
    (Winter 1978): 14–15.
Rosenfield, Geraldine. "The Polls: Attitudes Toward American Jews," *Public Opinion
    Quarterly*, 46 (1982): 431-443.

Rowan, Carl. "Controversy Had Little to Do with Ambassador Young," *New York Amsterdam News*, 8 September 1979.

———. "Moshe Dayan Insults Black GI's," *New York Amsterdam News*, 20 December 1980.

Royko, Mike. "It's Moshe-ly Racist," *Chicago Sun-Times*, 26 November 1980.

Ruby, Walter. "Fort Stony Brook," *Village Voice*, 20 December 1983: 21ff.

Salpeter, Eliahu. "Courting the PLO—Jesse Jackson's Pilgrimage," *The New Leader*, 22 October 1979: 3–5.

Savage, Gus. "America in the Wrong," *Freedomways*, 23, no. 3 (1983): 171–175.

Seltzer, Arthur. "The Dube Affair," *ADL Bulletin*, October 1984: 3–6.

Senghor, Leopold Sedar. "Africa, the Middle East and South Africa," *Africa Report* (September–October 1975): 18–20.

Shimoni, Yaacov. "Israel, the Arabs, and Africa," *Africa Report* (July-August 1976): 51–55.

Shipp, Bill. "Why Did Joe and Hosea Go to Mideast?" *Atlanta Constitution*, 21 September 1979.

Silverberg, David. "The D.C.-PLO Connection," *Baltimore Jewish Times*, 1 February 1980: 44–48.

Simon, Roger. "Jessie Raises $10,000 in Arab Cash," *Chicago Sun-Times*, 16 October 1979.

Smith, Gary V. "Perspectives on Zionism and the Arab-Jewish Conflict in the Black Establishment Press," *Arab Studies Quarterly*, 2, no. 1 (Winter 1980): 70–89.

"South Africa: Good Neighbor in Africa," no. 10/81. Washington, D.C.: Minister (Information), South African Embassy, 1981.

Squires, Gregory D. "South Africa, the Middle East and Iran: A Conversation with Jesse Jackson," *The Journal of Intergroup Relations* (Spring 1980): 4–12.

"Statement by Dr. Lowery...Following S.C.L.C.'s Middle East Peace Initiative," *S.C.L.C.* (November/December 1979).

Swan, Christopher. "Jesse Jackson—A Man with PUSH," *Christian Science Monitor*, 25 September 1979.

Thompson, Era Bell. "Are Black Americans Welcome in Africa," *Ebony* (January 1969): 44ff.

Tinney, James S. "Will Black Troops Have to Fight Africans in Mid-East War?" *Afro-American*, 3 November 1973.

Totenberg, Nina. "Discriminating to End Discrimination," *New York Times Magazine*, 14 April 1974: 9ff.

Walker, Wyatt Tee. "Liberation Theology and the Middle East Conflict," *Freedomways*, 23, no. 3 (1983): 147–152.

Walters, Ronald W. "The Black Initiatives in the Middle East," *Journal of Palestine Studies*, X, no. 2 (Winter 1981): 3–13.

———. "The Young Resignation: What Does It Mean?" *New Directions*, 6, no. 4 (October 1979): 6–14.

Washington, Booker T. "The Atlanta Exposition Address," *Booker T. Washington and His Critics—The Problem of Negro Leadership*. Edited by Hugh Hawkins. Boston: D. C. Heath and Co., 1962: 10–20.

Wilkins, Roy. "Israel's Time of Trial Also America's," *Afro-American*, 24 June 1967.

———. "Life Goes On in Israel," *Afro-American*, 1 April 1972.

———. "The State of Israel," *New York Post*, 18 March 1972.

Yette, Samuel. "Dr. King's Approach Pushed on Middle East Mission," *S.C.L.C.* (November/December 1979). (First published in *Afro-American*.)

Young, Lewis. "American Blacks and the Arab-Israeli Conflict," *Journal of Palestine Studies*, II, no. 1 (Autumn 1972): 70–85.

Young, Whitney. "A Black American Looks at Israel, the 'Arab Revolution,' Racism, Palestinians and Peace," An American Jewish Congress Report. 7 October 1970.

————. "Israel and Equality," *New America*, VIII, no. 18, 25 October 1969.

NEWSPAPERS AND PERIODICALS

Specific articles are cited under "Articles"

African Opinion, 1970.

Africa Report, July–August 1975.

Afro-American (Baltimore), 1956, 1972–1983.

Ann Arbor News, 27 August 1968.

Atlanta Constitution, 1979, 1982–1983.

Atlanta Daily World, 1979–1980.

The Atlanta Inquirer, 1979.

Atlanta Journal, 1979, 1982.

Baltimore Jewish Times, 1980.

Bay State Bannner, 1984.

Bilalian News, 1976, 1979–1981. (See also *Muhammad Speaks*).

Black Books Bulletin, Winter 1976.

The Blackman, 1933–1939.

The Black Panther, 1968–1970, 1975–1976.

Black Power, 1967.

Boston Globe, 1974, 1983–1984.

Chicago Defender, 1956, 1975, 1980, 1981.

Chicago Sun-Times, 1980.

Chicago Tribune, 1979, 1981.

Congressional Quarterly Weekly Report, 1984.

Congress Monthly, 1975, 1976–1977.

Crisis, 1918, 1919, 1929, 1956, 1970–1984.

Daily Worker, 1957.

Diamond Fields Advertiser (Kimberley), 1976.

Die Transvaler, 1961.

Ebony, 1968–1984.

The Facts (Seattle), 1982.

Freedomways, 1983.

India Today, 1 February–15 February 1980.

International Herald Tribune, (Paris), 1967, 1978.

Israel-South Africa Trade Review, 1980–1981.

Jerusalem Post (Local and International editions), 1961–1984.

Jewish Telegraph Agency's Daily News Bulletin, 1979–1982.

The Jewish-Week American Examiner, 1977.

Journal American, 27 October 1979.

Kansas City Call, 1975–1976, 1979–1980.

Kansas City Globe, 1979.

Liberian Star, 1967, 1969.
Los Angeles Herald-Dispatch, September 1972.
Los Angeles Herald-Examiner, 1979.
Los Angeles Sentinel, 1975–1976, 1978–1979, 1980.
Manhattan Tribune, 19 September 1970.
Metropolitan Star, (New York), 1969.
Muhammad Speaks, 1967, 1971.
National Guardian, 16 September 1967.
The National Jewish Monthly, 1979–1983.
Near East Report, 1983.
The Negro World, 31 July 1920.
Newsweek, 8 October 1979 and 9 April 1984.
New York Amsterdam News, 1967–1984.
New York Times, 1967–1984.
New York Voice, 7 March and 19 September 1981.
Norfolk Guide and Journal, 1956.
Philadelphia Tribune, 22 July 1975.
Pittsburgh Couurier, 1947, 1948, 1956, 1967, 1979, 1980.
Portland Observer, 1977–1979.
Pretoria News, 1976.
Providence Evening Bulletin, 1984.
Providence Journal, 1979.
Rand Daily Mail, 1974, 1976, 1978.
Rhode Island Herald, 28 February 1980.
SNCC Newsletter, June–July 1967 and September–October 1967.
South African Digest, 1977–1984.
South African Jewish Times, 1961.
The Star (Johannesburg), 1974, 1976.
Time, 1979, 1983.
U.S. News & World Report, 1979.
Voice News and Viewpoint (San Diego), 11 February 1976.
Washington Post, 1977, 1979–1984.
Washington Star, 1979.

REPORTS

United Nations General Assembly, Official Records, 16th sess., 1961; 26th sess., 1971; 27th sess., 1972; 28th sess., 1973; 29th sess., 1974; 30th sess., 1975; 31st sess., 1976; 32nd sess., 1977. Second Special Report on Relations between Israel and South Africa, 1977.

MANUSCRIPT COLLECTIONS

American Jewish Committee Files. New York City.
American Jewish Congress Files. New York City and Jerusalem.
CORE Papers. Martin Luther King Jr. Library and Archives, Atlanta.
Marcus Garvey Papers. UCLA, Los Angeles.
NAACP Papers. Microfilm.
SCLC Papers. Martin Luther King Jr. Library and Archives, Atlanta.

SNCC Papers. Martin Luther King Jr. Library and Archives, Atlanta.

South African Jewish Board of Deputies Files. Johannesburg.

South African Zionist Federation Files. Johannesburg and Cape Town.

W. E. B. Du Bois Papers. University of Massachusetts, Amherst, Mass.

Chaim Weizmann Archives, Rehovath, Israel.

OTHER UNPUBLISHED SOURCES

ABC News—Harris Survey, vol. I, no. 104, Released 24 August 1979; vol. I, no. 105, Released 27 August 1979; vol. I, no. 108, Released 3 September 1979.

"Ad Hoc Panel Report on the September 22 Event." Report, the Office of Science and Technology Policy of the Executive Office of the President of the United States, July 1980.

Allon, Yigal. Statement at the 31st General Assembly of the United Nations, 7 October 1976.

American Jewish Committee. "Currents—Fringe Movements and What They're Up To," no. 2, February 1972.

American Jewish Committee and the American Jewish Congress, "The Black Hebrews." An English Summary of the Special [Glass] Committee Report. Jerusalem, 1980.

"The Black Panther Party—The Anti-Semitic and Anti-Israel Component." Report of the American Jewish Committee, 23 January 1970.

Blum, Yehuda Z. Statement to the United Nations in the Plenary on Policies of Apartheid of the Government of South Africa, Item 32, 30 November 1981.

Brackman, Harold David. "The Ebb and Flow of Conflict. A History of Black-Jewish Relations Through 1900," Ph.D diss., UCLA, 1977.

Carmichael, Stokeley. Lecture at the University of Rhode Island, Kingston, Rhode Island, 5 December 1983.

Carson, Clayborne. "Blacks and Jews in the Civil Rights Movement." Paper presented at the spring symposium of the Afro-American Studies Program, Univeristy of Pennsylvania, 25–27 March 1982.

Chazan, Naomi. "The Fallacies of Pragmatism—Israeli Foreign Policy Towards South Africa." Paper presented at the spring symposium of the Afro-American Studies Program, University of Pennsylvania, 25–27 March 1982.

Decter, Moshe. "Arms Traffic with South Africa: Who Is Guilty?" Report, American Jewish Congress, 1976.

———. "South Africa and Black Africa—A Report on Growing Trade Relations." Report, American Jewish Congress, 1976.

Fauntroy, Walter E. Report, Fact-Finding Mission to Lebanon, September 17–21, 1979. Released 11 October 1979.

The Gallup Poll. "Attitudes of the American Public Toward American Jews and Israel, October 1980.

———. "Attitudes of the American Public Toward American Jews and Israel," March 1982.

Herzog, Chaim Amb. Address to the B'nai B'rith International Conference, Washington, D.C., 30 August 1976.

———. Address to the President's Conference of Major Jewish Organizations, New York, 19 October 1976.

————. Explanation of Vote Before the Vote on the Policies of Apartheid, 14 December 1977.

————. Statement to the Economic and Social Council, 60th sess. 29 April 1976.

————. Statement at the General Assembly in the Debate on the Policies of Apartheid, 1 November 1976.

————. Statement to the General Assembly on Item 27, Policies of Apartheid of the Government of South Africa, 17 November 1977.

————. Statement to the Security Council, 4 November 1976.

Hill, Robert A. "Jews and the Enigma of the Pan-African Congress of 1919." Paper presented at the spring symposium of the Afro-American Studies Program, University of Pennsylvania, 25–27 March 1982.

Hooks, Benjamin L. "Stand Up," Address, Boston, Mass., 29 June 1982.

"Israel's Programme for International Cooperation." Report, Division for International Cooperation of the Ministry of Foreign Affairs, n.d.

Jackson, Jesse. "A Quest for Peace in the Middle East—And the Vital Interests of Black People." A position paper, 20 August 1979.

King, Martin Luther, Jr. "An Address at the Synagogue Council of America." Waldorf-Astoria Hotel, New York, 5 December 1965.

————. "Statement on Soviet Jewry," 11 December 1966.

Lynch, Hollis R. "A Black Nineteenth Century Response to Jews and Zionism: The Case of Edward W. Blyden, 1832–1912." Paper presented at the spring symposium of the Afro-American Studies Program, University of Pennsylvania, 25–27 March 1982.

Report of the First Findings of the Delegation to Israel of BASIC and the A. Philip Randolph Educational Fund Regarding Human Rights As They Pertain to the Original Hebrew Israelite Nation, 17–28 January 1981.

Schneider, William. "Anti-Semitism and Israel: A Report on American Public Opinion," December 1978.

Schoenberg, Harris O. "South Africa's Silent Partners: A Study in Trade and Hypocrisy." Report, 1976.

Scott, William R. "Ethiopianism and Black Judaism: The Nexus." Paper presented at the spring symposium of the Afro-American Studies Program, University of Pennsylvania, 25–27 March 1982.

Sklar, Richard L. "Africa and the Middle East: What Blacks and Jews Owe to Each Other." Paper presented at the spring symposium of the Afro-American Studies Program, University of Pennsylvania, 25–27 March 1982.

"The South Atlantic Mystery Flash—Nuclear or Not?" DST–1510 D934–80 Rpt. 5. Report, Defense Intelligence Agency of the United States, June 1980.

Transcript of CBS' "Sixty Minutes," 18 March 1979 and 16 September 1979.

Transcript of WABC-TV's Eyewitness News Conference, 23 September 1979.

Transcript of WABC-TV's "Like It Is," 20 June 1976.

Walters, Ronald W. "South Africa's Nuclear Power Development: Political and Strategic Implications." Testimony before the Sub-Committee on Africa of the Committee on International Relations of the United States House of Representatives, 21 June 1977.

Weitz, Marvin. "Black Attitudes to Jews in the United States from World War II to 1976." Ph.D. diss., Yeshiva University, New York, 1977.

Yankelovich, Skelly and White, Inc. "A Study of the Attitudes of Grass Roots Black

Leaders Toward the Mideast Situation, Israel, The Arab Nations and American Jews.'' Prepared for the American Jewish Committee, May 1975.

INTERVIEWS

Abernathy, Rev. Ralph. Personal interview with author. Providence, R.I. 1 December 1982.

Agassi, Yitzhak. Personal interview with author. Jerusalem, Israel, 20 November 1972.

Allen, Alexander. Telephone interview with author. 27 May 1982.

Alperin, Micki. Personal interview with author. New York, 16 June 1983.

Avner, Gershon. Personal interview with author. Haifa, Israel, 6 July 1981.

Ben Israel, Nasi Ahsiel. Personal interview with author. Dimona, Israel, 15 November 1972.

Ben Zvi, Mina. Personal interview with author. Haifa, Israel, 15 March 1981,

Bond, Julian. Personal interview with author. Atlanta, Georgia, 17 March 1983.

Bookbinder, Hyman. Personal interview with author. Washington, D.C., 17 May 1983.

Clayman, David. Personal interview with author. Jerusalem, Israel, 14 June 1984.

Cummings, Robert. Telephone interview with author. 10 May 1983.

Dine, Thomas. Personal interview with author. Washington, D.C., 17 May 1983.

Eizenstat, Stuart. Personal interview with author. Washington, D.C., 18 May 1983.

Ellerin, Milton. Personal interview with author. New York City, 16 June 1983.

Fauntroy, Walter. Personal interview with author. Washington, D.C., 19 May 1983.

Fincham, Charles. Personal inverview with author. Cape Town, South Africa, 3 September 1983.

Frank, David. Personal interview with author. Jerusalem, Israel, 19 December 1980.

Frank, Leib. Personal interview with author. Kfar Shmaryahu, Israel, 31 May 1981.

Franklin, Derek Stuart. Personal interview with author. Pretoria, South Africa, 22 August 1983.

Gold, Bertram. Personal interview with author. New York City, 29 December 1982.

Goldberg, Aleck. Personal interview with author. Johannesburg, South Africa, 23 August 1983.

Goldreich, Arthur. Personal interview with author. Herzliya Pituah, Israel, 31 May 1981.

Jordan, Hamilton. Telephone interview with author. 17 March 1983.

Kahane, Rabbi Meir. Personal interview with author. Jerusalem, Israel, 20 November 1972.

Kahane, Yehoshua. Personal interview with author. Jerusalem, Israel, 17 June 1984.

Kenigsberg, K. R. Personal Interview with author. Johannesburg, South Africa, 23 August 1983.

Kennedy, Florynce. Personal interview with author. Kingston, R.I., 22 February 1983.

Kinlock, Rev. Robert M. Telephone interview with author. 22 March 1982.

Kirbo, Charles. Personal interview with author. Atlanta, Georgia, 17 March 1983.

Lewengrub, Stuart. Personal interview with author. Atlanta, Georgia, 17 March 1983.

Lipshutz, Robert. Personal interview with author. Atlanta, Georgia, 17 March 1983.

Lowery, Rev. Joseph. Personal interview with author. Atlanta, Georgia, 15 March 1983.

McCraw, Vincent. Personal interview with author. Atlanta, Georgia, 15 March 1983.

Montlana, N. H. Personal interview with author. Johannesburg, South Africa, 23 August 1983.

Naude, Marinus. Personal interview with author. Tel Aviv, Israel, 25 June 1981.

Nelson, William E., Jr. Telephone interview with author. 23 March 1983.

Respes, Rabbi Abel. Telephone interview with author. 20 March 1982.

Rustin, Bayard. Personal interview with author. New York City, 16 June 1983.

———. Telephone interview with author. 1 June 1982.

Shelef, Yitzhak. Personal interview with author. Jerusalem, Israel, 19 April 1981.

Shiloah, Betty. Personal interview with author. Jerusalem, Israel, 20 April 1981.

Sternstein, Rabbi Joseph. Telephone interview with author. 22 February 1983.

Suzman, Helen, M. P. Personal interview with author. Cape Town, South Africa, 31 August 1983.

Unna, Yitzhak. Personal interview with author. Jerusalem, Israel, 18 December 1980.

Vance, Cyrus. Telephone interview with author. 22 March 1983.

Williams, Rev. Hosea. Personal interview with author. Atlanta, Georgia, 17 March 1983.

Wittenstein, Charles. Personal interview with author. Atlanta, Georgia, 17 March 1983.

Wolman, Izzy. Personal interview with author. Cape Town, South Africa, 31 August 1983.

Index

Abourezk, James, 144, 145
Abram, Morris, 38-39
Accommodationism, 11, 13
Advocate Society, 135
Affirmative action, 133-36
Africa: Islamic cultural influences in, 46; Jewish colony in, 10. See also *names of specific countries*
African-Israeli relations, 94-96, 113-14; Israeli aid programs, 95, 98, 113; Six Day War and, 98, 102
African National Congress, 99
African Orthodox Church, 65
Afrikaners, 94, 101, 102. *See also* South African-Israeli relations
Afro-American, 30, 49, 50, 125
Afro-American Conference of 1955, 95
Afro-Americans: as God's chosen people, 65; Jewish exploitation of, 45-46; political power of, 156-57. *See also* Black-Israeli relations; Black-Jewish relations; *names of specific Black organizations*
Alexander, Clifford, 161
Al Fatah, 142, 147-48
Ali, Muhammed, 33, 35; anti-Zionism of, 46; Jewish support by, 46
Aliyah, 12, 18
Allon, Yigal, 100
Almogi, Yosef, 111

Altneuland (Herzl), 95
American-Arab Anti-Discrimination Committee, 182
American Council for Judaism, 56 n.15
American Israeli Public Affairs Committee, 184
American Jewish Committee: *Bakke* case and, 135; Black Muslims and, 46; on Dayan's "Black military" statement, 162-63; *DeFunis* case and, 134, 135
American Jewish Congress: *Bakke* case and, 135; Black press survey by, 49-50
Amin, Idi, 107
Amsterdam News, 49-50, 77
Anderson, Talmadge, 159
Angola, 105
Anti-Defamation League, 133; *Bakke* case and, 135; on Dayan's "Black military" statement, 163; *DeFunis* case and, 134-35; Martin Luther King, Jr., peace medal incident and, 159; proposed Begin-Jackson meeting and, 147; SNCC criticism by, 34
Anti-Israel resolutions: of National Black Political Convention, 48; of National Conference for New Politics, 37-39
Anti-Semitism: A. Philip Randolph's criticism of, 34; Bayard Rustin on, 34; of Black Panthers, 44; Martin Luther King, Jr.'s opposition to, 39; of

About the Authors

ROBERT G. WEISBORD is Professor of History at the University of Rhode Island. He is the author of several books on Jewish and Afro-American historical themes including *Genocide?: Birth Control and the Black American* (Greenwood Press, 1975), *Ebony Kinship: Africa, Africans and the Afro-American* (Greenwood Press, 1973), *Bittersweet Encounter: The Afro-American and the American Jew*, and *African Zion: The Attempt to Establish a Jewish Colony in the East Africa Protectorate 1903-1905*. In 1983 he was the recipient of Brown University's Charles H. Nichols Award for research in Afro-American history.

RICHARD KAZARIAN, JR., is History Department Coordinator and Instructor of American History at the College of Continuing Education at the University of Rhode Island. He holds a Ph.D. in History from Brown University.